Richard F. Burton

Personal Narrative of a Pilgrimage to Mecca and Medina in Three Volumes

Vol. 1

Richard F. Burton

Personal Narrative of a Pilgrimage to Mecca and Medina in Three Volumes
Vol. 1

ISBN/EAN: 9783741179013

Manufactured in Europe, USA, Canada, Australia, Japa

Cover: Foto ©Lupo / pixelio.de

Manufactured and distributed by brebook publishing software (www.brebook.com)

Richard F. Burton

Personal Narrative of a Pilgrimage to Mecca and Medina in Three Volumes

EACH VOLUME SOLD SEPARATELY.

COLLECTION OF BRITISH AUTHORS

TAUCHNITZ EDITION.

VOL. 1400.

A PILGRIMAGE TO MECCA AND MEDINA
BY RICHARD F. BURTON.

IN THREE VOLUMES. — VOL. 1.

LEIPZIG: BERNHARD TAUCHNITZ.
PARIS: C. REINWALD & CIE, 15, RUE DES SAINTS PÈRES.

This Collection is published with copyright for Continental circulation, but all

COLLECTION
OF
BRITISH AUTHORS

TAUCHNITZ EDITION.

VOL. 1400.

PERSONAL NARRATIVE OF A PILGRIMAGE TO
MECCA AND MEDINA BY R. F. BURTON.

IN THREE VOLUMES.

VOL. I.

"Our notions of Mecca must be drawn from the Arabians: as no unbeliever is permitted to enter the city, our travellers are silent."

GIBBON, chap. 50.

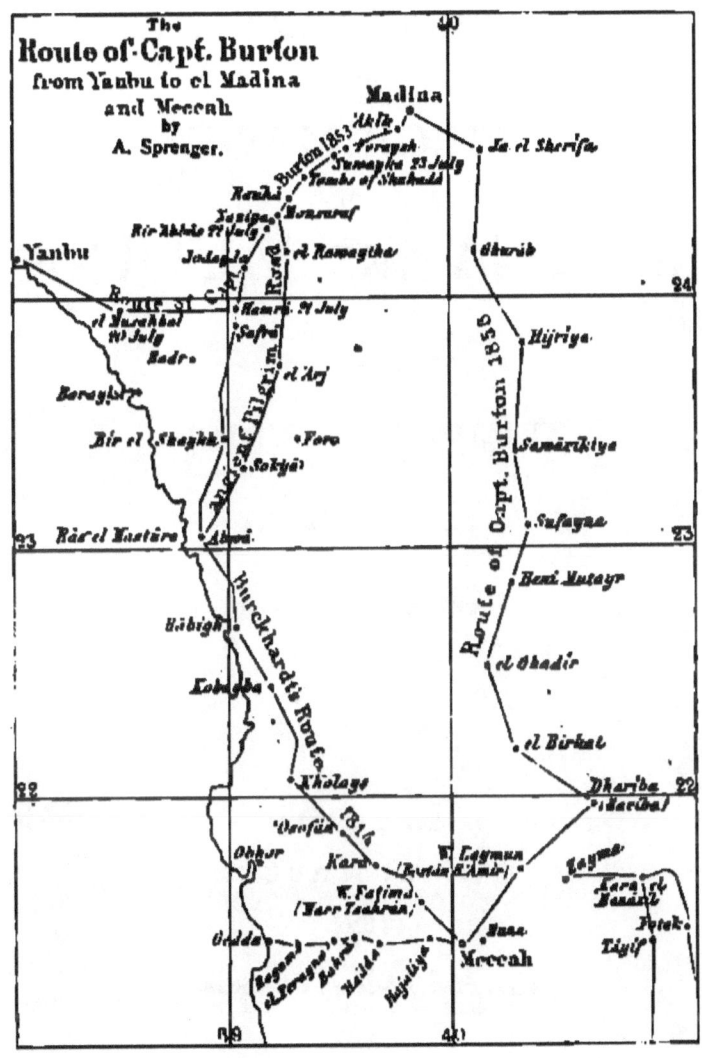

PERSONAL NARRATIVE
OF A
PILGRIMAGE
TO
MECCA AND MEDINA

BY

RICHARD F. BURTON.

COPYRIGHT EDITION.

IN THREE VOLUMES.—VOL. I.

LEIPZIG

BERNHARD TAUCHNITZ

1874.

The Right of Translation is reserved.

اَلْلَيْلُ وَالْخَيْلُ وَالْبَيْدَاءُ تَعْرِفُنِي
وَالسَّيْفُ وَالضَّيْفُ وَالْقِرْطَاسُ وَالْقَلَمُ

EL MUTANABBI.

TO

COLONEL WILLIAM SYKES,

F. R. SOC., M. R. G. SOC., M. R. A. SOC.,

AND LORD RECTOR OF THE MARISCHAL COLLEGE,

ABERDEEN.

I DO not parade your name, my dear Colonel, in the van of this volume, after the manner of that acute tactician who wore a Koran upon his lance in order to win a battle. Believe me it is not my object to use Your Orthodoxy as a cover to my heresies of sentiment and science, in politics, political economy and—what not?

But whatever I have done on this occasion, if I have done any thing, has been by the assistance of a host of friends, amongst whom you were ever the foremost. And the highest privilege I claim is this opportunity of publicly acknowledging the multitude of obligations owed to you and to them. Accept, my dear Colonel, this humble return for your kindness, and ever believe me,

The sincerest of your well wishers,

RICHARD F. BURTON.

PREFACE.

THE interest now felt in everything that relates to the East would alone be sufficient to ensure to the author of "El Medinah and Meccah" the favourable consideration of the Reading Public. But when it is borne in mind that since the days of William Pitts of Exeter (A. D. 1678—1688) no European travellers, with the exception of Burckhardt (1811) and Lieut. Burton, have been able to enter the city and to send us back an account of their travels there, it cannot be doubted but that the present work will be hailed as a welcome addition to our knowledge of these hitherto mysterious *penetralia* of Mohammedan superstition. In fact, El Medinah may be considered almost a virgin theme; for as Burckhardt was prostrated by sickness throughout the period of his stay in the Northern Hejaz, he was not able to describe it as satisfactorily or minutely as he did the southern country; he could not send a plan of the mosque, nor correct the popular but erroneous ideas which prevail concerning it and the surrounding city.

The reader may question the propriety of introducing in a work of description, anecdotes which may appear open to the charge of triviality. The author's object, however, seems to be to illustrate the peculiarities of the people; to dramatise, as it were, the dry journal of a journey, and to preserve the tone of the adventures, together with that local colouring in which mainly consists "*l'éducation d'un voyage.*" For the same reason, the prayers of the "Visitation" ceremony have been translated at length, despite the danger of inducing tedium; they are an essential part of the subject, and cannot be omitted, nor be represented by "specimens."

Mr. Burton is already known by his "History of Sindh." As if to mark their sense of the spirit of observation and daring evinced by him when in that country, and still more during his late journeyings in Arabia and East Africa, the Geographical Society, through their learned Secretary, Dr. Norton Shaw, have given valuable aid to this work in its progress through the press.

It was during a residence of many years in India that Mr. Burton had fitted himself for his late undertaking, by acquiring, through his peculiar aptitude for such studies, a thorough acquaintance with various dialects of Arabia and Persia; and, indeed, his Eastern cast of features seemed already to point him out as

PREFACE.

the very person of all others best suited for an expedition like that described in the following pages.

It will be observed that in writing Arabic, Hindoostanee, Persian, or Turkish words, the author has generally adopted the system proposed by Sir William Jones and modified by later Orientalists. But when a word has been "stamped" by general popular use, the conversational form has been preferred; and the same, too, may be said of the common corruptions, Cairo, Mohammed, &c., which, in any other form, would appear to us pedantic and ridiculous.

Let us hope that the proofs now furnished of untiring energy and capacity for observation and research by our author, as well as his ability to bear fatigue and exposure to the most inclement climate, will induce the Governments of this country and of India to provide him with men and means (evidently all that is required for the purpose) to pursue his adventurous and useful career in other countries equally difficult of access, and, if possible, of still greater interest, than the eastern shores of the Red Sea.

T. L. W.

Hampton Court Palace,
June, 1855.

PREFACE
TO THE THIRD (TAUCHNITZ) EDITION.

AFTER a lapse of nearly twenty years a third edition of my Pilgrimage has been called for by the public, to whom I take this opportunity of returning thanks.

The text has been carefully revised and the "baggage of notes" has been materially lightened. From the appendix I have removed matter which, though useful to the student, is of scant general interest. The quaint and interesting "Narrative and Voyages of Ludovicus Vertomannus, Gentleman of Rome," need no longer be read in extracts, when the whole has been printed by the Hakluyt Society. (The Travels of Ludovico di Varthema in Egypt, Syria, Arabia Deserta and Arabia Felix, in Persia, India and Ethiopia, A. D. 1503 to 1508. Translated from the original Italian edition of 1510, with a preface by John Winter Jones, Esq., F.S.A., and edited, with notes and an introduction, by George Percy Badger, late Government Chaplain in the Presidency of Bombay. London. Printed for the Hakluyt Society.) On the other hand

I have inserted, with the permission of the author, two highly interesting communications from Dr. Aloys Sprenger, the well-known Orientalist and Arabist, concerning the routes of the Great Caravans. My friend supports his suspicions that an error of direction has been made, and geographers will now enjoy the benefit of his conscientious studies, topographical and linguistic.

The truculent attacks made upon pilgrims and Darwayshes call for a few words of notice. Even the learned and amiable Dr. Wilson of Bombay (Lands of the Bible, vol. 2, p. 302) alludes in the case of the Spaniard Badia, alias Ali Bey el Abbásí, to the "unjustifiable disguise of a Mohammedan Pilgrim." The author of the Ruddy Goose Theory (Voice of Israel from Mount Sinai) and compiler of the Historical Geography of Arabia has dealt a foul blow to the memory of Burckhardt, the energetic and inoffensive Swiss traveller, whose name has ever been held in the highest repute. And now the "Government Chaplain" indites (Introduction p. xxvii) the following invidious remarks touching the travels of Ludovico di Varthema —the "vir Deo carus," be it remarked, of Julius Cæsar Scaliger:—

"This is not the place to discuss the morality of an act, involving the deliberate and voluntary denial of what a man holds to be truth in a matter so sacred as that of Religion. Such a violation of conscience is not justifiable by the end which the renegade may have in view, however abstractedly praiseworthy it may be; and even granting that his demerit should be gauged by the amount of knowledge which he possesses of what is true and what false, the conclusion is inevitable, that nothing short of utter ignorance of the precepts of his faith, or a conscientious disbelief in them, can fairly relieve the Christian, who conforms to Islamism without a corresponding persuasion of its verity, of the deserved odium which all honest men attach to apostasy and hypocrisy."

The reply to this tirade is simply, "judge not; especially when you are ignorant of the case which you are judging." Perhaps also the writer may ask himself, Is it right for those to cast stones who dwell in a tenement not devoid of fragility?

The second attack proceeds from a place whence no man would reasonably have expected it. The author of the "Narrative of a Year's Journey through Central and Eastern Arabia" (vol. I. pp. 258—59) thus expresses his opinions:—

"Passing oneself off for a wandering Darweesh, as some European explorers have attempted to do in the East, is for more reasons than one a very bad plan. It is unnecessary to dilate on that moral aspect of the proceeding which will always first strike unsophisticated minds. To feign a religion which the adventurer himself does not believe, to perform with scrupulous exactitude, as of the highest and holiest import, practices which he inwardly ridicules, and which he intends on his return to hold up to the ridicule of others, to turn for weeks and months together the most sacred and awful bearings of man towards his Creator into a deliberate and truthless mummery, not to mention other and yet darker touches,—all this seems hardly compatible with the character of a European gentleman, let alone that of a Christian."

This comes admirably à propos from a Christian who, born a Protestant, of Jewish descent, placed himself "in connection with," in plain words took the vows of, "the order of the Jesuits," an order "well-known in the annals of philanthropic daring"; a popular preacher who declaimed openly at Bayrút and elsewhere gainst his own nation, till the proceedings of a certain Father Michael Cohen were made the subject of an official report by Mr. Consul General Moore (Bayrút, November 11, 1857); an Englishman by birth who accepted French protection, a secret mission and the "liberality of the present Emperor of the French;" a military officer travelling in the garb of what he calls a native (Syrian) "quack" with a comrade who "by a slight but necessary fiction passed for his brother-in-law;"* a gentleman who by return to Protestantism

* The brother-in-law Barakat J'rayj'ray has since that time followed suit: educated at the Jesuit college of Mu' allakah (Libanus) he has settled as a Greek Catholic priest at the neighbouring town of Zahleh.

violated his vows, and a traveller who was proved by the experiment of Colonel Pelly to have brought upon himself all the perils and adventures that have caused his word to be considered so little worthy of trust. Truly this attack argues the sublime of daring: can it be accounted for by the principle of "vieille coquette, nouvelle dévote"?

Both writers certainly lack the "giftie" to see themselves as others see them.

In noticing these extracts my object is not to defend myself: I recognize no man's right to interfere between a human being and his conscience. But what is there, I would ask, in the Moslem Pilgrimage so offensive to Christians—what makes it a subject of "inward ridicule"? Do they not also venerate Abraham, the Father of the Faithful? Did not Locke, and even greater names, hold Mohammedans to be heterodox Christians, in fact Arians who, till the end of the 4th century, represented the mass of North-European Christianity? Did Mr. Lane never conform by praying at a Mosque in Cairo? did he ever fear to confess it? has he been called an apostate for so doing?

The fact is, there are honest men who hold that El Islam, in its capital tenets, approaches much nearer to the faith of Jesus than do the Pauline and Athanasian modifications which, in this our day, have divided the Indo-European mind into Catholic and Roman, Greek and Russian, Lutheran and Anglican. The disciples of Dr. Daniel Schenkel's school (A Sketch of the Character of Jesus. Longmans, 1869) will indeed find little difficulty in making this admission. Practically, a visit after Arab Meccah to Anglo-Indian Aden, with its "political" chaplain and its "priests after the order of Melchisedeck," suggested to me that the Moslem may be more tolerant, more enlightened, more charitable, than many societies of the so-called Christians.

And why rage so furiously against the "disguise of a wandering Darwaysh?" In what point is the Darwaysh more a mummer or show more of *"bêtise"* than the quack? Is the Darwaysh anything but an Oriental Freemason, and are Freemasons less Christians because they pray with Moslems and profess their belief in simple unitarianism?

I have said. And now to conclude.

After my return to Europe many enquired if I was not the only living European who has found his way to the Head Quarters of the Moslem Faith. I may answer in the affirmative, so far at least that when entering the penetralia of Moslem life my Eastern origin was never questioned, and my position was never what some would describe as "in loco apostatæ."

On the other hand any Jew, Christian or Pagan, after declaring before the Kazi and the Police Authorities at Cairo, or even at Damascus, that he embraces El Islam, may perform without fear of the so-called Mosaic institution "El Sunnah" his pilgrimage in all safety. It might be dangerous to travel down the desert line between Meccah and El Medinah during times of popular excitement; but the coast route is always safe. To the "new Moslem" however the old Moslem is rarely well affected; and the former, as a rule, returns home unpleasantly impressed by his experiences.

The Eastern world moves slowly "eppur si muove." Half a generation ago steamers were first started to Jeddah: now we hear of a railroad from that port to Meccah, the shareholders being all Moslems. And the example of Jerusalem encourages to hope that long before the end of the century a visit to Meccah will not be more difficult than a trip to Hebron. I shall have more to say upon this subject when writing about Damascus.

Ziyadeh hadd i adab.

RICHARD F. BURTON.

Trieste, 1873.

الحاج عباده

CONTENTS

OF THE FIRST VOLUME.

	Page
CHAPTER I.	
To Alexandria. A Few Words concerning what compelled me to a Pilgrimage	1
CHAPTER II.	
I leave Alexandria	16
CHAPTER III.	
The Little Asthmatic	29
CHAPTER IV.	
Life in the Wakaleh	42
CHAPTER V.	
The Ramazan	73
CHAPTER VI.	
The Mosque	88
CHAPTER VII.	
Preparations to quit Cairo	107
CHAPTER VIII.	
From Cairo to Suez	134
CHAPTER IX.	
Suez	153
CHAPTER X.	
The Pilgrim Ship	178

CONTENTS.

CHAPTER XI.
To Yambu' 200

CHAPTER XII.
The Halt at Yambu' 220

CHAPTER XIII.
From Yambu' to Bir Abbas 236

CHAPTER XIV.
From Bir Abbas to El Medinah 257

A PILGRIMAGE TO MECCA AND MEDINA.

CHAPTER I.
To Alexandria.

A few Words concerning what induced me to a Pilgrimage.

IN the autumn of 1852, through the medium of my excellent friend, the late General Monteith, I offered my services to the Royal Geographical Society of London, for the purpose of removing that opprobrium to modern adventure, the huge white blot which in our maps still notes the Eastern and the Central regions of Arabia. Sir Roderick I. Murchison, Colonel P. Yorke and Dr. Shaw, a deputation from that distinguished body, with their usual zeal for discovery and readiness to encourage the discoverer, honored me by warmly supporting, in a personal interview with the then Chairman of the then Court of Directors to the then Honorable East India Company, my application for three years' leave of absence on special duty from India to Muscat. But they were unable to prevail upon the said Chairman, Sir James Hogg, who, much disliking, if report spoke truly, my impolitic habit of telling political truths, and not unwilling to mortify my supporter, his colleague, Colonel W. Sykes, refused his sanction, alleging as a no-reason that the contemplated journey was of too dangerous a nature. In compensation, however, for the disappointment, I was allowed the additional furlough of a year, in order to pursue my Arabic studies in lands where the language is best learned.

What remained for me but to prove, by trial, that what might be perilous to other travellers was safe to me? The "experimentum crucis" was a visit to El Hejaz, at once the most difficult and the most dangerous point by which a European can enter Arabia. I had intended, had the period of leave originally applied for been granted, to land at Muscat—a favourable starting-place—and there to apply myself, slowly and surely, to the task of spanning the deserts. But now I was to hurry, in the midst of summer, after a four years' sojourn in Europe, during which many things Oriental had faded from my memory, and—after passing through the ordeal of Egypt, a country where the police is curious as in Rome or Milan—to begin with the Moslem's Holy Land, the jealously guarded and exclusive Haram. However, being liberally supplied with the sinews of travel by the Royal Geographical Society; thoroughly tired of "progress" and of "civilisation;" curious to see with my eyes what others are content to "hear with ears," namely, Moslem inner life in a really Mohammedan country; and longing, if truth be told, to set foot on that mysterious spot which no vacation tourist has yet described, measured, sketched and photographed, I resolved to resume my old character of a wandering "Dervish," and to make the attempt.

The principal object with which I started was this: —To cross the unknown Arabian Peninsula, in a direct line from either El Medinah to Muscat, or diagonally from Meccah to Makallah on the Indian Ocean. By what "circumstance, the miscreator" my plans were defeated, the reader will discover in the course of these volumes. The secondary objects were numerous. I was desirous to find out if any market for horses could be opened between Central Arabia and India, where the studs were beginning to excite general dissatisfaction; to obtain information concerning the Great Eastern wilderness, the vast expanse marked Ruba el Khali (the "Empty Abode") in our maps; to inquire into the hydrography of the Hejaz; its water-shed, the disputed slope of the country, and the existence or non-existence of perennial streams; and finally, to try, by actual observation, the truth of a theory proposed by Colonel W. Sykes, namely, that if tradition be true, in the population of the vast Peninsula there must exist certain physiological differences sufficient to warrant our questioning the common origin of the Arab family. As regards horses, I am satisfied that from the Eastern coast something might be done,— nothing on the Western, where the animals, though thorough-bred, are mere "weeds," of a foolish price and procurable only by chance. Of the Ruba el Khali I have heard enough, from credible relators, to conclude that its horrid depths swarm with a large and half-starving population; that it abounds in Wadys, valleys, gullies and ravines, partially fertilised by intermittent torrents; and therefore, that the land is open to the adventurous traveller. Moreover, I am satisfied, that in spite of all geographers, from Ptolemy to Jomard, Arabia, which abounds in Nullahs or Fiumaras, possesses not a single perennial stream worthy the name of river; and the testimony of the natives induces me to think, with Wallin, contrary to Ritter and others, that the Peninsula falls instead of rising towards the south. Finally, I have found proof, to be produced in a future part of this publication, for believing in three distinct races. 1. The aborigines of the country, driven, like the Bhíls and other autochthonic Indians, into the eastern and south-eastern wilds bordering upon the ocean. 2. A Syrian or Mesopotamian stock, typified by Shem and Joktan, that drove the Indigenæ from the choicest tracts of country; these invaders still enjoy their conquests, representing the great Arabian people. And 3. An impure Egypto-Arab clan —we personify it by Ishmael, his son Nebajoth and Edom (Esau, the son of Isaac)—that populated and still populates the Sinaitic Peninsula. And in most places, even in the heart of Meccah, I met with debris of heathenry, proscribed by Mohammed, yet still popular, though the ignorant observers of the old customs assign to them a modern and a rationalistic origin.

I have entitled this account of my summer's tour through El Hejaz, a Personal Narrative, and I have laboured to make its nature correspond with its name, simply because "it is the personal that interests mankind." Many may not follow my example; but some perchance will be curious to see what measures I adopted, in order to appear suddenly as an Eastern upon the stage of Oriental life; and as the recital may be found useful by future adventurers, I make no apology for the egotistical semblance of the narrative. Those who have felt the want of some "silent friend" to aid them with advice, when it must not be asked, will appreciate what may appear to the uninterested critic mere outpourings of a mind full of self.

On the evening of April 3, 1853, I left London for Southampton. By the advice of a brother officer —little thought at that time the adviser or the advised how valuable was the suggestion!—my Eastern dress was called into requisition before leaving town, and all my "impedimenta" were taught to look exceedingly Oriental. Early the next day a "Persian Prince," accompanied by Captain Henry Grindlay of the Bengal Cavalry, embarked on board the Peninsular and Oriental Company's magnificent screw steamer "Bengal."

A fortnight was profitably spent in getting into the train of Oriental manners. For what polite Chesterfield says of the difference between a gentleman and his reverse,—namely, that both perform the same offices of life, but each in a several and widely different way —is notably as applicable to the manners of the

Eastern as of the Western man. Look, for instance, at that Indian Moslem drinking a glass of water. With us the operation is simple enough, but his performance includes no less than five novelties. In the first place, he clutches his tumbler as though it were the throat of a foe; secondly, he ejaculates, "In the name of Allah the Compassionate, the Merciful!" before wetting his lips; thirdly, he imbibes the contents, swallowing them, not sipping them as he ought to do, and ending with a satisfied grunt; fourthly, before setting down the cup, he sighs forth, "Praise be to Allah!"—of which you will understand the full meaning in the Desert; and, fifthly, he replies, "May Allah make it pleasant to thee!" in answer to his friend's polite "Pleasurably and health!" Also he is careful to avoid the irreligious action of drinking the pure element in a standing position, mindful, however, of the three recognised exceptions, the fluid of the Holy Well Zem Zem, water distributed in charity, and that which remains after Wuzu, the lesser ablution. Moreover, in Europe, where both extremities are used indiscriminately, one forgets the use of the right hand, the manipulation of the rosary, the abuse of the chair,—your genuine Oriental gathers up his legs, looking almost as comfortable in it as a sailor upon the back of a high-trotting horse—the rolling gait with the toes straight to the front, the grave look and the habit of pious ejaculations.

Our voyage over the "summer sea" was eventless. In a steamer of two or three thousand tons you discover the once dreaded, now contemptible, "stormy waters" only by the band—a standing nuisance be it remarked—performing

> "There we lay
> All the day,
> In the Bay of Biscay, O!"

The sight of glorious Trafalgar excites none of the sentiments with which a tedious sail used to invest it. "Gib" is, probably, better known to you, by Theo. Gautier and Warburton, than the regions about Cornhill; besides which, you anchor under the Rock exactly long enough to land and to breakfast. Malta, too, wears an old familiar face, which bids you order a dinner and superintend the iceing of claret (beginning of Oriental barbarism), instead of galloping about on donkey-back through fiery air in memory of St. Paul and White-Cross Knights.

But though our journey was monotonous, there was nothing to complain of. The ship was in every way comfortable; the cook, strange to say, was good, and the voyage lasted long enough, and not too long. On the evening of the thirteenth day after our start, the big-trowsered pilot, so lovely in his deformities to western eyes, made his appearance, and the good screw "Bengal" found herself at anchor off the Headland of Figs—the promontory upon which immortal Pharos once stood.

Having been invited to start from the house of a kind friend, John Larking, I disembarked with him, and rejoiced to see that by dint of a beard and a shaven head I had succeeded, like the Lord of Geesh, in "misleading the inquisitive spirit of the populace." The mingled herd of spectators before whom we passed in review on the landing-place, hearing an audible "Alhamdulillah" (praise be to Allah, Lord of the [three] worlds!) whispered "Muslim!" The infant population spared me the compliments usually addressed to hatted heads; and when a little boy, presuming that the occasion might possibly open the hand of generosity, looked in my face and exclaimed "Bakhshish" (largesse!) he obtained in reply a "Mafish" (not a—bless!) which convinced the bystanders that the sheep-skin covered a real sheep. We then mounted a carriage, fought our way through the donkeys, and in half an hour found ourselves, chibouque in mouth and coffee-cup in hand, seated on the divan of my friend's hospitable home.

Wonderful was the contrast between the steamer and that villa on the Mahmudiyah canal! Startling the sudden change from presto to adagio life! In thirteen days we had passed from the clammy grey fog, that atmosphere of industry which kept us at anchor off the Isle of Wight, through the liveliest air of the Inland Sea, whose sparkling blue and purple haze spread charms even on N. Africa's beldame features, and now we are sitting silent and still, listening to the monotonous melody of the East—the soft night-breeze wandering through starlit skies and tufted trees, with a voice of melancholy meaning.

And this is the Arab's "Kayf." The savouring of animal existence; the passive enjoyment of mere sense;

the pleasant languor, the dreamy tranquillity, the airy castle-building, which in Asia stand in lieu of the vigorous, intensive, passionate life of Europe. It is the result of a lively, impressible, excitable nature, and exquisite sensibility of nerve; it argues a facility for voluptuousness unknown to northern regions, where happiness is placed in the exertion of mental and physical powers; where "Ernst ist das Leben;" where niggard earth commands ceaseless sweat of brow, and damp chill air demands perpetual excitement, exercise, or change, or adventure, or dissipation, for lack of something better. In the East, man wants but rest and shade: upon the bank of a bubbling stream, or under the cool shelter of a perfumed tree; he is perfectly happy, smoking a pipe, or sipping a cup of coffee, or drinking a glass of sherbet, but above all things deranging body and mind as little as possible; the trouble of conversations, the displeasures of memory, and the vanity of thought being the most unpleasant interruptions to his "Kayf." No wonder that "Kayf" is a word untranslatable in our mother-tongue!

* * * * * *

"Laudabunt alli claram Rhodon aut Mitylenen."

Let others describe this once famous Capital of Egypt, the City of Misnomers, whose dry docks are ever wet, and whose marble fountain is eternally dry, whose "Cleopatra's Needle" is not Cleopatra's; whose "Pompey's Pillar" never had any connection with Pompey; and whose Cleopatra's Baths are, according to veracious travellers, no baths at all. Yet is it a wonderful place, this "Libyan suburb" of our day, this outpost of civilisation planted upon the skirts of barbarism, this Osiris seated side by side with Typho, his great old enemy. Still may be said of it, "it ever beareth something new;" and Alexandria, a threadbare subject in Bruce's time, is even yet, from its perpetual changes, a fit field for modern description.

The better to blind the inquisitive eyes of servants and visitors, my friend Larking lodged me in an outhouse, where I could revel in the utmost freedom of life and manners. And although some Armenian Dragoman, a restless spy like all his race, occasionally remarked that "voilà un Persan diablement dégagé," none, except those who were entrusted with the secret, had any idea of the part I was playing. The domestics, devout Moslems, pronounced me to be an Ajami, a Persian as opposed to an Arab, not a good Mohammedan like themselves, but, still, better than nothing. I lost no time in securing the assistance of a Shaykh or private tutor, and plunged once more into the intricacies of the Faith, revived my recollections of religious ablution, read the Koran, and again became an adept in the art of prostration. My leisure hours were employed in visiting the baths, and coffee-houses, in attending the bazars, and in shopping,—an operation which hereabouts consists of sitting upon a chapman's counter, smoking, sipping coffee, and telling your beads the while, to show that you are not of the slaves for whom time is made; in fact, in pitting your

patience against that of your adversary, the vendor.
I found time for a short excursion to a country village
on the banks of the canal; nor was an opportunity of
seeing "El-nahl," the Bee-dance, neglected, for it would
be some months before my eyes might dwell on such
pleasant spectacle again.

"Delicias videam, Nile jocose, tuas!"

Careful also of graver matters, I attended the
mosque, and visited the venerable localities in which
modern Alexandria abounds. Pilgrimaging Moslems
are here shown the tomb of El-nabi Daniyal (Daniel
the Prophet), discovered upon a spot where the late
Sultan Mahmud dreamed that he saw an ancient man
at prayer. Sikandar El-Rumi, a Moslem Alexander the
Great, of course left his bones in the place bearing
his name, or—as he ought to have done so—bones
have been found for him. Alexandria also boasts of
two celebrated Walis—holy men. One is Mohammed
El-Busiri, the author of a poem called El-Burdah,
universally read by the world of Islam, and locally
recited at funerals, and on other solemn occasions. The other is Abu Abbas El-Andalusi, a sage
and saint of the first water, at whose tomb prayer is
never breathed in vain.

It is not to be supposed that the people of
Alexandria could look upon my phials and pill-boxes,
without a yearning for their contents. An Indian
doctor, too, was a novelty to them; Franks they despised, but a man who had come so far from East and

West! Then there was something infinitely seducing in the character of a magician, doctor, and fakir, each admirable of itself, thus combined to make "great medicine." Men, women, and children besieged my door, by which means I could see the people face to face, and especially the fair sex, of which Europeans, generally speaking, know only the worst. Even respectable natives, after witnessing a performance of the Magic mirror, opined that the stranger was a holy man, gifted with supernatural powers, and knowing everything. One old person sent to offer me his daughter in marriage;—he said nothing about dowry, —but I thought proper to decline the honor. And a middle-aged lady proffered me the sum of 100 piastres, one Napoleon, if I would stay at Alexandria, and superintend the restoration of her blind left eye.

But the reader must not be led to suppose that I acted "Carabin," or "Sangrado" without any knowledge of my trade. From youth I have always been a dabbler in medical and mystical study. Moreover, the practice of physic is comparatively easy amongst dwellers in warm latitudes, uncivilised peoples, where there is not that complication of maladies which troubles more polished nations. And further, what simplifies extremely the treatment of the sick in these parts is, the undoubted periodicity of disease, reducing almost all to one type—ague. Hence the origin of the Chronothermal System, a discovery which physic owes to my old friend, the late Dr. Samuel Dickson.

Many of the complaints of tropical climates, as medical men well know, display palpably intermittent symptoms little known to colder countries; and speaking from individual experience, I may safely assert that in all cases of suffering, from a wound to ophthalmia, this phenomenon has forced itself into my notice. So much by way of excuse. I therefore considered myself as well qualified for the work as if I had taken out a "buono per l'estero" diploma at Padua, and not more likely to do active harm than most of the regularly graduated young surgeons who start to "finish themselves" upon the frame of the British soldier.

After a month's hard work at Alexandria, I prepared to assume the character of a wandering Dervish, after reforming my title from "Mirza," the Persian "Mister," to "Shaykh" Abdullah. Arab Christians sometimes take the name of servant of God—"which," as a modern traveller observes, "all sects and religions might be equally proud to adopt." The Moslem Prophet said, "the names most approved of God are, Abdullah, Abd-el-rahman (Slave of the Compassionate), and such like." A reverend man, whose name I do not care to quote, some time ago initiated me into his order, the Kadiriyah, under the high-sounding name of Bismillah-Shah—"King-in-the-name-of-Allah," a manner of Oriental "Praise-God-Barebones"—and, after a due period of probation, he graciously elevated me to the proud position of Murshid* or Master in the mystic

* A Murshid is one allowed to admit Murids or apprentices into the order.

craft. I was therefore sufficiently well acquainted with the tenets and practices of these Oriental Freemasons. No character in the Moslem world is so proper for disguise as that of the Dervish. It is assumed by all ranks, ages, and creeds; by the nobleman who has been disgraced at court, and by the peasant who is too idle to till the ground; by Dives, who is weary of life, and by Lazarus, who begs his bread from to door to door. Further, the Dervish is allowed to ignore ceremony and politeness, as one who ceases to appear upon the stage of life; he may pray or not, marry or remain single as he pleases, be respectable in cloth of frieze as in cloth of gold, and no one asks him—the chartered vagabond—Why he comes here? or Wherefore he goes there? He may wend his way on foot or alone, or ride his Arab mare followed by a dozen servants; he is equally feared without weapons, as swaggering through the streets armed to the teeth. The more haughty and offensive he is to the people, the more they respect him; a decided advantage to the traveller of choleric temperament. In the hour of imminent danger, he has only to become a maniac, and he is safe; a madman in the East, like a notably eccentric character in the West, is allowed to say or do whatever the spirit directs. Add to this character a little knowledge of medicine, a "moderate skill in magic and a reputation for caring for nothing but study and books," together with capital sufficient to save you from the chance of starving, and you appear in the East to peculiar advantage. The only danger of the "Mystic Path" which leads, or is supposed to lead, to heaven, is, that the Dervish's ragged coat not unfrequently covers the cut-throat, and, if seized in the society of such a "brother," you may reluctantly become his companion, under the stick or on the stake. For be it known, Dervishes are of two orders, the Sharai, or those who conform to religion, and the Bi-Sharai, or Luti, whose practices are hinted at by their own tradition that "he we daurna name" once joined them for a week, but at the end of that time left them in dismay, and returned to whence he came.

CHAPTER II.
I leave Alexandria.

THE thorough-bred wanderer's idiosyncrasy I presume to be a composition of what phrenologists call "inhabitiveness" and "locality" equally and largely developed. After a long and toilsome march, weary of the way, he drops into the nearest place of rest to become the most domestic of men. For awhile he smokes the "long pipe of permanence" with an infinite zest; he delights in various siestas during the day, relishing withal deep sleep through the dark hours; he enjoys dining at a fixed dinner-hour, and he wonders at the demoralisation of the mind which cannot find means of excitement in chit-chat or small talk, in a novel or a newspaper. But soon the passive fit has passed away; again a paroxysm of ennui coming on by slow degrees, Viator loses appetite, he walks about his room all night, he yawns at conversations, and a book acts upon him as a narcotic. The man wants to wander, and he must do so or he shall die.

After about a month most pleasantly spent at Alexandria, I perceived the approach of the enemy, and as nothing hampered my incomings and outgoings, I surrendered. The world was "all before me," and there was pleasant excitement in plunging single-handed into its chilling depths. My Alexandrian Shaykh, whose heart fell victim to a new "jubbah" or cloak of broad cloth, which I had given in exchange for his tattered "za'abut," woollen cloak, offered me, in consideration of a certain monthly stipend, the affections of a brother and religious refreshment, proposing to send his wife back to her papa, and to accompany me, in the capacity of private chaplain, to the other side of Kaf, the mountain that encircles the world. I politely accepted the "Bruderschaft," but many reasons induced me to decline his society and services. In the first place, he spoke the detestable Egyptian jargon. Secondly, it was but prudent to lose the "spoor" between Alexandria and Suez. And, thirdly, my "brother" had shifting eyes (symptoms of fickleness), close together (indices of cunning); a flat-crowned head, and large ill-fitting lips; signs which led me to think lightly of his honesty, firmness, and courage. Phrenology and physiognomy, be it observed, disappoint you often amongst civilised people, the proper action of whose brains upon the features is impeded by the external pressure of education, accident, example, habit, and necessity. But they are tolerably safe guides when groping your way through the mind of man in his so-called natural state, a being of impulse in that chrysalis state of mental development which is rather instinct than reason.

Before my departure, however, there was much to be done.

The land of the Pharaohs is becoming civilised, and unpleasantly so: nothing can be more uncomfortable than its present middle-state between barbarism and the reverse. The prohibition against carrying arms is rigid as in Italy; all "violence" is violently denounced, and beheading being deemed cruel, the most atrocious crimes, as well as those small political offences, which in the days of the Mamelukes would have led to a beyship or a bow-string, receive fourfold punishment by deportation to Faizoghli, the local Cayenne. If you order your peasant to be flogged, his friends gather in threatening hundreds at your gates; when you scold your boatman, he complains to your consul; the dragomans afflict you with strange wild notions about honesty; a government order prevents you from using vituperative language to the "natives" in general; and the very donkey boys are becoming cognisant of the right of man to remain unbastinadoed. Still the old leaven remains behind: here, as elsewhere in "Morning-land," you cannot hold your own without employing the *voie de fait*. The passport system, now dying out of Europe, has sprung up, or rather has revived in Egypt, with peculiar vigour. Its good effects claim for it our respect; still we cannot but lament its inconvenience. *We*, I mean real Easterns. As strangers—even those whose beards have whitened in the land—know absolutely nothing of what unfortunate natives must endure, I am tempted to subjoin a short sketch of my adventures in search of a Tezkirah, or passport, at Alexandria.

Through ignorance which might have cost me dear but for friend Larking's weight with the local authorities, I had neglected to provide myself with a passport in England, and it was not without difficulty, involving much unclean dressing and an unlimited expenditure of broken English, that I obtained from H. B. M's Consul at Alexandria a certificate, declaring me to be an Indo-British subject named Abdullah, by profession a doctor, aged thirty, and not distinguished—at least so the frequent blanks seemed to denote—by any remarkable conformation of eyes, nose, or cheek. For this I disbursed a dollar. And here let me record the indignation with which I did it. That mighty Britain —the mistress of the seas—the ruler of one-sixth of mankind—should charge five shillings to pay for the shadow of her protecting wing! That I cannot speak my modernised "civis sum Romanus" without putting my hand into my pocket, in order that these officers of the Great Queen may not take too ruinously from a revenue of 70 millions! O the meanness of our magnificence! the littleness of our greatness!

My new passport would not carry me without the Zabit or Police Magistrate's counter-signature, said H. B. M's Consul. Next day I went to the Zabit, who referred me to the Muhafiz (Governor) of Alexandria, at whose gate I had the honor of squatting at least three hours, till a more compassionate clerk vouchsafed the information that the proper place to apply to was the Diwan Kharijiyah (the Foreign-Office). Thus a second day was utterly lost. On the morning of the third I started, as directed, for the palace, which crowns the Headland of Figs. It is a huge and couthless shell of building in parallelogrammic form containing all kinds of public offices in glorious confusion, looking with their glaring whitewashed faces upon a central court, where a few leafless wind-wrung trees seem struggling for the breath of life in an eternal atmosphere of clay-dust and sun-blaze.

The first person I addressed was a Kawwas or police officer, who, coiled comfortably up in a bit of shade fitting his person like a robe, was in full enjoyment of the Asiatic "Kayf." Having presented the consular certificate and briefly stated the nature of my business, I ventured to inquire what was the right course to pursue for a visa.

They have little respect for Dervishes, it appears, at Alexandria!

M'adri—"Don't know," growled the man of authority without moving any thing but the quantity of tongue necessary for articulation.

Now there are three ways of treating Asiatic officials,—by bribe, by bullying, or by bothering them with a dogged perseverance into attending to you and your concerns. The latter is the peculiar province of the poor; moreover, this time I resolved, for other reasons, to be patient. I repeated my question in almost the same words. Ruh! "Be off," was what I obtained for all reply. But this time the questioned went so far as to open his eyes. Still I stood twirling the paper in my hands, and looking very humble and very persevering, till a loud Ruh ya Kalb! "Go, O dog!" converted into a responsive curse the little speech I was preparing about the brotherhood of El-Islam and the mutual duties obligatory on true believers. I then turned away slowly and fiercely, for the next thing might have been a cut with the Kurbaj or *cravache* of hippopotamus hide, and, by the hammer of Thor! British flesh and blood could never have stood *that*.

After which satisfactory scene,—for satisfactory it was in one sense, proving the complete fitness of the Dervish's costume,—I tried a dozen other promiscuous sources of information,—policemen, grooms, scribes, donkey boys, and idlers in general. At length, wearied of patience, I offered a soldier some pinches of tobacco, and promised him an oriental sixpence if he would manage the business for me. The man was interested by the tobacco and the pence; he took my hand, and inquiring the while he went along, led me from place to place, till, mounting a grand staircase, I stood in the presence of Abbas Effendi, Naib or deputy to the Governor.

It was a little, whey-faced, black-bearded Turk, coiled up in the usual conglomerate posture upon a calico-covered divan, at the end of a long bare large-windowed room. Without deigning even to nod the head, which hung over his shoulder with transcendent listlessness and affectation of pride, in answer to my salams and benedictions, he eyed me with wicked eyes, and faintly ejaculated "Min ent?" for "man anta?" who art thou? Then hearing that I was a Dervish and doctor—he must be an Osmanli Voltairian, that little Turk—the official snorted a contemptuous snort. He condescendingly added, however, that the proper source to seek was "Taht," which meaning simply "below," conveyed to an utter stranger rather imperfect information in a topographical point of view.

At length, however, my soldier guide found out that a room in the custom-house bore the honorable appellation of "Foreign Office." Accordingly I went there, and, after sitting at least a couple of hours at the bolted door in the noon-day sun, was told, with a fury which made me think I had sinned, that the officer in whose charge the department was, had been presented with an olive branch in the morning, and consequently that business was not to be done that day. The angry-faced official communicated the intelligence to a large group of Anadolian, Caramanian, Boshniac, and Roumelian Turks,—sturdy, undersized, broad-shouldered, bare-legged, splay-footed, horny-fisted, dark-browed, honest-looking mountaineers, who were lounging about with long pistols and yataghans stuck in their broad sashes, head-gear composed of immense tarbooshes with proportionate turbans coiled round them, and two or three suits of substantial clothes, even at this season of the year, upon their shoulders. Like myself they had waited some hours, but they were not so patient under disappointment: they bluntly told the angry official that he and his master were a pair of idlers, and the curses that rumbled and gurgled in their hairy throats as they strode towards the door, sounded like the growling of wild beasts.

Thus was another day truly orientally lost. On the morrow, however, I obtained permission, in the character of Dr. Abdullah, to visit any part of Egypt I pleased, and to retain possession of my dagger and pistols.

And now I must explain what induced me to take so much trouble about a passport. The home reader naturally inquires, why not travel under your English name?

For this reason. In the generality of barbarous countries you must either proceed, like Bruce, preserving the "dignity of manhood," and carrying matters with a high hand, or you must worm your way by timidity and subservience; in fact, by becoming an animal too contemptible for man to let or injure. But to pass through the Holy Land, you must either be a born believer, or have become one; in the former case you may demean yourself as you please, in the latter a path is ready prepared for you. My spirit could not bend to own myself a Burmah, a renegade—to be pointed at and shunned and catechised, an object of suspicion to the many and of contempt to all. Moreover, it would have obstructed the aim of my wanderings. The convert is always watched with Argus eyes, and men do not willingly give information to a "new Moslem," especially a Frank: they suspect his conversion to be feigned or forced, look upon him as a spy, and let him see as little of life as possible. Firmly as was my heart set upon travelling in Arabia, by Heaven! I would have given up the dear project rather than purchase a doubtful and partial success at such a price. Consequently, I had no choice but to appear as a born believer, and part of my birthright in that respectable character was toil and trouble in obtaining a Tezkirah.*

Then I had to provide myself with certain necessaries for the way. These were not numerous. The silver-mounted dressing-case is here supplied by a rag containing a Miswak or tooth-stick, a bit of soap and a comb, wooden, for bone and tortoiseshell are not, religiously speaking, correct. Equally simple was my wardrobe; a change or two of clothing. It is a great mistake to carry too few clothes, and those who travel as Orientals should always have at least one very grand suit on critical occasions. Throughout the East a badly dressed man is a pauper, and, as in England, a pauper—unless he belongs to an order having a right to be poor—is a scoundrel. The only article of canteen description was a Zemzemiyeh, a goat-skin water-bag, which, especially when new, communicates to its contents a ferruginous aspect and a wholesome, though hardly an attractive, flavour of tanno-gelatine. This was a necessary; to drink out of a tumbler, possibly fresh from pig-eating lips, would have entailed a certain loss of reputation. For bedding and furniture I had a coarse Persian rug—which, besides being couch, acted as chair, table, and oratory—a cotton-stuffed chintz-covered pillow, a blanket in case of cold, and a sheet, which did duty for tent and mosquito curtains

* During my journey, and since my return, some Indian papers conducted by jocose editors made merry upon an Englishman "turning Turk." Once for all, I beg leave to point above for the facts of the case; it must serve as a general answer to any pleasant little fictions which may hereafter appear.

in nights of heat. Almost all Easterns sleep under a cloth, which becomes a kind of respirator, defending them from the dews and mosquitos by night and the flies by day. The "rough and ready" traveller will learn to follow the example, remembering that "Nature is founder of Customs in savage countries;" whereas, amongst the soi-disant civilised, Nature has no deadlier enemy than Custom. As shade is a convenience not always procurable, another necessary was a huge cotton umbrella of Eastern make, brightly yellow, suggesting the idea of an overgrown marigold. I had also a substantial housewife, the gift of a kind relative Miss Elizabeth Stisted; it was a roll of canvas, carefully soiled, and garnished with needles and thread, cobblers'-wax, buttons, and other such articles. These things were most useful in lands where tailors abound not; besides which, the sight of a man darning his coat or patching his slippers teems with pleasing ideas of humility. A dagger, a brass inkstand and pen-holder stuck in the belt, and a mighty rosary, which on occasion might have been converted into a weapon of offence, completed my equipment. I must not omit to mention the proper method of carrying money, which in these lands should never be entrusted to box or bag. A common cotton purse secured in a breast pocket, (for Egypt now abounds in that civilised animal the pickpocket,) contained silver pieces and small change. My gold, of which I carried twenty-five sovereigns, and papers, were committed to a substantial leathern belt of Maghrabi manufacture, made to be strapped round the waist under the dress. This is the Asiatic method of concealing valuables, and one more civilised than ours in the last century, when Roderic Random and his companion, "sewed their money between the lining and the waistband of their breeches, except some loose silver for immediate expense on the road." The great inconvenience of the belt is its weight, especially where dollars must be carried, as in Arabia, causing chafes and discomfort at night. Moreover, it can scarcely be called safe. In dangerous countries wary travellers will adopt surer precautions. Some prefer a long chain of pure gold divided into links and covered with leather, so as to resemble the twisted girdle which the Arab fastens round his waist. It is a precaution well known to the wandering knights of old.

A pair of common native Khúrjin or saddle-bags contained my wardrobe, the bed was readily rolled up into a bundle, and for a medicine chest I bought a pea-green box with red and yellow flowers, capable of standing falls from a camel twice a day.

The next step was to find out when the local steamer would start for Cairo, and accordingly I betook myself to the Transit Office. No vessel was advertised; I was directed to call every evening till satisfied. At last the fortunate event took place: a "weekly departure," which, by the by, occurred once every fortnight or so, was in orders for the next day. I hurried to the office, but did not reach it till past noon—the hour of idleness. A little, dark gentleman—Mr. G.

—so formed and dressed as exactly to resemble a liver-and-tan bull-terrier, who with his heels on the table was dozing, cigar in mouth, over the last "Galignani," positively refused, after a time,—for at first he would not speak at all,—to let me take my passage till three P.M. I inquired when the boat started, upon which he referred me, as I had spoken bad Italian, to the advertisement. I pleaded inability to read or write, whereupon he testily cried "Alle nove! alle nove!"—at nine! at nine! Still appearing uncertain, I drove him out of his chair, when he rose with a curse and read 8 A.M. An unhappy Eastern, depending upon what he said, would have been precisely one hour too late.

Thus were we lapsing into the real good old East-Indian style of doing business. Thus Anglo-Indicus orders his first clerk to execute some commission; the senior, having "work" upon his hands, sends a junior; the junior finds the sun hot, and passes on the word to a "peon;" the "peon" charges a porter with the errand, and the porter quietly sits or dozes in his place, trusting that Fate will bring him out of the scrape, but firmly resolved, though the shattered globe fall, not to stir an inch.

The reader, I must again express a hope, will pardon the egotism of these descriptions,—my object is to show him how business is carried on in these hot countries. Business generally. For had I not been Abdullah the Dervish, but a rich native merchant, it would have been the same. How many complaints of similar treatment have I heard in different parts of the Eastern world! and how little can one realise them without having actually experienced the evil! For the future I shall never see a "nigger" squatting away half a dozen mortal hours in a broiling sun patiently waiting for something or for some one, without a lively remembrance of my own cooling of the calces at the custom-house of Alexandria.

At length, about the end of May (1853) all was ready. Not without a feeling of regret I left my little room among the white myrtle blossoms and the rosy oleander flowers with the almond smell. I kissed with humble ostentation my good host's hand in presence of his servants,—he had become somewhat unpleasantly anxious, of late, to induce in me the true Oriental feeling, by a slight administration of the bastinade—I bade adieu to my patients, who now amounted to about fifty, shaking hands with all meekly and with religious equality of attention, and, mounted in a "trap" which looked like a cross between a wheel-barrow and a dog-cart, drawn by a kicking, jibbing, and biting mule, I set out for the steamer, the "Little Asthmatic."

CHAPTER III.

The Little Asthmatic.

In the days of the Pitts we have invariably a "Relation" of Egyptian travellers who embark for a place called "Roseet" on the "River Nilus." Wanderers of the Brucean age were wont to record their impressions of voyage upon land subjects observed between Alexandria and Cairo. A little later we find every one inditing rhapsodies about, and descriptions of, his or her Dahabiyeh (barge) on the canal. After this came the steamer. And after the steamer will come the railroad, which may disappoint the author tourist, but will be delightful to that class of men who wish to get over the greatest extent of ground with the least inconvenience to themselves and others. Then shall the Mahmudiyeh—ugliest and most wearisome of canals—be given up to cotton boats and grain barges, and then will note-books and the headings of chapters clean ignore its existence.

I saw the canal at its worst, when the water was low: I have not one syllable to say in its favour. Instead of thirty hours, we took three mortal days and nights to reach Cairo, and we grounded with painful regularity four or five times between sunrise and sunset. In the scenery on the banks sketchers and describers have left you nought to see. From Pompey's Pillar to the Maison Carrée, Kariom and its potteries, El Birkah of the night birds, Bastarah with the alleys of trees, even unto Atfeh, all things are perfectly familiar to us, and have been so years before the traveller actually sees them. The Nil el Mubarak itself—the Blessed Nile,—as notably fails too at this season to arouse enthusiasm. You see nothing but muddy waters, dusty banks, a sand mist, a milky sky, and a glaring sun: you feel nought but a breeze like the blast from a potter's furnace. You can only just distinguish through a veil of reeking vapours the village Shibr Katt from the village Kafr el Zayyat, and you steam too far from Wardan town to enjoy the Timonic satisfaction of enraging its male population with "Haykall ya ibn Haykall"—O Haykal! O son of Haykal! "Haykal" was a pleasant fellow, who, having basely abused the confidence of the fair ones of Wardan, described their charms in sarcastic verse, and stuck his scroll upon the door of the village mosque, taking at the same time the wise precaution to change his lodgings without delay. The very mention of his name affronts the brave Wardanenses to the last extent, making them savage as Oxford bargees. You are nearly wrecked, as a matter of course, at the Barrage; and you are certainly dumbfounded by the sight of its ugly little Gothic crenelles. The Pyramids of Cheops and Cephren, "rearing their majestic heads above the margin of the Desert," only suggest of remark that they have been remarkably well-sketched; and thus you proceed till with a real feeling of satisfaction you moor alongside of the tumble-down old suburb, "Bulak."

To me there was double dulness in the scenery: it seemed to be Sind over again—the same morning mist and noon-tide glare; the same hot wind and heat clouds, and fiery sunset, and evening glow; the same pillars of dust and "devils" of sand sweeping like giants over the plain; the same turbid waters of a broad, shallow stream studded with sand-banks and silt-isles, with crashing earth slips and ruins nodding over a kind of cliff, whose base the stream gnaws with noisy tooth. On the banks, saline ground sparkled and glittered like hoar-frost in the sun; and here and there mud villages, solitary huts, pigeon-towers, or watch turrets, whence little brown boys shouted and slung stones at the birds, peeped out from among bright green patches of palm-tree, tamarisk, and mimosa; maize, tobacco, and sugar-cane. Beyond the narrow tongue of land on the river banks lay the glaring, yellow desert, with its low hills and sand slopes bounded by innumerable pyramids of Nature's architecture. The boats, with their sharp bows, preposterous sterns, and lateen sails, might have belonged to the Indus. So might the chocolate-skinned, blue-robed peasantry; the women carrying progeny on their hips, with the eternal waterpot on their heads; and the men sleeping in the shade, or following the plough, to which probably Osiris first put hand. The lower animals, like the higher, are the same; gaunt, mange-stained camels, muddy buffaloes, scurvied donkeys, sneaking jackals, and fox-like dogs. Even the feathered creatures were perfectly familiar to my eye

—paddy birds, pelicans, giant cranes, kites, and wild water-fowl.

I had taken a third-class or deck passage, whereby the evils of the journey were exasperated. A roasting sun pierced the canvas awning like hot water through a gauze veil, and by night the cold dews fell raw and thick as a Scotch mist. The cooking was abominable, and the dignity of Dervish-hood did not allow me to sit at meat with Infidels or to eat the food which they had polluted. So the Dervish squatted apart, smoking perpetually, with occasional interruptions to say his prayers and to tell his beads upon the mighty rosary; and he drank the muddy water of the canal out of a leathern bucket, and he munched his bread and garlic with a desperate sanctimoniousness. Those skilled in simples, Eastern as well as Western, praise garlic highly, declaring that it "strengthens the body, prepares the constitution for fatigue, brightens the sight, and, by increasing the digestive power, obviates the ill effects arising from sudden change of air and water." The traveller inserts it into his dietary in some pleasant form, as "Provence-butter," because he observes that, wherever fever and ague abound, the people, ignorant of cause but observant of effect, make it a common article of food. The old Egyptians highly esteemed this vegetable, which, with onions and leeks, enters into the list of articles so much regretted by the Hebrews (Numbers, xi. 5.; Koran, chap. 2.). The modern people of the Nile, like the Spaniards, delight in onions, which, as they contain between 25 and

30 per cent. of gluten, are highly nutritive. In Arabia, however, the stranger must use this vegetable sparingly. The city people despise it as the food of a Fellah—a boor. The Wahhabis have a prejudice against onions, leeks, and garlic, because the Prophet disliked their strong smell, and all strict Moslems refuse to eat them immediately before visiting the mosque or meeting for public prayer.

The "Little Asthmatic" was densely crowded, and discipline not daring to mark out particular places, the scene on board of her was motley enough. There were two Indian officers, who naturally spoke to none but each other, drank bad tea, and smoked their cigars, exclusively like Britons. A troop of Kurd policemen, escorting treasure, was surrounded by a group of noisy Greeks; these men's gross practical jokes sounding anything but pleasant to the solemn Moslems, whose saddle-bags and furniture were at every moment in danger of being defiled by abominable drinks and the ejected juices of tobacco. There was one pretty woman on board, a Spanish girl, who looked strangely misplaced—a rose in a field of thistles. Some silent Italians, with noisy interpreters, sat staidly upon the benches. It was soon found out, through the communicative dragoman, that their business was to buy horses for H. M. of Sardinia: they were exposed to a volley of questions delivered by a party of French tradesmen returning to Cairo, but they shielded themselves and fought shy with Machiavellian dexterity. Besides these was a German—a "beer-bottle in the morning and a bottle of beer in the evening," to borrow a simile from his own nation—a Syrian merchant, the richest and ugliest of Alexandria, and a few French house-painters going to decorate the Pasha's palace at Shoobra. These last were the happiest of our voyagers, veritable children of Paris, Montagnards, Voltairiens, and thorough-bred Sans-Soucis. All day they sat upon deck chattering as only their lively nation can chatter, indulging in ultra-gallic maxims, such as "on ne vieillit jamais à table;" now playing écarté for love or nothing, then composing "des ponches un peu chiques;" now reciting adventures of the category "Mirabolant," then singing, then dancing, then sleeping and rising to play, to drink, talk, dance, and sing again. One chaunted:

> "Je n'ai pas connu mon père,
> Ce respectable vieillard;
> Je suis né trois ans trop tard, &c."

Whilst another trolled out:

> "Qu'est ce que je vois?
> Un canard en robe de chambre!"

They, being new comers, free from the disease morgue so soon caught by Oriental Europeans, were particularly civil to me, even wishing to mix me a strong draught; I was not so fortunate, however, with all on board. A large shopkeeper threatened to "briser" my "figure" for putting my pipe near his pantaloons; but seeing me finger my dagger curiously, though I did not shift my pipe, he forgot to remember his threat. I had taken charge of a parcel for one M. P——, a student of Coptic, and remitted it to him on board;

of this little service the only acknowledgment was a stare and a petulant inquiry why I had not given it to him before. And one of the Englishmen, half publicly, half privily, as though communing with himself, condemned my organs of vision because I happened to touch his elbow. He was a man in my own service; I pardoned him in consideration of the compliment paid to my disguise.

Two fellow-passengers were destined to play an important part in my comedy of Cairo. Just after we had started, a little event afforded us some amusement. On the bank appeared a short, crummy, pursy kind of man, whose efforts to board the steamer were notably ridiculous. With attention divided between the vessel and a carpet-bag carried by his donkey boy, he ran along the sides of the canal, now stumbling into hollows, then climbing heights, then standing shouting upon the projections with the fierce sun upon his back, till every one thought his breath was completely gone. But no! game to the back-bone, he would have perished miserably rather than lose his fare: "perseverance," say the copy-books, "accomplishes great things:" at last he was taken on board, and presently he lay down to sleep. His sooty complexion, lank black hair, features in which appeared beaucoup de finesse, that is to say, abundant rascality; an eternal smile and treacherous eyes; his gold ring, dress of showy colours, fleshy stomach, fat legs, round back and a peculiar manner of frowning and fawning simultaneously, marked him an Indian. When he awoke he introduced himself to me as Miyan Khudabakhsh Namdar, a native of Lahore: he had carried on the trade of a shawl merchant in London and Paris, where he had lived two years, and after a pilgrimage intended to purge away the sins of civilised lands, he had settled at Cairo.

My second friend, Haji Wali, I will introduce to the reader in a future chapter.

Long conversations in Persian and Hindostani abridged the tediousness of the voyage, and when we arrived at Bulak, the polite Khudabakhsh insisted upon my making his house my home. I was unwilling to accept the man's civility, disliking his looks, but he advanced cogent reasons for changing my mind. His servants cleared my luggage through the custom-house, and a few minutes after our arrival I found myself in his abode near the Ezbekiyeh Gardens, sitting in a cool Mashrabiyah—the projecting latticed window of richly-carved wood, for which Cairo was once so famous —that gracefully projected over a garden, and sipping the favourite glass of pomegranate syrup.

As the Wakalehs or caravanserais were at that time full of pilgrims, I remained with Khudabakhsh ten days or a fortnight. But at the end of that time my patience was thoroughly exhausted. My host had become a civilised man, who sat on chairs, who ate with a fork, who talked European politics, and who had learned to admire, if not to understand liberty—liberal ideas! and was I not flying from such things? Besides which, we English have a peculiar national quality, which the Indians, with their characteristic acuteness, soon perceived, and described by an opprobrious name. Observing our solitary habits, that we could not, and would not, sit and talk and sip sherbet and smoke with them, they called us "Jangli"—wild men, fresh caught in the jungle and sent to rule over the land of Hind. Certainly nothing suits us less than perpetual society, an utter want of solitude, when one cannot retire into oneself an instant without being asked some puerile question by a companion, or look into a book without a servant peering over one's shoulder; when from the hour you rise to the time you rest, you must ever be talking or listening, you must converse yourself to sleep in a public dormitory, and give ear to your companion's snores and mutterings at midnight.

The very essence of Oriental hospitality, however, is this family style of reception, which costs your host neither money nor trouble. You make one more at his eating tray, and an additional mattress appears in the sleeping-room. When you depart, you leave if you like a little present, merely for a memorial, with your entertainer; he would be offended if you offered it him openly as a remuneration, and you give some trifling sums to the servants. Thus you will be welcome wherever you go. If perchance you are detained perforce in such a situation,—which may easily happen to you, medical man,—you have only to make yourself as disagreeable as possible, by calling for all manner of impossible things. Shame is a passion with

Eastern nations. Your host would blush to point out to you the indecorum of your conduct; and the laws of hospitality oblige him to supply the every want of a guest, even though he be a détenu.

But of all orientals, the most antipathetical companion to an Englishman is, I believe, an East-Indian. Like the fox in the fable, fulsomely flattering at first, he gradually becomes easily friendly, disagreeably familiar, offensively rude—which ends by rousing the "spirit of the British lion." Nothing delights the Hindi so much as an opportunity of safely venting the spleen with which he regards his victors.* He will sit in the presence of a magistrate, or an officer, the very picture of cringing submissiveness. But after leaving the room, he is as different from his former self as a counsel in

---

* The Calcutta Review (No. 41.), noticing "L'Inde sous la Domination Anglaise," by the Baron Barchou de Penhoën, delivers the following sentiment: "Whoever states, as the Baron B. de P. states and repeats again and again, that the natives generally entertain a bad opinion of the Europeans generally, states what is decidedly untrue."

The reader will observe that I differ as decidedly from the Reviewer's opinion. Popular feeling towards the English in India was "at first one of fear, afterwards of horror: Hindoos and Moslems considered the strangers a set of cow-eaters and fire-drinkers, tetræ belluæ ac molossis suis ferociores, who would fight like Eblis, cheat their own fathers, and exchange with the same readiness a broadside of shots and thrusts of boarding-pikes, or a bale of goods and a bag of rupees." (The English in Western India.) We have risen in a degree above such low standard of estimation; still, incredible as it may appear to the Frank himself, it is no less true, that the Frank everywhere in the East is considered a contemptible being, and dangerous withal. As regards Indian opinion concerning our government, my belief is, that in and immediately about the three presidencies, where the people owe every thing to and hold every thing by our rule, it is popular. At the same time I am convinced that in other places the people would most willingly hail any change. And how can we hope it to be otherwise,—we, a nation of strangers, aliens to the country's customs and creed, who, even while resident in India, act the part which absentees do in other lands? Where, in the history of the world, do we read that such foreign dominion ever made itself loved?

court from a counsel at a concert, a sea captain at a club dinner from a sea captain on his quarter deck. Then he will discover that the English are not brave, nor clever, nor generous, nor civilised, nor anything but surpassing rogues; that every official takes bribes, that their manners are utterly offensive, and that they are rank infidels. Then he will descant complacently upon the probability of a general Bartholomew's day in the East, and look forward to the hour when enlightened young India will arise and drive the "foul invader" from the land.* Then he will submit his political opinions nakedly, that India should be wrested from the Company and given to the Queen, or taken from the Queen and given to the French. If the Indian has been a European traveller, so much the worse for you. He has blushed to own,—explaining, however, conquest by bribery,—that 50,000 Englishmen hold 150,000,000 of his compatriots in thrall, and for aught you know, republicanism may have become his idol. He has lost all fear of the white face, and, having been accustomed to unburden his mind in

"The land where, girt by friend or foe,
A man may say the thing he will,"

he pursues the same course in other countries, where it is exceedingly misplaced. His doctrines of liberty and equality he applies to you personally and practically, by not rising when you enter or leave the room,—at first you could scarcely induce him to sit

* Note to Third Edition.—This was written three years before the Indian Mutiny. I also sent in to the Court of Directors a much stronger report—for which I duly suffered.

down,—by not offering you his pipe, by turning away when you address him,—in fact, by a variety of similar small affronts which none know better to manage skilfully and with almost impalpable gradations. If,—and how he prays for it!—an opportunity of refusing you any thing presents itself, he does it with an air.

> "In rice strength,
> In an Indian manliness,"

say the Arabs. And the Persians apply the following pithy tale to their neighbours. "Brother," said the leopard to the jackal, "I crave a few of thy cast-off hairs; I want them for medicine (for an especial purpose, an urgent occasion); where can I find them?" "Wallah!" replied the jackal, "I don't exactly know— I seldom change my coat—I wander about the hills. Allah is bounteous—('Allah Karim!' said to a beggar when you do not intend to be bountiful)—brother! hairs are not so easily shed."

Woe to the unhappy Englishman, Pasha, or private soldier, who must serve an Eastern lord! Worst of all, if the master be an Indian who, hating all Europeans, adds an especial spite to Oriental coarseness, treachery, and tyranny. Even the experiment of associating with them is almost too hard to bear. But a useful deduction may be drawn from such observations; and as few have had greater experience than myself, I venture to express my opinion with confidence, however unpopular or unfashionable it may be.

I am convinced that the natives of India cannot respect a European who mixes with them familiarly, or especially who imitates their customs, manners, and dress. The tight pantaloons, the authoritative voice, the pococurante manner, and the broken Hindostani impose upon them—have a weight which learning and honesty, which wit and courage, have not. This is to them the master's attitude: they bend to it like those Scythian slaves that faced the sword but fled from the horsewhip. Such would never be the case amongst a brave people, the Afghan for instance. And for the same reason it is not so, we read, with "White Plume" the North American Indian. "The free trapper combines in the eye of an Indian (American) girl, all that is dashing and heroic, in a warrior of her own race, whose gait and garb and bravery he emulates, with all that is gallant and glorious in the white man." There is but one cause for this phenomenon; the "imbelles Indi" are still, with few exceptions, a cowardly and slavish people, who would raise themselves by depreciating those superior to them in the scale of the creation. The Afghans and American aborigines, being chivalrous races, rather exaggerate the valour of their foes, because by so doing they exalt their own.

CHAPTER IV.

Life in the Wakaleh.

THE "Wakaleh," as the Caravanserai or Khan is called in Egypt, combines the offices of hotel, lodging-house, and store. It is at Cairo, as at Constantinople, a massive pile of buildings surrounding a quadrangular "Hosh" or court-yard. On the ground-floor are rooms like caverns for merchandise, and shops of different kinds—tailors, cobblers, bakers, tobacconists, fruiterers, and others. A roofless gallery or a covered verandah, into which all the apartments open, runs round the first and sometimes the second story; the latter, however, is usually exposed to the sun and wind. The accommodations consist of sets of two or three rooms, generally an inner one and an outer; the latter contains a hearth for cooking, a bathing-place, and similar necessaries. The staircases are high, narrow, and exceedingly dirty, dark at night and often in bad repair; a goat or donkey is tethered upon the different landings; here and there a fresh skin is stretched in process of tanning, and the smell reminds the veteran traveller of those closets in the old French inns where cat used to be prepared for playing the part of jugged hare. The interior is unfurnished; even the pegs upon which clothes are hung have been pulled down for firewood: the walls are bare but for stains, thick cobwebs depend in festoons from the blackened rafters of the ceiling, and the stone floor would disgrace a civilised prison: the windows are huge apertures carefully barred with wood or iron, and in rare places show remains of glass or paper pasted over the framework. In the court-yard the poorer sort of travellers consort with tethered beasts of burden, beggars howl, and slaves lie basking and scratching themselves upon mountainous heaps of cotton bales and other merchandise.

This is not a tempting picture, yet is the Wakaleh a most amusing place, presenting a succession of scenes which would delight lovers of the Dutch school —a rich exemplification of the grotesque, and what is called by artists the "dirty picturesque."

I could find no room in the Wakaleh Khan Khalil (the Long's, or Meurice's, of native Cairo); I was therefore obliged to put up with the Jemaliyeh, a Greek quarter, swarming with drunken Christians, and therefore about as fashionable as Oxford Street or Covent Garden. Even for this I had to wait a week. The pilgrims were flocking to Cairo, and to none other would the prudent hotel keepers open their doors, for the following sufficient reasons. When you enter a Wakaleh, the first thing you have to do is to pay a small sum, varying from two to five shillings, for the Miftah (the key). This is generally equivalent to a month's rent; so the sooner you leave the house the better for it. I was obliged to call myself a Turkish pilgrim in order to get possession of two most comfortless rooms, which I afterwards learned were celebrated for making travellers ill, and I had to pay eighteen piastres for the key and eighteen ditto per mensem for rent, besides five piastres to the man who swept and washed the place. So that for this month my house hire amounted to nearly four-pence a day.

But I was fortunate enough in choosing the Jemaliyeh Wakaleh, for I found a friend there. On board the steamer a fellow-voyager, seeing me sitting alone and therefore as he conceived in discomfort, placed himself by my side and opened a hot fire of kind inquiries. He was a man about forty-five, of middle size, with a large round head closely shaven, a bull-neck, limbs sturdy as a Saxon's, a thin red beard, and handsome features beaming with benevolence. A curious dry humour he had, delighting in "quizzing," but in so quiet, solemn, and quaint a way that before you knew him you could scarcely divine his drift.

"Thank Allah, we carry a doctor!" said my friend more than once, with apparent fervour of gratitude, after he had discovered my profession. I was fairly taken in by the pious ejaculation, and some days elapsed before the drift of his remark became apparent.

"You doctors," he explained when we were more intimate, "what do you do? a man goes to you for ophthalmia. It is a purge, a blister, and a drop in the eye! Is it for fever? well! a purge and Kinakina (quinine). For dysentery? a purge and extract of opium. Wallah! I am as good a physician as the best of you," he would add with a broad grin, "if I only knew the

Dirhambirhams — drams and drachms — and a few break-jaw Arabic names of diseases."

Haji Wali therefore emphatically advised me to make bread by honestly teaching languages. "We are doctor-ridden," said he, and I found it was the case.

When we lived under the same roof, the Haji and I became fast friends. During the day we called on each other frequently, we dined together, and passed the evening in a Mosque, or some other place of public pastime. Coyly at first, but less guardedly as we grew bolder, we smoked the forbidden weed "Hashish," conversing lengthily the while about that world of which I had seen so much. Originally from Russia, he also had been a traveller, and in his wanderings he had cast off most of the prejudices of his people. "I believe in Allah and his Prophet, and in nothing else," was his sturdy creed; he rejected alchemy, genii and magicians, and truly he had a most unoriental distaste for tales of wonder. When I entered the Wakaleh, he constituted himself my Cicerone, and especially guarded me against the cheating of tradesmen. By his advice I laid aside the Dervish's gown, the large blue pantaloons, and the short shirt, in fact all connection with Persia and the Persians. "If you persist in being an Ajemi," said the Haji, "you will get yourself into trouble; in Egypt you will be cursed, in Arabia you will be beaten because you are a heretic, you will pay the treble of what other travellers do, and if you fall sick you may die by the road-side." After long deliberation about the choice of nations I became a "Pathan." Born in India of Afghan parents, who had settled in the country, educated at Rangoon, and sent out to wander, as men of that race frequently are, from early youth, I was well guarded against the danger of detection by a fellow-countryman. To support the character requires a knowledge of Persian, Hindostani, and Arabic, all of which I knew sufficiently well to pass muster; any trifling inaccuracy was charged upon my long residence at Rangoon. This was an important step: the first question at the shop, on the camel, and in the Mosque, is "What is thy name?" the second "Whence comest thou?" This is not generally impertinent, nor intended to be annoying; if, however, you see any evil intention in the questioner, you may rather roughly ask him, "What may be his maternal parent's name"—equivalent to inquiring, Anglicè, in what church his mother was married—and escape your difficulties under cover of the storm. But this is rarely necessary. I assumed the polite pliant manners of an Indian physician, and the dress of a small Effendi or gentleman, still, however, representing myself to be a Dervish, and frequenting the places where Dervishes congregate. "What business," asked the Haji, "have those reverend men with politics or statistics, or any of the information which you are collecting? Call yourself a religious wanderer if you like, and let those who ask the object of your peregrinations know that you are under a vow to visit all the holy places in Islam. Thus you will persuade them that you are a man of rank under a cloud, and you will receive much more civility than perhaps you deserve," concluded my friend with a dry laugh. The remark proved his sagacity, and after ample experience I had not to repent having been guided by his advice.

Haji Wali, by profession a merchant at Alexandria, had accompanied Khudabakhsh the Indian, to Cairo, on law-business. He soon explained his affairs to me, and as his case brought out certain Oriental peculiarities in a striking light, with his permission I offer a few of its details.

My friend was defendant in a suit instituted against him in H. B. M's Consular court, Cairo, by one Mohammed Shafi'a, a scoundrel of the first water. This man lived, and lived well, by setting up in business at places where his name was not known; he enticed the unwary by artful displays of capital, and after succeeding in getting credit, he changed residence, carrying off all he could lay hands upon. But swindling is a profession of personal danger in uncivilised countries, where law punishes pauper debtors by a short imprisonment; and where the cheated prefer to gratify their revenge by the cudgel or the knife. So Mohammed Shafi'a, after a few narrow escapes, hit upon a prime expedient. Though known to be a native of Bokhara—he actually signed himself so in his letters—and his appearance at once bespoke his origin, he determined to protect himself by a British passport. Our officials are sometimes careless enough in distributing these documents, and by so doing, they expose themselves to a certain loss of reputation at Eastern courts*; still Mohammed Shafi'a found some difficulties in effecting his fraud. To recount all his Reynardisms would weary the reader; suffice it to say that by proper management of the subalterns in the consulate, he succeeded without ruining himself. Armed with this new defence, he started boldly for Jeddah on the Arabian coast. Having entered into partnership with Haji Wali, whose confidence he had won by prayers, fastings, and pilgrimages, he openly trafficked in slaves, sending them to Alexandria for sale, and writing with matchless impudence to his correspondent that he would dispose of them in person, but for fear of losing his British passport and protection.

An unlucky adventure embroiled this worthy British subject with Faraj Yusuf, the principal merchant of Jeddah, and also an English protégé. Fearing so powerful an adversary, Mohammed Shafi'a packed up his spoils and departed for Egypt. Presently he quarrels with his former partner, thinking him a

---

* For the simple reason that no Eastern power confers such an obligation except for value received. In old times, when official honor was not so rigorous as it is now, the creditors of Eastern powers and principalities would present high sums to British Residents and others for the privilege of being enrolled in the list of their subjects or servants. This they made profitable; for their claims, however exorbitant, when backed by a name of fear, were certain to be admitted, unless the Resident's conscience would allow of his being persuaded by weightier arguments of a similar nature to abandon his protégé.

It is almost needless to remark that nothing of the kind can occur in the present day, and at the same time that throughout the Eastern world it is firmly believed that such things are of daily occurrence. Ill fame descends to distant generations; whilst good deeds, if they blossom, as we are told, in the dust, are at least as short lived as they are sweet.

soft man, and claims from him a debt of 165*l*. He supports his pretensions by a document and four witnesses, who are ready to swear that the receipt in question was "signed, sealed, and delivered" by Haji Wali. The latter adduces his books to show that accounts have been settled, and he can prove that the witnesses in question are paupers, therefore, not legal; moreover, each has received from the plaintiff two dollars, the price of perjury.

Now had such a suit been carried into a Turkish court of justice, it would very sensibly have been settled by the bastinado, for Haji Wali was a respectable merchant, and Mohammed Shafi'a a notorious swindler. But the latter was a British subject, which notably influenced the question. The more to annoy his adversary, he went up to Cairo, and began proceedings there, hoping by this acute step to receive part payment of his demand.

Arrived at Cairo Mohammed Shafi'a applied himself stoutly to the task of bribing all who could be useful to him, distributing shawls and piastres with great generosity. He secured the services of an efficient lawyer, and, determining to enlist heaven itself in his cause, he passed the Ramazan ostentatiously, he fasted, and he slaughtered sheep to feed the poor.

Meanwhile Haji Wali, a simple truth-telling man, who could never master the rudiments of that art, which teaches man to blow hot and to blow cold with the same breath, had been persuaded to visit Cairo by Khudabakhsh, the wily Indian, who promised to introduce him to influential persons, and to receive him in his house till he could provide himself with a lodging at the Wakaleh. But Mohammed Shafi'a, who had once been in partnership with the Indian, and who possibly knew more than was fit to meet the public ear, found this out, and, partly by begging, partly by bullying, persuaded Khudabakhsh to transfer the influential introductions to himself. Then the Hakim Abdullah—your humble servant—appears upon the scene: he has travelled in Feringistan, he has seen many men and their cities, he becomes an intimate and an adviser of the Haji, and he finds out evil passages in Mohammed Shafi'a's life. Upon which Khudabakhsh ashamed, or rather afraid of his duplicity, collects his Indian friends. The Hakim Abdullah draws up a petition addressed to Mr. Walne, H. B. M's Consul, by the Indian merchants and others resident at Cairo, informing him of Mohammed Shafi'a's birth, character, and occupation as a vendor of slaves, offering proof of all assertions, and praying him for the sake of their good name to take away his passport. And all the Indians affix their seals to this paper. Then Mohammed Shafi'a threatens to waylay and to beat the Haji. The Haji, not loud or hectoringly, but with a composed smile, advises his friends to hold him off.

One would suppose that such a document would have elicited some inquiry.

But Haji Wali was a Persian protégé, and proceedings between the consulates had commenced before the petition was presented. The pseudo-British subject, having been acknowledged as a real one, must be supported. Consuls, like kings, may err, but must not own to error. No notice was taken of the Indian petition; worse still, no inquiry into the slave-affair was set on foot, and it was discovered that the passport having been granted by a Consul-general could not with official etiquette be resumed by a Consul. Yet at the time there was at Alexandria an acting Consul-general, to whom the case could with strict propriety have been referred.

Thus matters were destined to proceed as they began. Mohammed Shafi'a had offered 5,000 piastres to the Persian Consul's interpreter; this of course was refused, but still somehow or other all the Haji's affairs seemed to go wrong. His statements were mistranslated, his accounts were misunderstood, and the suit was allowed to drag on to a suspicious length. When I left Cairo in July Haji Wali had been kept away nearly two months from his business and family, though both parties—for the plaintiff's purse was rapidly thinning—appeared eager to settle the difference by arbitration: when I returned from Arabia in October matters were almost in statu quo ante, and when I started for India in January, the proceedings had not closed.

Such is a brief history, but too common, of a case in which the subject of an Eastern state has to contend against British influence. It is doubtless a point of honor to defend our protégés from injustice, but the higher principle should rest upon the base of common honesty. The worst part of such a case is, that the injured party has no redress.

"Fiat injustitia, ruat cœlum,"

is the motto of his "natural protectors," who would violate every law to gratify the false pride of a petty English official. And, saving the rare exceptions where rank or wealth command consideration, with what face, to use the native phrase, would a hapless Turk appeal to the higher powers, our ministers or our Parliament?

After lodging myself in the Wakaleh, my first object was to make a certain stir in the world. In Europe your travelling doctor advertises the loss of a diamond ring, the gift of a Russian autocrat, or he monopolises a whole column in a newspaper, feeing perhaps a title for the use of a signature; the large brass plate, the gold-headed cane, the rattling chariot, and the summons from the sermon complete the work. Here, there is no such royal road to medical fame. You must begin by sitting with the porter, who is sure to have blear eyes, into which you drop a little nitrate of silver, whilst you instil into his ear the pleasing intelligence that you never take a fee from the poor. He recovers; his report of you spreads far and wide, crowding your doors with paupers. They come to you as though you were their servant, and when cured, they turn their backs upon you for ever. Hence it is that European doctors generally complain of ingratitude on the part of their Oriental patients. It is true that if you save a man's life he naturally asks you for the means of preserving it. Moreover, in none of the Eastern languages with which I am acquainted, is there a single term conveying the meaning of our "gratitude," and none but Germans have ideas unexplainable by words. But you must not condemn this absence of a virtue without considering the cause. An Oriental deems that he has a right to your surplus. "Daily bread is divided" (by heaven), he asserts, and eating yours, he considers it his own. Thus it is with other things. He is thankful to Allah for the gifts of the Creator, but he has a claim to the good offices of a fellow creature. In rendering him a service you have but done your duty, and he would not pay you so poor a compliment as to praise you for the act. He leaves you, his benefactor, with a short prayer for the length of your days. "Thank you," being expressed by "Allah increase thy weal!" or the selfish wish that your shadow (with which you protect him and his fellows) may never be less. And this is probably the last you hear of him.

There is a discomfort in such proceedings, a reasonable, a metaphysical coldness, uglily contrasting in theory with the genial warmth which a little more heart would infuse into them. In theory, I say, not in practice. What can be more troublesome than, when you have obliged a man, to run the gauntlet of his and his family's thanksgivings,—to find yourself become a master from being a friend, a great man when you were an equal; not to be contradicted, where shortly before every one gave his opinion freely? You must be unamiable if these considerations deter you from benefiting your friend, yet, I humbly opine, you still may fear his gratefulness.

To resume. When the mob has raised you to fame, patients of a better class will slowly appear on the scene. After some coquetting about "etiquette," whether you are to visit them, or they are to call upon you, they make up their minds to see you, and to judge with their eyes whether you are to be trusted or not; whilst you, on your side, set out with the determination that they shall at once cross the Rubicon,—in less classical phrase, swallow your drug. If you visit the house, you insist upon the patient's servants attending you; he must also provide and pay an ass for your conveyance, no matter if it be only to the other side of the street. Your confidential man accompanies you, primed for replies to the "fifty searching questions" of the servants' hall. You are lifted off the saddle tenderly, as nurses dismount their charges, when you arrive at the gate, and you waddle up stairs with dignity. Arrived at the sick room, you salute those present with a general "Peace be upon you!" to which they respond, "And upon thee be the peace and the mercy of Allah, and his blessing!" To the invalid you say, "There is nothing the matter, please Allah, except the health;" to which the proper answer—for here every sign of ceremony has its countersign—is, "May Allah give thee health!" Then you sit down, and acknowledge the presence of the company by raising your right hand to your lips and forehead, bowing the while circularly; each individual returns the civility by a similar gesture. Then inquiry about the state of your health ensues. Then you are asked what refreshment you will take: you studiously mention something not likely to be in the house, but at last you rough it with a pipe and a cup of coffee. Then you proceed to the patient, who extends his wrist, and asks you what his complaint is. Then you examine his tongue, you feel his pulse, you look learned, and—he is talking all the time—after hearing a detailed list of all his ailments, you gravely discover them, taking for the same as much praise to yourself as does the practising phrenologist, for a similar simple exercise of the reasoning faculties. The disease, to be respectable, must invariably be connected with one of the four temperaments, or the four elements, or the "humors of Hippocrates." Cure is easy, but it will take time, and you, the doctor, require attention; any little rudeness it is in your power to punish by an alteration in the pill, or the powder, and, so unknown is professional honor, that none will brave your displeasure.

If you would pass for a native practitioner, you must finally proceed to the most uncomfortable part of your visit, bargaining for fees. Nothing more effectually arouses suspicion than disinterestedness in a doctor. I once cured a rich Hazramaut merchant of rheumatism, and neglected to make him pay for treatment; he carried off one of my coffee cups, and was unceasingly wondering where I came from. So I made him produce five piastres, a shilling, which he threw upon the carpet, cursing Indian avarice. "You will bring on another illness," said my friend, the Haji, when he heard of it. Properly speaking, the fee for a visit to a respectable man is 20 piastres, but with the rich patient you begin by making a bargain. He complains, for instance, of dysentery and sciatica. You demand 10*l*. for the dysentery, and 20*l*. for the sciatica. But you will rarely get it. The Eastern pays a doctor's bill as an Oirishman does his "rint," making a grievance of it. Your patient will show indisputable signs of convalescence: he will laugh and jest half the day; but the moment you appear, groans and a lengthened visage, and pretended complaints welcome you. Then your way is to throw out some such hint as

"The world is a carcass, and they who seek it are dogs."

And you refuse to treat the second disorder, which conduct may bring the refractory one to his senses.

"Dat Galenus opes," however, is a Western apothegm: the utmost "Jalinus" can do for you here is to provide you with the necessaries and the comforts of life. Whatever you prescribe must be solid and material, and if you accompany it with something painful, such as rubbing unto scarification with a horse brush, so much the better. Easterns, as our peasants in Europe, like the doctor to "give them the value of their money." Besides which, rough measures act beneficially upon their imagination. So the Hakim of the King of Persia cured fevers by the bastinado; patients are beneficially baked in a bread-oven at Baghdad; and an Egyptian at Alexandria, whose quartan resisted the strongest appliances of European physic, was effectually healed by the actual cautery, which a certain Arab Shaykh applied to the crown of his head.

When you administer with your own hand the remedy—half-a-dozen huge bread pills, dipped in a solution of aloes or cinnamon water, flavoured with assafœtida, which in the case of the dyspeptic rich often suffice, if they will but diet themselves—you are careful to say, "In the name of Allah, the Compassionate, the Merciful." And after the patient has been dosed, "Praise be to Allah, the Curer, the Healer;" you then call for pen, ink, and paper, and write some such prescription as this—

"A

(A monogram generally placed at the head of writings. It is the initial letter of "Allah," and the first of the Alphabet, used from time immemorial to denote the origin of creation. "I am Alpha and Omega, the first and the last.")

"In the name of Allah, the Compassionate, the Merciful, and blessings and peace be upon our Lord the Apostle, and his family, and his companions one and all! But afterwards let him take bees'-honey and cinnamon and album græcum, of each half a part, and of ginger a whole part, which let him pound and mix with the honey, and form boluses, each bolus the weight of a Miskal, and of it let him use every day a Miskal on the saliva (that is to say, fasting—the first thing in the morning). Verily its effects are wonderful! And let him abstain from flesh, fish, vegetables, sweetmeats, flatulent food, acids of all descriptions, as well as the major ablution, and live in perfect quiet. So shall he be cured by the help of the King the Healer (*i. e.* the Almighty). And the peace (W'assalam, *i. e.* adieu)."

The diet, I need scarcely say, should be rigorous; nothing has tended more to bring the European system of medicine into contempt among orientals than our inattention to this branch of the therapeutic art. When a Hindi or Hindu "takes medicine," he prepares himself for it by diet and rest two or three days before adhibition, and as gradually, after the dose, he relapses into his usual habits; if he break though the régime it is concluded that fatal results must ensue. The ancient Egyptians, we learn from Herodotus, devoted a certain number of days in each month to the use of alteratives, and the period was consecutive, doubtless in order to graduate the strength of the medicine. The Persians, when under salivation, shut themselves up in a warm room; never undress, and so carefully guard against cold that they even drink tepid water. When the Afghan princes find it necessary to employ Chob-Chini, (the Jin-seng, or China root so celebrated as a purifier, tonic, and aphrodisiac) they choose the spring season; they remove to a garden, where flowers and trees and bubbling streams soothe their senses; they carefully avoid fatigue and trouble of all kinds, and will not even hear a letter read, lest it should contain bad news.

When the prescription is written out, you affix an impression of your ring seal to the beginning and to the end of it, that no one may be able to add to or to take from its contents. And when you send medicine to a patient of rank, who is sure to have enemies, you adopt some similar precaution against the box or the bottle being opened. One of the Pashas whom I attended,—a brave soldier who had been a favourite with Mohammed Ali, and therefore was degraded by his successor,—kept an impression of my ring in wax, to compare with that upon the phials. Men have not forgotten how frequently, in former times, those who became obnoxious to the state were seized with sudden and fatal cramps in the stomach. In the case of the doctor it is common prudence to adopt these precautions, as all evil consequences would be charged upon him, and he would be exposed to the family's revenge.

Cairo, though abounding in medical practitioners, can still support more; but to thrive they must be Indians, or Chinese, or Maghrabis. The Egyptians are thoroughly disgusted with European treatment, which is here about as efficacious as in India—that is to say, not at all. But they are ignorant of the medicine of

Hind, and therefore great is its name; deservedly perhaps, for skill in simples and dietetics. Besides which the Indian may deal in charms and spells,—things to which the latitude gives such force that even Europeans learn to put faith in them. The traveller who, on the banks of the Seine, scoffs at Sights and Sounds, Table-turning and Spirit-rapping, in the wilds of Tartary and Thibet sees a something supernatural and diabolical in the bungling Sie-fa of the Bokte.* Some sensible men, who pass for philosophers among their friends, have been caught by the incantations of the turbaned and bearded Cairo magician. In our West African colonies the phrase "growing black," was applied to colonists, who, after a term of residence, became thoroughly imbued with the superstitions of the land. And there are not wanting old English Indians, intelligent men, that place firm trust in tales and tenets too puerile even for the Hindus to believe. As a "Hindi" I could use animal magnetism, taking care, however, to give the science a specious supernatural appearance. Haji Wali, who, professing positive scepticism, showed the greatest interest in the subject as a curiosity, advised me not to practise pure mesmerism; otherwise, that I should infallibly become a "Companion of Devils." "You must call this an Indian secret," said my friend, "for it is clear that you are no Mashaikh (holy man), and people will ask, where are your drugs, and what business have you with charms?" It is useless to say that I followed his counsel; yet

* See M. Huc's Travels.

patients would consider themselves my disciples, and delighted in kissing the hand of the Sahib Nafas or minor saint.

The Haji repaid me for my docility by vaunting me everywhere as the very phœnix of physicians. My first successes were in the Wakaleh; opposite to me there lived an Arab slave dealer, whose Abyssinians constantly fell sick. A tender race, they suffer when first transported to Egypt from many complaints, especially consumption, dysentery and varicose veins. I succeeded in curing one girl. As she was worth at least fifteen pounds, the gratitude of her owner was great, and I had to dose half a dozen others in order to cure them of the pernicious and price-lowering habit of snoring. Living in rooms opposite these slave girls, and seeing them at all hours of the day and night, I had frequent opportunities of studying them. They were average specimens of the steatopygous Abyssinian breed, broad-shouldered, thin-flanked, fine-limbed, and with haunches of a prodigious size. None of them had handsome features, but the short curly hair that stands on end being concealed under a kerchief, there was something pretty in the brow, eyes and upper part of the nose, coarse and sensual in the pendent lips, large jowl and projecting mouth, whilst the whole had a combination of piquancy with sweetness. Their style of flirtation was peculiar.

"How beautiful thou art, O Maryam!—what eyes! —what—"

"Then why,"—would respond the lady—"don't you buy me?"

"We are of one faith—of one creed—formed to form each other's happiness."

"Then why don't you buy me?"

"Conceive, O Maryam, the blessing of two hearts—"

"Then why don't you buy me?"

And so on. Most effectual gag to Cupid's eloquence! Yet was not the plain-spoken Maryam's reply without its moral. How often is it our fate in the West, as in the East, to see in bright eyes and to hear from rosy lips an implied, if not an expressed, "Why don't you buy me?" or, worse still, "Why *can't* you buy me?".

All I required in return for my services from the slave dealer, whose brutal countenance and manners were truly repugnant, was to take me about the town, and explain to me certain mysteries in his craft, which knowledge might be useful in time to come. I have, however, nothing new to report concerning the present state of bondsmen in Egypt. England has already learned that slaves are not necessarily the most wretched and degraded of men. Some have been bold enough to tell the British public, that, in the generality of Oriental countries, the serf fares far better than the servant, or indeed than the poorer orders of freemen. "The laws of Mahomet enjoin his followers to treat slaves with the greatest mildness, and the Moslems are in general scrupulous observers of the Prophet's recommendation. Slaves are considered members of the family, and in houses where free servants are kept besides, they seldom do any other work than filling the pipes, presenting the coffee, accompanying their master when going out, rubbing his feet when he takes his nap in the afternoon, and driving away the flies from him. When a slave is not satisfied, he can legally compel his master to sell him. He has no care for food, lodging, clothes and washing, and has no taxes to pay; he is exempt from military service and socage, and in spite of his bondage is freer than the freest Fellah in Egypt." This is, I believe, a true statement, but of course it in nowise affects the question of slavery in the abstract. A certain amount of reputation was the consequence of curing the Abyssinian girls: my friend Haji Wali carefully told the news to all the town, and before fifteen days were over, I found myself obliged to decline extending a practice which threatened me with fame.

Servants are most troublesome things to all Englishmen in Egypt, but especially to one travelling as a respectable native, and therefore expected to have slaves. After much deliberation, I resolved to take a Berberi or Native of Upper Egypt, and accordingly summoned a Shaykh—there is a Shaykh for every thing down to thieves in Asia—and made known my want. The list of sine quâ nons was necessarily rather extensive, good health and a readiness to travel anywhere, a little skill in cooking, sewing and washing, willingness to fight, and a habit of regular prayers.

After a day's delay the Shaykh brought me a

specimen of his choosing, a broad-shouldered, bandy-legged fellow, with the usual bull-dog expression of the Berberis, in his case rendered doubly expressive by the drooping of an eyelid—an accident brought about with acrid juice in order to avoid conscription. He responded sturdily to all my questions. Some Egyptian donkey boys and men were making a noise in the room at the time, and the calm ferocity with which he ejected them commanded my approval. When a needle, thread, and an unhemmed napkin were handed to him, he sat down, held the edge of the cloth between his big toe and its neighbour, and finished the work in superior style. Walking out he armed himself with a Kurbaj, which he used, now lightly, then heavily, upon all laden animals, biped and quadruped, that came in the way. His conduct proving equally satisfactory in the kitchen, after getting security from him, and having his name registered by the Shaykh,—who becomes responsible, and must pay for any theft his protégé may commit,—I closed with him for eighty piastres a month. But Ali the Berberi and I were destined to part. Before a fortnight he stabbed his fellow servant—a Surat lad, who wishing to return home forced his services upon me, and for this trick he received, with his dismissal, 400 blows on the feet by order of the Zabit, or police magistrate.

After this failure I tried a number of servants, Egyptians, Saidis, and clean- and unclean-eating Berberis. Recommended by different Shaykhs all had some fatal defect: one cheated recklessly, another robbed me, a third drank, a fourth was always in scrapes for infringing the Julian edict, and the last, a long-legged Nubian, after remaining two days in the house, dismissed me for expressing my determination to travel by sea from Suez to Yambu. I kept one man; he complained that he was worked to death: two—they did nothing but fight; and three—they left me, as Mr. Elwes said of old, to serve myself.

At last, thoroughly tired of Egyptian domestics, and one servant being really sufficient for comfort, as well as suitable to my assumed rank, I determined to keep only the Indian boy. He had all the defects of his nation; a brave at Cairo, he was an arrant coward at El Medina; and the Bedawin despised him heartily for his effeminacy in making his camel kneel to dismount. But the choice had its advantages: his swarthy skin and chubby features made the Arabs always call him an Abyssinian slave, which, as it favoured my disguise, I did not care to contradict; he served well, he was amenable to discipline and, being completely dependent upon me, he was therefore less likely to watch and especially to prate about my proceedings. As master and man we performed the pilgrimage together; but, on my return to Egypt after the pilgrimage, Shaykh, become Haji Nur, finding me to be a Sahib or English official, changed for the worse. He would not work, and he reserved all his energy for the purpose of pilfering, which he practised so audaciously upon my friends, as well as upon myself, that he could not be kept in the house.

Perhaps the reader may be curious to see the necessary expenses of a bachelor residing at Cairo. He must, observe, however, in the following list that I was not a strict economist, and, besides that, I was a stranger in the country: inhabitants and old settlers would live as well for little more than two-thirds the sum.

		Piastres.	Faddeh.
House rent at 18 piastres per mensem		0	24
Servant at 80 piastres per do.		2	26
Breakfast for self and servant.	10 eggs	0	5
	Coffee	0	10
	Water melon	1	0
	Two rolls of bread	0	10
Dinner.	2 lbs. of meat	2	20
	Two rolls of bread	0	10
	Vegetables	0	20
	Rice	0	5
	Oil and clarified butter.	1	0
Sundries.	A skin of Nile water	1	0
	Tobacco	1	0
	Hammam, (hot bath)	3	20
	Total	12	50

equal to about two shillings and sixpence.

In these days who at Cairo without a Shaykh? I thought it right to conform to popular custom, and accordingly, after having secured a servant, my efforts were directed to finding a teacher—the pretext being that as an Indian doctor I wanted to read Arabic works on medicine, as well as to perfect myself in divinity and pronunciation. My theological studies were in the Shafe'i school for two reasons: in the first place, it is the least rigorous of the Four Orthodox, and, secondly, it most resembles the Shi'ah heresy, with which long intercourse with Persians had made me familiar. My choice of doctrine, however, confirmed those around me in their conviction that I was a rank heretic, for the Ajemi, taught by his religion to conceal offensive tenets in lands where the open expression would be dangerous, always represents himself to be a Shafe'i. This, together with the original mistake of appearing publicly at Alexandria as a Mirza in a Persian dress, caused me infinite small annoyance at Cairo, in spite of all precautions and contrivances. And throughout my journey, even in Arabia, though I drew my knife every time an offensive hint was thrown out, the ill-fame clung to me like the shirt of Nessus.

It was not long before I happened to hit upon a proper teacher, in the person of Shaykh Mohammed el Attar, or the druggist. He had known prosperity, having once been a Khatib (preacher) in one of Mohammed Ali's mosques. But H. H. the late Pasha had dismissed him, which disastrous event, with its subsequent train of misfortunes, he dates from the melancholy day when he took to himself a wife. He talks of her abroad as a stern and rigid master dealing with a naughty slave, though, by the look that accompanies his rhodomontade, I am convinced that at home he is the very model of "managed men." His dismissal was the reason that compelled him to fall back upon the trade of a druggist, the refuge for the once wealthy, though now destitute, Sages of Egypt.

His little shop in the Jemeliyeh Quarter is a perfect gem of Nilotic queerness. A hole pierced in the wall of some house, about five feet long and six deep, it is divided into two compartments separated by a thin partition of wood, and communicating by a kind of arch cut in the boards. The inner box, germ of a back parlour, acts store-room, as the pile of empty old baskets tossed in dusty confusion upon the dirty floor shows. In the front is displayed the stock in trade, a matting full of Persian tobacco and pipe bowls of red clay, with a palm-leaf bag, containing vile coffee and large lumps of coarse, whity-brown sugar wrapped up in browner paper. On the shelves and ledges are rows of well-thumbed wooden boxes, labelled with the greatest carelessness, pepper for rhubarb, arsenic for Tafl or wash-clay, and sulphate of iron where sal ammoniac should be. There is also a square case containing, under lock and key, small change and some choice articles of commerce, damaged perfumes, bad antimony for the eyes, and pernicious rouge. And dangling close above it is a rusty pair of scales, ill poised enough for Egyptian Justice herself to use. To hooks over the shop front are suspended reeds for pipes, tallow candles, dirty wax tapers and cigarette paper; instead of plate-glass windows and brass-handled doors, a ragged net keeps away the flies when the master is in, and the thieves when he goes out to recite in the Hasanayn mosque his daily Chapter, "Ya Sin." A wooden shutter which closes down at night-time, and by day two palm-stick stools intensely dirty and full of fleas, occupying the place of the Mastabah, or earthen bench, which once accommodated purchasers, complete the furniture of my preceptor's establishment.

There he sits or rather lies (for verily I believe he sleeps through three-fourths of the day), a thin old man, about fifty-eight, with features once handsome and regular, a sallow face, shaven head, deeply wrinkled cheeks, eyes hopelessly bleared, and a rough grey beard ignorant of oil and comb. His turban, though large, is brown with wear, his coat and small-clothes display many a hole, and though his face and hands must be frequently washed preparatory to devotion, still they have the quality of always looking unclean. It is wonderful how fierce and gruff he is to the little boys and girls who flock to him grasping farthings for pepper and sugar. On such occasions I sit admiring to see him, when forced to exertion, wheel about on his place, making a pivot of that portion of our organisation which mainly distinguishes our species from the other families of the Simiadæ, to reach some distant drawer, or to pull down a case from its accustomed shelf. How does he manage to say his prayers, to kneel and to prostrate himself over that two feet of ragged rug, scarcely sufficient for a British infant to lie upon? He hopelessly owns that he knows nothing of his craft, and the seats before his shop are seldom occupied. His great pleasure appears to be when the Haji and I sit by him a few minutes in the evening, bringing with us pipes, which he assists us to smoke, and ordering coffee, which he insists upon sweetening with a lump of sugar from his little store. There we make him talk and laugh, and occasionally quote a few lines strongly savouring of the jovial: we provoke him to long stories about the love borne him in his student-days by the great and holy Shaykh Abdul Rahman, and the antipathy with which he was regarded by the equally great and holy Shaykh Nasr el Din, his memorable single imprisonment for contumacy, and the temperate but effective lecture, beginning with "O almost entirely destitute of shame!" delivered on that occasion in presence of other undergraduates by the Right Reverend principal of his college. Then we consult him upon matters of doctrine, and quiz him tenderly about his powers of dormition, and flatter him, or rather his age, with such phrases as, "the water from thy hand is of the waters of Zem Zem," or, "we have sought thee to deserve the blessings of the wise upon our undertakings." Sometimes, with interested motives it must be owned, we induce him to accompany us to the Hammam, where he insists upon paying the smallest sum, quarrelling with every thing and every body, and giving the greatest trouble. We are generally his only visitors; acquaintances he appears to have few, and no friends; he must have had them once, for he was rich, but he is now poor, so they have fallen away from the old man.

When the Shaykh Mohammed sits with me, or I climb up into his little shop for the purpose of receiving a lesson from him, he is quite at his ease, reading when he likes, or making me read, and generally beginning each lecture with some such preamble as this:—

"Aywa! aywa! aywa!"—"even so, even so, even so!

we take refuge with Allah from the Stoned Fiend! In the name of Allah, the Compassionate, the Merciful, and the blessings of Allah upon our lord Mohammed, and his family, and his companions one and all. Thus saith the author, may Almighty Allah have mercy upon him! 'Section I. of chapter two, upon the orders of prayers,' &c."

He becomes fiercely sarcastic when I differ with him in opinion, especially upon a point of the grammar, or the theology over which his beard has grown grey.

"Subhan Allah! Allah be glorified!—this is of course ironical, 'Allah be praised for creating such a prodigy of learning as thou art!'—What words are these? If thou be right, enlarge thy turban (*i. e.* set up as a learned man), and throw away thy drugs, for verily it is better to quicken men's souls than to destroy their bodies, O Abdullah!"

Oriental-like, he revels in giving good counsel.

"Thou art always writing, O my brave!" (this is said on the few occasions when I venture to make a note in my book,) "what evil habit is this! Surely thou hast learned it in the lands of the Frank. Repent!"

He loathes my giving medical advice gratis.

"Thou hast two servants to feed, O my son! The doctors of Egypt never write A, B, without a reward. Wherefore art thou ashamed? Better go and sit upon the mountain at once (*i. e.* go to the desert), and say thy prayers day and night!"

And finally he is prodigal of preaching upon the subject of household expenses.

"Thy servant did write down 2 lbs. of flesh yesterday! What words are these, O he!—Ya hu, a common interpellative, not, perhaps, of the politest description—Dost thou never say, 'Guard us, Allah, from the sin of extravagance!'"

He delights also in abruptly interrupting a serious subject when it begins to weigh upon his spirits. For instance,

"Now the waters of ablution being of seven different kind, it results that——hast thou a wife? No? Then verily thou must buy thee a female slave, O youth! This conduct is not right, and men will say of thee—— Repentance: I take refuge with Allah——'of a truth his mouth watereth for the spouses of other Moslems.'"

But sometimes he nods over a difficult passage under my very eyes, or he reads it over a dozen times in the wantonness of idleness, or he takes what schoolboys call a long "shot" most shamelessly at the signification. When this happens I lose my temper, and raise my voice, and shout, "Verily there is no power nor might save in Allah, the High, the Great!" Then he looks at me, and with passing meekness whispers—

"Fear Allah, O man!"

CHAPTER V.

The Ramazan.

THIS year the Ramazan befel in June, and a fearful infliction was that "blessed month," making the Moslem unhealthy and unamiable. For the space of sixteen consecutive hours and a quarter, we were forbidden to eat, drink, smoke, snuff, and even to swallow our saliva designedly. I say forbidden, for although the highest orders of Turks,—the class popularly described as

> "Turco fino
> Mangia porco e beve vino"—

may break the ordinance in strict privacy, popular opinion would condemn any open infraction of it with uncommon severity. In this, as in most human things, how many are there who hold that

> "Pécher en secret n'est pas pécher,
> Ce n'est que l'éclat qui fait le crime."

The middle and lower ranks observe the duties of the season, however arduous, with exceeding zeal: of all who suffered severely from such total abstinence, I found but one patient who would eat even to save his life. And among the vulgar, sinners who habitually drink when they should pray, will fast and perform their devotions through the Ramazan.

Like the Latin, Anglo-Catholic and Greek fasts, the chief effect of the "blessed month" upon True

Believers is to darken their tempers into positive gloom. Their voices, never of the softest, acquire, especially after noon, a terribly harsh and creaking tone. The men curse one another and beat the women. The women slap and abuse the children, and these in their turn cruelly entreat, and use bad language to, the dogs and cats. You can scarcely spend ten minutes in any populous part of the city without hearing some violent dispute. The "Karakun," or station-houses, are filled with lords who have administered an undue dose of chastisement to their ladies, and with ladies who have scratched, bitten, and otherwise injured the persons of their lords. The Mosques are crowded with a sulky, grumbling population, making themselves offensive to one another on earth, whilst working their way to heaven; and in the shade, under the outer walls, the little boys who have been expelled the church attempt to forget their miseries in spiritless play. In the bazars and streets, pale long-drawn faces, looking for the most part intolerably cross, catch your eye, and at this season a stranger will sometimes meet with positive incivility. A shopkeeper, for instance, usually says when he rejects an insufficient offer, Yaftah Allah, "Allah opens" viz., the door of daily bread, a polite way of informing a man that you and he are not likely to do business; in other words, that you are not in want of his money. In the Ramazan, he will grumble about the bore of Ghashim ("Johnny raws"), and gruffly tell you not to stand there wasting his time. But as a rule the shops are either shut or destitute of shopmen, merchants will not purchase, and students will not study. In fine, the Ramazan, for many classes, is one twelfth of the year wantonly thrown away.

The following is the routine of a fast day. About half an hour after midnight, the gun sounds its warning to faithful men that it is time to prepare for the Sahur (early breakfast). My servant then wakes me, if I have slept, brings water for ablution, spreads the Sufrah or leather cloth, and places before me certain remnants of the evening's meal. It is some time before the stomach becomes accustomed to such hours, but in matters of appetite, habit is everything, and for health's sake one should strive to eat as plentifully as possible. Then sounds the Salam, or Blessings on the Prophet, an introduction to the Call of Morning Prayer. Smoking sundry pipes with tenderness, as if taking leave of a friend, and until the second gun, fired at about half past two A.M., gives the Imsak,—the order to abstain from food,—I wait the Azan, or summons to prayer, which in this month is called somewhat earlier than usual. Then, after a ceremony termed the Niyat (intention) of fasting, I say my prayers, and prepare for repose. At 7 A.M. the labors of the day begin for the working classes of society; the rich spend the night in revelling, and rest in down from dawn till noon.

The first thing on rising is to perform the Wuzu, or lesser ablution, which invariably follows sleep in a reclining position; without this it would be improper to pray, to enter the Mosque, to approach a religious man, or to touch the Koran. A few pauper patients usually visit me at this hour, report the phenomena of their complaints,—which they do, by-the-by, with unpleasant minuteness of detail,—and receive fresh instructions. At 9 A.M. Shaykh Mohammed enters, with "lecture" written upon his wrinkled brow, or I pick him up on the way, and proceed straight to the Mosque el Azhar. After three hours' hard reading with little interruption from bystanders,—most of the students being at home,—comes the call to mid-day prayer. The founder of Islam ordained but few devotions for the morning, which is the business part of the Eastern day, but during the afternoon and evening they succeed one another rapidly, and their length increases. It is then time to visit my rich patients, and afterwards, by way of accustoming myself to the sun, to wander among the bookshops for an hour or two, or simply to idle in the street. At 3 P.M. I return home, recite the afternoon prayers, and re-apply myself to study.

This is the worst part of the day. In Egypt the summer nights and mornings are, generally speaking, pleasant, but the forenoons wax sultry, and the afternoons become serious. A wind wafting the fine dust and furnace heat of the desert blows over the city, the ground returns with interest the showers of caloric from above, and not a cloud or a vapour breaks the dreary expanse of splendor on high. There being no such comforts as Indian tatties, and few but the wealthiest houses boasting glass windows, the interior of your room is somewhat more fiery than the street.

Weakened with fasting, the body feels the heat trebly, and the disordered stomach almost affects the brain. Every minute is counted with morbid fixity of idea as it passes on towards the blessed sunset, especially by those whose terrible lot is manual labor at such a season. A few try to forget their afternoon miseries in slumber, but most people take the Kaylulah, or Siesta, shortly after the meridian, holding it unwholesome to sleep late in the day.

As the Maghrib, the sunset hour, approaches—and how slowly it comes!—the town seems to recover from a trance. People flock to the windows and balconies, in order to watch the moment of their release. Some pray, others tell their beads, while others, gathering together in groups or paying visits, exert themselves to while away the lagging time.

O gladness! at length it sounds, that gun from the citadel. Simultaneously rises the sweet cry of the Muezzin, calling men to prayer, and the second cannon booms from the Abbasiyeh Palace. "El Fitar! el Fitar!" fast-breaking! fast-breaking! shout the people, and a hum of joy rises from the silent city. Your acute ears waste not a moment in conveying the delightful intelligence to your parched tongue, empty stomach, and languid limbs. You exhaust a pot full of water, no matter its size. You clap hurried hands for a pipe, you order coffee, and, provided with these comforts, you sit down, and calmly contemplate the coming pleasures of the evening.

Poor men eat heartily at once. The rich break

their fast with a light meal,—a little bread and fruit, fresh or dry, especially water-melon, sweetmeats, or such digestible dishes as "Muhallabeh"—a thin jelly of milk, starch, and rice-flour. They then smoke a pipe, drink a cup of coffee or a glass of sherbet, and recite the evening prayers; for the devotions of this hour are delicate things, and while smoking a first pipe after sixteen hours' abstinence, time easily slips away. Then they sit down to the Fatur (breakfast), *the* meal of the twenty-four hours, and eat plentifully, if they would avoid illness.

There are many ways of spending a Ramazan evening. The Egyptians have a proverb, like ours of the Salernitan school.

"After El-Ghada (early dinner) rest, if it be but for two moments:
After El-Asha (early supper) walk, if it be but two steps."

The streets are now crowded with a good-humoured throng of strollers, the many bent on pleasure, the few wending their way to mosque, where the Imam recites "Tarawih," or extra prayers. They saunter about, the accustomed pipe in hand, shopping, for the stalls are open till a late hour, or they sit in crowds at the coffee-house entrance, smoking Shishahs (water-pipes), chatting, and listening to storytellers, singers and itinerant preachers. Here, a barefooted girl trills and quavers, accompanied by a noisy tambourine and a "scrannel pipe" of abominable discordance, in honor of a perverse saint whose corpse insisted upon being buried inside some respectable man's dwelling-house. The scene reminds you strongly of the Sonneurs of

Brittany and the Zampognari from the Abruzzian Highlands bagpiping before the Madonna. There, a tall gaunt Maghrabi displays upon a square yard of dirty paper certain lines and blots, supposed to represent the venerable Kaabah, and collects coppers to defray the expenses of his pilgrimage. A steady stream of loungers sets through the principal thoroughfares towards the Ezbekiyeh Gardens, which skirt the Frank quarter: there they sit in the moonlight, listening to Greek and Turkish bands, or making merry with cakes, toasted grains, coffee, sugared-drinks, and the broad pleasantries of Kara-Gyuz, the local Punch and Judy. Here the scene is less thoroughly oriental than within the city, but the appearance of Frank dress amongst the varieties of Eastern costume, the moonlit sky, and the light mist hanging over the deep shade of the Acacia trees—whose rich scented yellow-white blossoms are popularly compared to the old Pasha's beard—make it passing picturesque. And the traveller from the far East remarks with wonder the presence of certain ladies, whose only mark of modesty is the Burka', or face-veil: upon this laxity the police looks with lenient eyes, inasmuch as, until very lately, it paid a respectable tax to the state.

Returning to the Moslem quarter, you are bewildered by its variety of sounds. Everyone talks, and talking here is always in extremes, either in a whisper, or in a scream; gesticulation excites the lungs, and strangers cannot persuade themselves that men so converse without being or becoming furious. All the street-cries, too, are in the soprano key. "In thy protection! in thy protection!" shouts a Fellah (peasant) to a sentinel, who is flogging him towards the station-house, followed by a tail of women, screaming, "Yá Ghárati—Yá Dahwati—Yá Hasrati—Yá Nidámati"—"O my calamity! O my shame!" The boys have elected a Pasha, whom they are conducting in procession, with wisps of straw for Mashals, or cressets, and outrunners, all huzzaing with ten-schoolboy power. "O thy right! O thy left! O thy face! O thy heel! O thy back, thy back!" cries the panting footman, who, huge torch on shoulder, runs before the grandee's carriage; "Bless the Prophet, and get out of the way!" "O Allah, bless him!" respond the good Moslems, some shrinking up to the walls to avoid the stick, others rushing across the road, so as to give themselves every chance of being knocked down. The donkey boy beats his ass with a heavy palm-cudgel,—he fears no treadmill here, —cursing him at the top of his voice for a "pander," a "Jew," a "Christian," and a "son of the One-eyed, whose portion is Eternal Punishment." "O chick pease! O pips!" sings the vender of parched grains, rattling the unsavoury load in his basket. "Out of the way, and say, 'There is one God,'" pants the industrious water-carrier, laden with a skin, fit burden for a buffalo. "Sweet-water, and gladden thy soul, O lemonade!" pipes the seller of that luxury, clanging his brass cups together. Then come the beggars, intensely Oriental. "My supper is in Allah's hands, my supper is in Allah's hands! whatever thou givest, that will go with thee!"

chaunts the old vagrant, whose wallet perhaps contains more provision than the basket of many a respectable shopkeeper. "Naal 'abuk—drat thy father*—O brother of a naughty sister!" is the response of some petulant Greek to the touch of the old man's staff. "The grave is darkness, and good deeds are its lamp!" sings the blind woman, rapping two sticks together: "upon Allah! upon Allah! O daughter!" cry the bystanders, when the obstinate "bint" of sixty years seizes their hands, and will not let go without extorting a farthing. "Bring the sweet (*i. e.* fire) and take the full" (*i. e.* empty cup, euphuistically), cry the long-mustachioed, fierce-browed Arnauts to the coffee-house keeper, who stands by them charmed by the rhyming repartee that flows so readily from their lips.

"Hanien," may it be pleasant to thee! is the signal for encounter.

"Thou drinkest for *ten*," replies the other, instead of returning the usual religious salutation.

"I am the cock and thou art the *hen!*" is the rejoinder,—a tart one.

"Nay, I am the thick one and thou art the *thin!*" resumes the first speaker, and so on till they come to equivoques which will not bear a literal English translation.

And sometimes, high above the hubbub, rises the melodious voice of the blind muezzin, who, from his balcony in the beetling tower rings forth, "Hie ye to

---

* For Laan 'abuk, curse thy father. So in Europe pious men have sworn per Diem instead of per Deum.

devotion! Hie ye to salvation! Devotion is better than sleep! Devotion is better than sleep!" Then good Moslems piously stand up, and mutter, previous to prayer, "Here am I at thy call, O Allah! here am I at thy call!"

Sometimes I walked with my friend to the citadel, and sat upon a high wall, one of the outworks of Mohammed Ali's mosque, enjoying a view which, seen by night, when the summer moon is near the full, has a charm no power of language can embody. Or escaping from "stifled Cairo's filth," we passed, through the Gate of Victory, into the wilderness beyond the City of the Dead. Seated upon some mound of ruins, we inhaled the fine air of the desert, inspiriting as a cordial, when starlight and dew-mists diversified a scene, which, by day, is one broad sea of yellow loam with billows of chalk rock, thinly covered by a spray of sand surging and floating in the fiery wind. There, within a mile of crowded life, all is desolate; the town walls seem crumbling to decay, the hovels are tenantless, and the paths untrodden; behind you lies the wild; before you, the thousand tomb-stones, ghastly in their whiteness, while beyond them the tall dark forms of the Mameluke Sultans' towers rise from the low and hollow ground like the spirits of kings guarding ghostly subjects in the Shadowy Realm. Or we spent the evening at some Takiyeh (Dervish's Oratory), generally preferring that called the "Gulshani," near the Muayyid Mosque outside the Mutawalli's saintly door. There is nothing attractive in its appearance. You mount a flight of ragged steps, and enter a low verandah enclosing an open stuccoed terrace, where stands the holy man's domed tomb; the two stories contain small dark rooms in which the Dervishes dwell, and the ground-floor doors open into the verandah. During the fast-month, zikrs (forms of Dervish worship) are rarely performed in the Takiyehs; the inmates pray there in congregation, or they sit conversing upon benches in the shade. And a curious medley of men they are, composed of the choicest vagabonds from every nation of Islam. Beyond this I must not describe the Takiyeh or the doings there, for the "path" of the Dervish may not be trodden by feet profane.

Curious to see something of my old friends the Persians, I called with Haji Wali upon one Mirza Husayn, who by virtue of his dignity as "Shahbandar,"—"consul-general,"—ranks with the dozen little quasi-diplomatic kings of Cairo. He suspends over his lofty gate a sign-board in which the Lion and the Sun, Iran's proud ensign, are by some Egyptian limner's art metamorphosed into a preternatural tabby-cat grasping a scimitar, with the jolly fat face of a "gay" young lady, curls and all complete, resting fondly upon her pet's concave back. This high dignitary's reception room was a court-yard "sub dio:" fronting the door were benches and cushions composing the Sadr or high place, with the parallel rows of Divans spread down the less dignified sides, and a line of naked boards, the lowest seats, ranged along the door-wall. In the middle stood three little tables supporting three huge lanterns—as is their size so is the owner's dignity—each of which contained three of the largest spermaceti candles.

The Haji and I entering took our seats upon the side benches with humility, and exchanged salutations with the great man on the Sadr. When the Darbar or levee was full, in stalked the Mirza, and all arose as he calmly divested himself of his shoes and with all due solemnity ascended his proper cushion. He is a short thin man about thirty-five, with regular features and the usual preposterous lamb-skin cap and beard, two peaked black cones at least four feet in length, measured from the tips, resting on a slender basement of pale yellow face. After a quarter of an hour of ceremonies, polite mutterings and low bendings with the right hand on the left breast, the Mirza's pipe was handed to him first, in token of his dignity—at Teheran he was probably an under-clerk in some government office. In due time we were all served with Kaliuns (Persian hookahs) and coffee by the servants, who made royal congees whenever they passed the great man, and more than once the janissary in dignity of belt and crooked sabre, entered the court to quicken our awe.

The conversation was the usual oriental thing. It is, for instance, understood that you have seen strange things in strange lands.

"Voyaging—is—victory," quotes the Mirza; the quotation is a hackneyed one, but it steps forth majestic as to pause and emphasis.

"Verily," you reply with equal ponderousness of pronunciation and novelty of citation, "in leaving home one learns life, yet a journey is a bit of Jehannum."

Or if you are a physician the "lieu commun" will be,

> "Little-learn'd doctors the body destroy:
> Little-learn'd parsons the soul destroy."

To which you will make answer, if you would pass for a man of belles lettres, by the well-known lines,

> "Of a truth, the physician hath power with drugs,
> Which, long as the patient hath life, may relieve him:
> But the tale of our days being duly told,
> The doctor is daft, and his drugs deceive him."

After sitting there with dignity, like the rest of the guests, I took my leave, delighted with the truly Persian "apparatus" of the scene. The Mirza, having no salary, lives by fees extorted from his subjects, who pay rather than lack protection; and his dragoman for a counter-fee will sell their interests shamelessly. He is a hidalgo of blue blood in pride, pompousness and poverty. There is not a sheet of writing paper in the "consulate"—when they want one a farthing is sent to the grocer's—yet the consul drives out in an old carriage with four out-riders, two tall-capped men preceding and two following the crazy vehicle. And the Egyptians laugh heartily at this display, being accustomed by sensible Mohammed Ali to consider all such parade obsolete.

About half an hour before midnight sounds the Abrar or call to prayer, at which time the latest wanderers return home to prepare for their dawn-meal. You are careful on the way to address each sentinel with a "Peace be upon thee!" especially if you have no lantern, otherwise you may chance to sleep in the guard-house. And, "chemin faisant," you cannot but stop to gaze at streets as little like what civilised Europe understands by that name as is an Egyptian temple to the new Houses of Parliament.

There are certain scenes, cannily termed "Kenspeckle," which print themselves upon memory, and which endure as long as memory lasts,—a thundercloud bursting upon the Alps, a night of stormy darkness off the Cape, an African tornado, and, perhaps, most awful of all, a solitary journey over the sandy Desert.

Of this class is a stroll through the thoroughfares of old Cairo by night. All is squalor in the brilliancy of noon-day. In darkness you see nothing but a silhouette. When however the moon is high in the heavens, and the summer stars rain light upon God's world, there is something not of earth in the view. A glimpse at the strip of pale blue sky above scarcely reveals three ells of breadth: in many places the interval is less; here the copings meet, and there the outriggings of the houses seem to interlace. Now they are parted by a pencil, then by a flood of silvery splendor; while under the projecting cornices and the huge hanging-windows of fantastic wood-work, supported by gigantic corbels, and deep verandahs, and gateways vast enough for Behemoth to pass through, and blind wynds and long cul-de-sacs, lie patches of thick darkness, made visible by the dimmest of oil lights. The arch is a favourite form: in one place you see it a mere skeleton of stone opening into some huge deserted hall; in another it is full of fretted stone and carved wood. Not a line is straight, the tall dead walls of the mosques slope over their massy buttresses, and the thin minarets seem about to fall across your path. The cornices project crookedly from the houses, while the great gables stand merely by force of cohesion. And that the Line of Beauty may not be wanting, the graceful bending form of the palm, on whose topmost feathers, quivering in the cool night breeze, the moonbeam glistens, springs from a gloomy mound, or from the darkness of a mass of houses almost level with the ground. Briefly, the whole view is so fantastic, so ghostly, that it seems rather preposterous to imagine that in such places human beings like ourselves can be born, and live through life, to carry out the command "increase and multiply," and die.

CHAPTER VI.

The Mosque.

WHEN the Byzantine Christians, after overthrowing the temples of Paganism, meditated re-building and remodelling them, poverty of invention and artistic impotence reduced them to group the spoils in a heterogeneous mass. The seaports of Egypt and the plains of Syria abounding in pillars of granite, syenite, and precious marbles, in Pharaonic, Greek, and Roman statuary, and in all manner of structural ornaments, the architects were at no loss for material. Their Syncretism, the result of chance and precipitancy, of extravagance and incuriousness, fell under eyes too ignorant to be hurt by the hybrid irregularity: it was perpetuated in the so-called Saracenic style, a plagiarism from the Byzantine, and it was reiterated in the Gothic, an off-shoot from the Saracenic. This fact accounts in the Gothic style for the manifold incongruities in the architecture, and for the phenomenon, —not solely attributable to the buildings having been erected piece-meal,—of its most classic period being that of its greatest irregularity.

Such "architectural lawlessness," such disregard for symmetry,—the result, I believe, of an imperfect "amalgamation and enrichment,"—may doubtless be defended upon the grounds both of cause and of effect.

Architecture is of the imitative arts, and Nature, the Myriomorphous, everywhere delighting in variety, appears to abhor nothing so much as perfect similarity and precise uniformity. To copy her exactly we must therefore seek that general analogy compatible with individual variety; in fact, we should avoid the over-display of order and regularity. And again, it may be asserted that, however incongruous these disorderly forms may appear to the conventional eye, we find it easy to surmount our first antipathy. Perhaps we end in admiring them the more, as we love those faces in which irregularity of feature is compensated for by diversity and piquancy of expression.

There is nothing, I believe, new in the Arab Mosque; it is an unconscious revival of the forms used from the earliest ages to denote by symbolism the worship of the generative and the creative gods. The reader will excuse me if I only glance at a subject of which the investigation would require a volume, and which, discussed at greater length, would be out of place in such a narrative as this.

The first mosque in El-Islam was erected by Mohammed at Kuba near El Medina: shortly afterwards, when he entered Mecca as a conqueror, he destroyed the 360 idols of the Arab pantheon, and he purified that venerable building from its abominations. He had probably observed in Syria the two forms appropriated by the Christians to their places of worship, the cross and the parallelogramic Basilica; he therefore preferred for the prayers of the "Saving Faith" a square, some authors say with, others without, an arcade. At length in the reign of El Walid (about A.H. 90) the cupola, the niche, and the minaret made their appearance, and what is called the Saracenic style became for ever the order of the Moslem world.

The Hindoos I believe to have been the first who symbolised by an equilateral triangle their peculiar cult, the Yoni-Lingam: in their temple architecture it became either a conoid or a perfect pyramid. Egypt denoted it by the obelisk, peculiar to that country; and the form appeared in different parts of the world: —thus in England it was a mere upright stone, and in Ireland a round tower. This we might expect to see. D'Hancarville and Brotier have successfully traced the worship itself, in its different modifications, to all people: the symbol would therefore be found everywhere. The old Arab minaret is a plain conical or polygonal tower, without balcony or stages, widely different from the Turkish, Modern-Egyptian, and Hejazi combinations of cylinder and prism, happily compared by a French traveller to "une chandelle coiffée d'un éteignoir." And finally the ancient minaret, made solid as all Gothic architecture is, and provided with a belfry, became the spire and steeple of our ancestors.

From time immemorial, in hot and rainy lands, a hypæthral court, either round or square, surrounded by a covered portico, was used for the double purpose of church and mart,—a place where God and Mammon were worshipped turn by turn. In some places we find rings of stones, like the Persian Pyrœtheia; in others, circular concave buildings representing the vault of heaven, where Fire, the divine symbol, was worshipped; and in Arabia, columnar aisles, which, surmounted by the splendid blue vault, resemble the palm-grove. The Greeks adopted this area in the fanes of Creator Bacchus; and at Puzzuoli, near Naples, it may be seen in the building vulgarly called the Temple of Serapis. It was equally well known to the Celts: in some places the Temenos was a circle, in others a quadrangle. And such to the present day is the Mosque of El-Islam.

Even the Riwak or porches surrounding the area in the Mosque are revivals of older forms. "The range of square buildings which enclose the temple of Serapis are not, properly speaking, parts of the fane, but apartments of the priests, places for victims, and sacred utensils, and chapels dedicated to subordinate deities, introduced by a more complicated and corrupt worship, and probably unknown to the founders of the original edifice." The cloisters in the Mosque became cells, used as lecture rooms, and stores for books bequeathed, to the college. They are unequal, because some are required to be of larger, others to be of smaller dimensions. The same reason causes difference of size when the building is distributed into four hyposteles opening upon the area: the porch in the direction of the Kaabah, where worshippers mostly congregate, demands greater depth than the other three. The wings were not unfrequently made unequal, either from want of building materials, or because the same extent of accommodation was not required in both. The columns were of different substances; some of handsome marble, others of rough stone meanly plastered over with dissimilar capitals, vulgarly cut shafts of various sizes, here with a pediment, there without; now turned upside down, then joined together by halves in the centre, and almost invariably nescient of intercolumnar rule. This is the result of Byzantine syncretism, carelessly and ignorantly grafted upon Arab ideas of the natural and the sublime. Loving and admiring the great, or rather the big in plan, they care little for the execution of mere details, and they have not the acumen to discern the effect which clumsy workmanship, crooked lines, and visible joints,—parts apparently insignificant,—exercise upon the whole of an edifice. Their use of colors was a false taste, commonly displayed by mankind in their religious houses, and statues of the gods. The Hindus paint their pagodas inside and outside; and rub vermilion, in token of honor, over their deities. The Persian Colossi of Kaiomars and his consort on the Balkh road, and the Sphinx of Egypt, as well as the temples of the Nile, still show traces of artificial complexion. The fanes in classic Greece have been dyed. In the Forum Romanum, one of the finest buildings still bears stains of the Tyrian purple. And to mention no other instances, in the churches and belfries of Modern Italy, we see alternate bands of white and black material so disposed as to give them the appearance of giant zebras. The origin of "Arabesque" ornament must be referred to one of the principles of El-Islam. The Moslem, forbidden by his law to decorate his Mosque with statuary and pictures, supplied their place with quotations from the Koran, and inscriptions, "plastic metaphysics," of marvellous perplexity. His alphabet lent itself to the purpose, and hence probably arose that almost inconceivable variety of lace-like fretwork, of incrustations, of Arabesques, and of geometric flowers, in which his eye delights to lose itself.

The Meccan mosque became a model to the world of El-Islam, and the nations that embraced the new faith copied the consecrated building, as religiously as Christendom produced imitations of the Holy Sepulchre. The Mosque of Omar at Jerusalem, of Amru at Babylon on the Nile, and of Taylun at Cairo were erected with some trifling improvements, such as arched cloisters and inscribed cornices, upon the plan of the Kaabah. From Egypt and Palestine the ichnography spread far and wide. It was modified, as might be expected, by national taste; what in Arabia was simple and elegant became highly ornate in Spain, florid in Turkey, and effeminate in India. Still divergence of detail has not, even after the lapse of twelve centuries, materially altered the fundamental form.

Perhaps no Eastern city affords more numerous or more accessible specimens of Mosque architecture than Cairo. Between 300 or 400 places of worship, some stately piles, others ruinous hovels, many new, more decaying and earthquake-shaken, with minarets that rival in obliquity the Pisan monster, are open to the traveller's inspection. And Europeans by following the advice of their hotelkeeper have penetrated, and can penetrate, into any one they please. If architecture be really what I believe it to be, the highest expression of a people's artistic feeling,—highest because it includes all others,—to compare the several styles of the different epochs, to observe how each monarch building his own Mosque, and calling it by his own name, identified the manner of the monument with himself, and to trace the gradual decadence of art through twelve hundred years, down to the present day, must be a work of no ordinary interest to orientalists. The limits of my plan, however, compel me to place only the heads of the argument before the reader. May I be allowed to express a hope that it will induce some learned traveller to investigate a subject in every way worthy his attention!

The Jami Taylun (9th cent.) is simple and massive, yet elegant, and in some of its details peculiar. One of the four colonnades still remains to show the original magnificence of the building; the other porches are walled and inhabited by paupers. In the centre of a quadrangle about 100 paces square is a domed building springing from a square which occupies the proper place of the Kaabah. This "Jami" (cathedral) is interesting as a point of comparison. If it be an exact copy of the Meccan temple, as it stood in A.D. 879, it shows that the latter has greatly altered in this our modern day.

Next in date to the Taylun Mosque is that of the Sultan El Hakim, third Caliph of the Fatimites, and founder of the Druze mysteries. The minarets are remarkable in shape, as well as size; they are unprovided with the usual outer gallery, they are based upon a cube of masonry, and they are pierced above with apertures apparently meaningless. A learned Cairene informed me that these spires were devised by the eccentric monarch to disperse, like large censers, fragrant smoke over the city during the hours of prayer. The Azhar and Hasanayn Mosques are simple and artless piles, celebrated for sanctity, but remarkable for nothing save ugliness. Few buildings, however, are statelier in appearance, or give a nobler idea of both founder and architect than that which bears Sultan Hasan's name. The stranger stands awe-struck before walls high towering without a single break, a hypæthral court severe in masculine beauty, a gateway that might suit the palace of the Titans, and a lofty minaret of massive grandeur. This Mosque, with its fortress aspect, owns no more relationship to the efforts of a later age than does Canterbury Cathedral to an Anglo-Indian "Gothic." For dignified beauty and refined taste, the mosque and tomb of Kaid Bey and the other Mameluke kings are admirable. Even in their present state picturesqueness presides over decay, and the traveller has seldom seen aught more striking than the rich light of the stained glass pouring through the first shades of evening upon the marble floor.

The modern Mosques must be visited, to see

Egyptian architecture in its decline and fall. That of Sittna Zaynab (our Lady Zaynab), founded by Murad Bey, the Mameluke, and interrupted by the French invasion, shows, even in its completion, some lingering traces of taste. But nothing can be more offensive than the building which every tourist flogs donkey in his hurry to see—old Mohammed Ali's "Folly" in the citadel. Its Greek architect has toiled to caricature a Mosque, to emulate the glories of our English "Oriental Pavilion." Outside, as Monckton Milnes sings,

"The shining minarets, thin and high,"

are so thin, so high above the lumpy domes, that they look like the spindles of crouching crones, and are placed in full sight of Sultan Hasan the Giant, so as to derive all the disadvantages of the contrast. Is the pointed arch forgotten by man, that this hapless building should be disgraced by large and small parallelograms of glass and wood, so placed and so formed as to give its exterior the appearance of a European theatre coiffé with oriental cupolas? Inside, money has been lavished upon alabaster full of flaws; round the bases of pillars run gilt bands; in places the walls are painted with streaks to mock marble, and the woodwork is overlaid with tinsel gold. After a glance at these abominations, one cannot be surprised to hear the old men of Egypt lament that, in spite of European education, and of prizes encouraging geometry and architecture, modern art offers a melancholy contrast to antiquity. It is said that H. H. Abbas Pasha proposed to erect for himself a mosque that shall far surpass the boast of the last generation. I venture to hope that his architect will light the "sacred fire" from Sultan Hasan's, not from Mohammed Ali's Turco-Grecian splendors. The former is like the genuine Osmanli of past ages, fierce, cold, with a stalwart frame, index of a strong mind—there was a sullen grandeur about the man. The latter is the pert and puny modern Turk in pantaloons, frock coat, and Fez, ill-dressed, and ill-bred, body and soul.

We will now enter the Mosque El Azhar. At the dwarf wooden railing we take off our slippers, hold them in the left hand, sole to sole, that no dirt may fall from them, and cross the threshold with the right foot, ejaculating, Bismillah, &c. Next we repair to the Mayza'ah, or large tank, for ablution, without which it is unlawful to appear in the House of Allah. We then seek some proper place for devotion, place our slippers on some other object in front of us to warn the lounger, and perform a two-bow prayer in honour of the Mosque. This done, we may wander about, and inspect the several objects of curiosity.

The moon shines splendidly upon a vast open court, paved with stones which are polished like glass by the feet of the Faithful. There is darkness in the body of the building, a large oblong hall, at least twice too lengthy for its height, supported by a forest of pillars, thin, poor-looking, crooked marble columns, planted avenue-like, upon torn and dirty matting. A few oil lamps shed doubtful light over scanty groups, who are debating some point of grammar, or are listening to the words of wisdom that fall from the mouth of a Wa'iz (lecturer). Presently they will leave the hypostyle, and throw themselves upon the flags of the quadrangle, where they may enjoy the open air, and avoid some fleas. It is now "long vacation:" so the holy building has become a kind of caravanserai for travellers; perhaps a score of nations meet in it; there is a confusion of tongues, and the din at times is deafening. Around the court runs a tolerably well-built colonnade, whose entablature is garnished with crimson arabesques, and in the inner wall are pierced apartments, now closed with plank doors. Of the Riwak, as the porches are called, the Azhar contains twenty-four, one for each recognised nation in El-Islam, and of these, fifteen are still open to students. Inside them we find nothing but matting, and a pile of large dingy wooden boxes, which once contained the college library: they are now, generally speaking, empty.

There is nothing worth seeing in the cluster of little dark chambers that form the remainder of the Azhar. Even the Zawiyat el Umyan (or the Blind Men's Oratory), a place whence so many "gown-rows" have emanated, is rendered interesting only by the fanaticism of its inmates, and the certainty that, if recognised in this sanctum, we shall run the gauntlet under the staves of its proprietors, the angry blind.

The Azhar is the grand collegiate Mosque of this city,—the Christ Church, in fact, of Cairo,—once celebrated through the world of El-Islam. It was built, I was told, originally in poor style by one Jauhar, the slave of a Moorish merchant, in consequence of a dream that ordered him to erect a place whence the light of science should shine upon El-Islam. It gradually increased by "Wakf" (entailed bequests) of lands, money, and books; and pious rulers made a point of adding to its size and wealth. Of late years it has considerably declined, the result of sequestrations, and of the diminished esteem in which the purely religious sciences are held in the land of Egypt. Yet it is calculated that between 2000 and 3000 students of all nations and ages here receive instruction gratis. Each one is provided with bread, in a quantity determined by the amount of endowment, at the Riwak set apart for his nation, with some article of clothing on festival days, and with a few piastres once a year. The professors, who are about 150 in number, may not take fees from their pupils; some lecture on account of the religious merit of the action, others to gain the high title of "Teacher in El Azhar." Six officials receive stipends from the government,—the Shaykh el Jami or dean, the Shaykh el Sakka, who regulates the provision of water for ablution, and others that may be called heads of departments.

The following is the course of study in the Azhar. The school-boy of four or five years' standing has been taught, by a liberal application of the maxim "the Green Rod is of the Trees of Paradise," to chaunt the Koran without understanding it, the elementary rules of arithmetic, and, if he is destined to be a learned man, the art of writing. He then registers his name in El Azhar, and applies himself to the branches of study most cultivated in El-Islam, namely Nahw (syntax), Fikh (the Law), Hadis (the Traditions of the Prophet), and Tafsir, or Exposition of the Koran.

The young Egyptian reads at the same time Sarf, or Inflexion, and Nahw (syntax). But as Arabic is his mother-tongue, he is not required to study the former so deeply as are the Turks, the Persians, and the Indians. If he desire, however, to be a proficient, he must carefully peruse five books in Sarf, and six in Nahw.

Master of grammar, our student now applies himself to its proper end and purpose, Divinity. Of the four schools those of Abu Hanifah and El Shafe'i are most common in Cairo; the followers of Ibn Malik abound only in Southern Egypt and the Berberah country, and the Hanbali is almost unknown. The theologian begins with what is called a Matn or text, a short, dry, and often obscure treatise, a mere string of precepts; in fact, the skeleton of the subject. This he learns by repeated perusal, till he can quote almost every passage literatim. He then passes to its "Sharh," or commentary, generally the work of some other savant, who explains the difficulty of the text, amplifies its Laconicisms, enters into exceptional cases, and deals with principles and reasons, as well as with mere precept. A difficult work will sometimes require

"Hashiyah," or marginal notes; but this aid has a bad name.

> "Who readeth with note,
> But learneth by rote,"

says a popular doggrel. The reason is, that the student's reasoning powers being little exercised, he learns to depend upon the dixit of a master rather than to think for himself. It also leads to the neglect of another practice, highly advocated by the eastern pedagogue.

> "The lecture is one.
> The dispute (upon the subject of the lecture) is one thousand."

In order to become a Fakih, or divine of distinguished fame, the follower of Abu Hanifah must peruse about ten volumes, some of huge size, written in a diffuse style: the Shafe'i's reading is not quite so extensive. Theology is much studied, because it leads directly to the gaining of daily bread, as priest or tutor; and other scientific pursuits are neglected for the opposite reason.

The theologian in Egypt, as in other parts of El-Islam, must have a superficial knowledge of the Prophet's traditions. Of these there are eight well known collections, but only the three first are generally read.

School-boys are instructed, almost when in their infancy, to intone the Koran; at the university they are taught a more exact system of chaunting. The style called "Hafs" is the most common in Egypt, as it is indeed throughout the Moslem world. And after learning to read the holy volume, some savans are ambitious enough to wish to understand it: under these circumstances they must dive into the Ilm el Tafsir, or the Exegesis of the Koran.

Our student is now a perfect Fakih or Mulla. But the poor fellow has no scholarship or fellowship—no easy tutorship—no fat living to look forward to. After wasting seven years, or twice seven years, over his studies, and reading till his brain is dizzy, his digestion gone, and his eyes half blind, he must either starve upon college alms, or squat, like my old Shaykh Mohammed, in a druggist's shop, or become pedagogue and preacher in some country place, on the pay of 8*l.* per annum. With such prospects it is wonderful how the Azhar can present any attractions; but the southern man is essentially an idler, and many become Olema, like Capuchins, in order to do nothing. A favoured few rise to the degree of Mudarris (professors), and thence emerge Kazis and Muftis. This is another inducement to matriculate; every undergraduate having an eye upon the Kazi-ship, with as much chance of obtaining it as the country Parocco has of becoming a cardinal. Others again devote themselves to laical pursuits, degenerate into Wakils (lawyers), or seek their fortunes as Katibs—public or private accountants.

To conclude this part of the subject, I cannot agree with Dr. Bowring when he harshly says, upon the subject of Moslem education: "The instruction given by the Doctors of the Law in the religious schools, for the formation of the Mohammedan priesthood, is of the most worthless character." Would not a superficial, hasty, and somewhat prejudiced Turk say exactly the same thing about the systems of Christ Church and Trinity College? His opinion is equally open to objection with that of those who depreciate the law itself because it deals rather in precepts than in principle, in ceremonies and ordinances rather than in ethics and æsthetics. Both are what Eastern faiths and Eastern training have ever been,—both are eminently adapted for the Oriental mind. When the people learn to appreciate ethics, and to understand psychics and æsthetics, the demand will create a supply. Meanwhile they leave transcendentalism to their poets and philosophers, and they busy themselves with preparing for heaven by practising the only part of their faith now intelligible to them—the material.

It is not to be supposed that a nation in this stage of civilisation could be so fervently devout as the Egyptians are, without the bad leaven of bigotry. The same tongue which is employed in blessing the Almighty, is, it is conceived, doing its work equally well in cursing his enemies. Wherefore the Kafir is denounced by every sex, age, class, and condition, by the man of the world as by the boy at school; and out of, as well as in, the Mosque. If you ask your friend who is the person with a black turban, he replies,

"A Christian. Allah make his Countenance cold!"

If you inquire of your servant, who are the people

singing in the next house, it is ten to one that his answer will be,

"Jews. May their lot be Jehannum!"

It appears unintelligible, still it is not less true, that Egyptians who have lived as servants under European roofs for years, retain the liveliest loathing for the manners and customs of their masters. Few Franks, save those who have mixed with the Egyptians in Oriental disguise, are aware of their repugnance to, and contempt for, Europeans,—so well is the feeling veiled under the garb of innate politeness, and so great is their reserve, when conversing with those of strange religions. I had a good opportunity of ascertaining the truth when the first rumour of a Russian war arose. Almost every able-bodied man spoke of hastening to the Jihad or holy war, and the only thing that looked like apprehension was the too eager depreciation of their foes. All seemed delighted at the idea of French cooperation, for, somehow or other, the Frenchman is everywhere popular. When speaking of England, they were not equally easy: heads were rolled, pious sentences were ejaculated, and finally out came the old Eastern cry, "Of a truth they are Shaytans, those English." The Austrians are despised, because the East knows nothing of them since the days when Osmanli hosts threatened the gates of Vienna. The Greeks are hated as clever scoundrels, ever ready to do El-Islam a mischief. The Maltese, the greatest of cowards off their own ground, are regarded with a profound contempt: these are the protégés which bring the British nation into disrepute at Cairo. And Italians are known only as "istruttori" and "distruttori"—doctors, druggists, and pedagogues.

Yet Egyptian human nature is, like human nature everywhere, contradictory. Hating and despising Europeans, they still long for European rule. This people admire an iron-handed and lion-hearted despotism; they hate a timid and a grinding tyranny. Of all foreigners, they would prefer the French yoke,—a circumstance which I attribute to the diplomatic skill and national dignity of our neighbours across the Channel. But whatever European nation secures Egypt will win a treasure. Moated on the north and south by seas, with a glacis of impassable deserts to the eastward and westward, capable of supporting an army of 180,000 men, of paying a heavy tribute, and yet able to show a considerable surplus of revenue, this country in western hands will command India, and by a ship-canal between Pelusium and Suez would open the whole of Eastern Africa.*

---

* As this canal has become a question of national interest, its advisability is surrounded with all the circumstance of unsupported assertion and bold denial. The English want a railroad, which would confine the use of Egypt to themselves. The French desire a canal that would admit the hardy cruisers of the Mediterranean into the Red Sea. The cosmopolite will hope that both projects may be carried out. Even in the seventh century Omar forbade Amru to cut the Isthmus of Suez for fear of opening Arabia to Christian vessels.

Note to Third Edition. The Canal is now a fact. As late as April 1864 Lord Palmerston informed the House of Commons that labourers might be more usefully employed in cultivating cotton than in "digging a canal through a sandy desert, and in making two harbours in deep mud and shallow waters." It is however understood that the Premier was the only one of his cabinet who took this view. Mr. Robert Stephenson, C.E., certainly regretted before his death the opinion which he had been induced to express—by desire.

There is no longer much to fear from the fanaticism of the people, and a little prudence would suffice to command the interests of the Mosque. The chiefs of corporations, in the present state of popular feeling, would offer even less difficulty to an invader or a foreign ruler than the Olema. Briefly, Egypt is the most tempting prize which the East holds out to the ambition of Europe, not excepted even the Golden Horn.

CHAPTER VII.

Preparations to quit Cairo.

AT length the slow "month of blessings" passed away. We rejoiced like Romans finishing their Quaresima, when a salvo of artillery from the citadel announced the end of our Lenten woes. On the last day of Ramazan all gave alms to the poor, at the rate of a piastre and a half for each member of the household—slave, servant, and master.

The next day, first of the three composing the Eed, or Lesser Festival, we arose before dawn, performed our ablutions, and repaired to the Mosque, to recite the peculiar prayer of the season, and to hear the sermon which bade us be "merry and wise." After which we ate and drank heartily; then with pipes and tobacco-pouches in hand, we sauntered out, to enjoy the contemplation of smiling faces and street scenery.

The favourite resort on this occasion is the large cemetery beyond the Bab el Nasr—that stern, old, massive gateway which opens upon the Suez road. There we found a scene of jollity. Tents and ambulant coffee-houses were full of men equipped in their "Sunday best," listening to singers and musicians, smoking, chatting, and looking at jugglers, buffoons, snake-charmers, Dervishes, ape-leaders, and dancing boys habited in women's attire. Eating-stalls and lollipop-shops, booths full of playthings, and sheds for lemonade and syrups, lined the roads, and disputed with swings and merry-go-rounds the regards of the little Moslems and Moslemahs. The chief item of the crowd,—fair Cairenes,—carried in their hands huge palm branches, intending to ornament therewith the tombs of parents and friends. Yet, even on this solemn occasion, there is, they say, not a little flirtation and love-making; parties of policemen are posted, with orders to interrupt all such irregularities with a long cane; but their vigilance is notoriously unequal to the task. I could not help observing that frequent pairs —doubtless cousins or other relations—wandered to unusual distances among the sand-hills, and that sometimes the confusion of a distant bastinado struck the ear. These trifles did not, however, by any means interfere with the general joy. Every one wore something new; most people were in the fresh suits of finery intended to last through the year, and so strong is personal vanity in the breasts of Orientals, men and women, young and old, that from Cairo to Calcutta it would be difficult to find a sad heart under a handsome coat. The men swaggered, the women minced their steps, rolled their eyes, and were eternally arranging, and coquetting with their head-veils. The little boys strutting about foully abused any one of their number who might have a richer suit than his neighbours. And the little girls ogled every one in the ecstacy of conceit, and glanced contemptuously at other little girls their rivals.

Weary of the country, the Haji and I wandered about the city, paying visits, which at this time are like new-year calls in continental Europe. I can describe the operation of calling in Egypt only as the discussion of pipes and coffee in one place, and of coffee and pipes in another. But on this occasion whenever we meet a friend we throw ourselves upon each other's breast, placing right arms over left shoulders, and vice versâ, squeezing like wrestlers, with intermittent hugs, then laying cheek to cheek delicately, at the same time making the loud noise of many kisses in the air. You are bound also to meet even your enemies in the most friendly way—for which mortification you afterwards hate them more cordially than before. The compliment of the season is, "Kull'am antum bil khair"—"Every year may you be well!"—in fact, our "Many happy returns of the day!" After this come abundant good wishes, and kindly prophecies, and from a "religious person" a blessing, and a short prayer. To complete the resemblance between a Moslem and a Christian festival, we have dishes of the day, fish, Shurayk the cross-bun, and a peculiarly indigestible cake, called in Egypt Kahk, the plum-pudding of El-Islam.

This year's Eed was made gloomy, comparatively speaking, by the state of politics. Report of war with Russia, with France, with England, who was going to land 3,000,000 men at Suez, and with Infideldom in general, rang through Egypt, and the city of Mars[*] became unusually martial. The government armouries, arsenals, and manufactories, were crowded with kidnapped workmen. Those who purposed a pilgrimage feared forcible detention. Wherever men gathered together, in the Mosques, for instance, or the coffeehouses, the police closed the doors, and made forcible capture of the able-bodied. This proceeding, almost as barbarous as our old impressment law, filled the main streets with detachments of squalid-looking wretches, marching to be made soldiers with collars round their necks and irons on their wrists. The dismal impression of the scene was deepened by crowds of women, who, habited in mourning, and scattering dust and mud over their rent garments, followed their sons, brothers, and husbands, with cries and shrieks. The death-wail is a peculiar way of cheering on the patriot departing "pro patriâ mori," and the origin of the custom is characteristic of the people. The principal public amusements allowed to Oriental women are those that come under the general name of "Fantasia," —birth-feasts, marriage festivals, and funerals. And the early campaigns of Mohammed Ali's family in Syria and El Hejaz having, in many cases, deprived the bereaved of their sex-right to "keen" for the dead, they have now determined not to waste the opportunity,

[*] With due deference to the many of a different opinion, I believe "Kahirah" (corrupted through the Italian into Cairo) to mean, not the "victorious," but the "City of Kahir," or Mars. It was so called because, as Richardson has informed the world, it was founded in A.D. 968 by one Jauhar when the warlike planet was in the ascendant.

but to revel in the luxury of woe at the live man's wake.

Another cloud hung over Cairo. Rumors of conspiracy were afloat. The Jews and Christians,—here as ready to take alarm as the English in Italy,— trembled at the fancied preparations for insurrection, massacre, and plunder. And even the Moslems whispered that some hundred desperadoes had resolved to fire the city, beginning with the bankers' quarter, and to spoil the wealthy Egyptians. Of course H. H. Abbas Pasha was absent at the time, and, even had he been at Cairo, his presence would have been of little use: the ruler can do nothing towards restoring confidence to a panic-stricken Oriental nation.

At the end of the Eed, as a counter-irritant to political excitement, the police magistrates began to bully the people. There is a standing order in the chief cities of Egypt, that all who stir abroad after dark without a lantern shall pass the night in the station-house. But in certain quarters at Cairo, the Ezbekiyeh for instance, a little laxity is usually allowed. Before I left the capital the licence was withdrawn, and the sudden strictness caused many ludicrous scenes.

If by chance you (clad in Oriental garb) had sent on your lantern to a friend's house by your servant, and had leisurely followed it five minutes after the hour of eight—you were sure to be met, stopped, collared, questioned, and captured by the patrol. You probably punched three or four of them, but found the dozen too strong for you. Held tightly by the sleeves, skirts, and collar of your wide outer garment, you were hurried away on a plane of about nine inches above the ground, your feet mostly treading the air. You were dragged along with a rapidity which scarcely permitted you to answer strings of questions concerning your name, nation, dwelling, faith, profession, and self in general,—especially concerning the present state of your purse. If you lent an ear to the voice of the charmer that began by asking a crown to release you, and gradually came down to two-pence half-penny, you fell into a simple trap; the butt-end of a musket applied à posteriori, immediately after the transfer of property, convicted you of wilful waste. But if, more sensibly, you pretended to have forgotten your purse, you were reviled, and dragged with increased violence of shaking to the office of the Zabit, or police magistrate. You were spun through the large archway leading to the court, every fellow in uniform giving you, as you passed, a Kafa, "cuff," on the back of the neck. Despite your rage, you were forced up the stairs to a long gallery full of people in a predicament like your own. Again your name, nation—I suppose you to be masquerading—offence, and other particulars were asked, and carefully noted in a folio by a ferocious-looking clerk.

If you knew no better, you were summarily thrust into the Hasil, or condemned cell, to pass the night with pickpockets and ruffians, pell-mell. But if an adept in such matters, you insisted upon being conducted before the "Pasha of the night," and, the clerk fearing to refuse, you were hurried to the great man's office hoping for justice, and dealing out ideal vengeance to your captors,—the patrol. Here you found the dignitary sitting with pen, ink, and paper before him, and pipe and coffee-cup in hand, upon a wide Divan of dingy chintz, in a large dimly-lit room, with two guards by his side, and a semicircle of recent seizures vociferating before him. When your turn came, you were carefully collared, and led up to the presence, as if even at that awful moment you were mutinously and murderously disposed. The Pasha, looking at you with a vicious sneer, turned up his nose, ejaculated "Ajemi," and prescribed the bastinado. You observed that the mere fact of being a Persian did not give mankind a right to capture, imprison, and punish you; you declared moreover that you were no Persian, but an Indian under British protection. The Pasha, a man accustomed to obedience, then stared at you, to frighten you, and you, we will suppose, stared at him, till, with an oath, he turned to the patrol, and asked them your offence. They all simultaneously swore by Allah, that you had been found without a lantern, dead-drunk, beating respectable people, breaking into houses, robbing and invading harems.

You openly told the Pasha, that they were eating abominations; upon which he directed one of his guards to smell your breath,—the charge of drunkenness being tangible. The fellow, a comrade of your capturers, advanced his nose to your lips; as might be expected, cried, "Kikh,"—Fie! or Ugh!—contorted his countenance, and answered, by the beard of "Effendina"—"Our lord," *i. e.* H. H. the Pasha—that he perceived a pestilent odour of distilled waters. This announcement probably elicited a grim grin from the "Pasha of the night," who loves Curaçoa, and who is not indifferent to the charms of Cognac. Then by his favour (for you improved the occasion), you were allowed to spend the hours of darkness on a wooden bench, in the adjacent long gallery, together with certain little parasites, for which polite language has no name.

In the morning the janissary of your consulate was sent for; he came, and claimed you; you were led off criminally; again you gave your name and address, and if your offence was merely sending on your lantern, you were dismissed with advice to be more careful in future. And assuredly your first step was towards the Hammam.

But if, on the other hand, you had declared yourself a European, you would either have been dismissed at once, or sent to your consul, who is here judge, jury, and jailor. Egyptian authority has of late years lost half its prestige. When Mr. Lane first settled at Cairo, all Europeans accused of aggression against Moslems were, he tells us, surrendered to the Turkish magistrates. Now, the native powers have no jurisdiction over strangers, nor can the police enter their houses. If the West would raise the character of its Eastern co-religionists, it will be forced to push the system a point further, and to allow all bonâ-fide Christian subjects to register their names at the different consulates whose protection they might prefer. This is what Russia has so "unwarrantably and outrageously" attempted. We confine ourselves to a lesser injustice, which deprives Eastern states of their right as independent Powers to arrest, and to judge foreigners, who for interest or convenience settle in their dominions. But we still shudder at the right of arrogating any such claim over the born lieges of Oriental Powers. What, however, would be the result were Great Britain to authorise her sons resident at Paris, or Florence, to refuse attendance at a French or an Italian court of justice, and to demand that the police should never force the doors of an English subject? I commend this consideration to all those who "stickle for abstract rights" when the interest and progress of others are concerned, and who become somewhat latitudinarian and concrete in cases where their own welfare and aggrandisement are at stake.

Besides patients I made some pleasant acquaintances at Cairo. Antun Zananire, a young Syrian of considerable attainments as a linguist, paid me the compliment of permitting me to see the fair face of his "Hareem." Mr. Hatchadur Nury, an Armenian gentleman, well known in Bombay, amongst other acts of kindness, introduced me to one of his compatriots, Khwajah Yusuf, whose advice was most useful to me. The Khwajah had wandered far and wide, picking up everywhere some scrap of strange knowledge, and his history was a romance. Expelled for a youthful peccadillo from Cairo, he started upon his travels, qualified himself for sanctity at Mecca and El Medina, became a religious beggar at Baghdad, studied French in Paris, and finally settled down as a professor of languages, under an amnesty, at Cairo. In his house I saw an Armenian marriage. The occasion was memorable: after the gloom and sameness of Moslem society, nothing could be more gladdening than the unveiled face of a pretty woman. Some of the guests were undeniably charming brunettes, with the blackest possible locks, and the brightest conceivable eyes. Only one pretty girl wore the national costume; yet they all smoked chibouques and sat upon the Divans, and, as they entered the room, they kissed with a sweet simplicity the hands of the priest, and of the other old gentlemen present.

Among the number of my acquaintances was a Meccan boy, Mohammed el Basyuni, from whom I bought the pilgrim-garb called "El Ihram" and the Kafan or shroud, with which the Moslem usually starts upon such a journey as mine. He, being in his way homewards after a visit to Constantinople, was most anxious to accompany me in the character of a "companion." But he had travelled too much to suit me; he had visited India, he had seen Englishmen, and he had lived with the "Nawab Balu" of Surat. Moreover he showed signs of over-wisdom. He had been a regular visitor, till I cured one of his friends of an ophthalmia, after which he gave me his address at

Mecca, and was seen no more. Haji Wali described him and his party to be "Nas jarrár" (extractors), and certainly he had not misjudged them. But the sequel will prove how "der Mensch denkt und Gott lenkt," and as the boy, Mohammed, eventually did become my companion throughout the pilgrimage, I will place him before the reader as summarily as possible.

He is a beardless youth, of about eighteen, chocolate-brown, with high features, and a bold profile; his bony and decided Meccan cast of face is lit up by the peculiar Egyptian eye, which seems to descend from generation to generation. His figure is short and broad, with a tendency to be obese, the result of a strong stomach and the power of sleeping at discretion. He can read a little, write his name, and is uncommonly clever at a bargain. Mecca had taught him to speak excellent Arabic, to understand the literary dialect, to be eloquent in abuse, and to be profound at prayer and pilgrimage. Constantinople has given him a taste for Anacreontic singing, and female society of the questionable kind, a love of strong waters,—the hypocrite looked positively scandalised when I first suggested the subject,—and an off-hand latitudinarian mode of dealing with serious subjects in general. I found him to be the youngest son of a widow, whose doting fondness had moulded his disposition; he was selfish and affectionate, as spoiled children usually are, volatile, easily offended and as easily pacified (the Oriental), coveting other men's goods, and profuse of his own (the Arab), with a matchless intrepidity of countenance (the traveller), brazen lunged, not more than half brave, exceedingly astute, with an acute sense of honor, especially where his relations were concerned (the individual). I have seen him in a fit of fury because some one cursed his father; and he and I nearly parted because on one occasion I applied to him an epithet which etymologically considered might be exceedingly insulting to a high-minded brother, but which in popular parlance signifies nothing. This "point d'honneur" was the boy Mohammed's strong point.

During the Ramazan I laid in my stores for the journey. These consisted of tea, coffee, loaf-sugar, rice, dates, biscuit, oil, vinegar, tobacco, lanterns, and cooking pots, a small bell-shaped tent, costing twelve shillings, and three water-skins for the desert. The provisions were placed in a "Kafas" or hamper artistically made of palm sticks, and in a huge Sahharah, or wooden box, about three feet each way, covered with leather or skin, and provided with a small lid fitting into the top. The former, together with my green box containing medicines, and saddle-bags full of clothes, hung on one side of the camel, a counterpoise to the big Sahharah on the other flank, Bedawin, like muleteers, always requiring a balance of weight. On the top of the load was placed transversely a Shibriyah or cot, on which Shaykh Nur squatted like a large crow. This worthy had strutted out into the streets armed with a pair of horse-pistols and a sword almost as long as himself. No sooner did the mischievous boys of Cairo—they are as bad as the gamins of Paris and London—catch sight of him than they began to scream with laughter at the sight of the "Hindi (Indian) in arms," till like a vagrant owl pursued by a flight of larks he ran back into the caravanserai.

Having spent all my ready money at Cairo I was obliged to renew the supply. My native acquaintances advised me to take at least eighty pounds sterling, and considering the expense of outfit for desert travelling, the sum did not appear excessive. I should have found some difficulty in raising the money had it not been for the kindness of a friend at Alexandria, John Thurburn, and Mr. Shepherd, then of Shepherd's Hotel, Cairo, presently a landed proprietor near Rugby, and now no more. My Indians scrutinised the diminutive square of paper—the letter of credit—as a raven may sometimes be seen peering, with head askance, into the interior of a suspected marrow-bone. "Can this be a bonâ fide draft?" they mentally inquired. And finally they offered, most politely, to write to England for me, to draw the money, and to forward it in a sealed bag directed "El Medina." I need scarcely say that such a style of transmission would, in the case of precious metals, have left no possible chance of its safe arrival.

When the difficulty was overcome, I bought fifty pounds' worth of German dollars (Maria Theresas), and invested the rest in English and Turkish sovereigns. The gold I myself carried; part of the silver I sewed up in Shaykh Nur's leather waist-belt, and part was packed in the boxes, for this reason. When Bedawin begin plundering a respectable man, if they find a certain amount of ready money in his baggage, they do not search his person: if they find none they proceed to a bodily inspection, and if his waist-belt be empty they are rather disposed to rip open his stomach, in the belief that he must have some peculiarly ingenious way of secreting valuables.

Having passed through this trouble I immediately fell into another. My hardly-earned Alexandrian passport required a double visa, one at the Police office, the other at the Consul's. After returning to Egypt I found it was the practice of travellers who required any civility from Dr. Walne, then the English official at Cairo, to enter the "presence" furnished with an order from the Foreign Office. I had neglected the precaution, and had ample reason to regret having done so. Failing at the British consulate, and unwilling to leave Cairo without being "en règle,"—the Egyptians warned me that Suez was a place of obstacles to pilgrims—I was obliged to look elsewhere for protection. My friend Haji Wali was the first consulted: after a long discussion he offered to take me to his consul, the Persian, and to find out for what sum I could become a temporary subject of the Shah. We went to the sign of the "Lion and the Sun," and we found the dragoman,* a subtle Syrian Christian,

* The consular dragoman is one of the greatest abuses I know. The tribe is, for the most part, Levantine and Christian, and its connections are extensive.

who, after a rigid inquiry into the state of my purse (my country was no consideration at all), introduced me to the Great Man. I have described this personage once already, and he merits not a second notice. The interview was truly ludicrous. He treated us with exceeding hauteur, motioned me to sit almost out of hearing, and after rolling his head in profound silence for nearly a quarter of an hour, vouchsafed the information that though my father *might* be a Shirazi, and my mother an Afghan, he had not the honor of my acquaintance. His companion, a large old Persian with Polyphemean eyebrows and a mulberry beard, put some gruff and discouraging questions. I quoted the verses

"He is a man who benefits his fellow-men,
Not he who says 'why?' and 'wherefore?' and 'how much?'"

upon which an imperious wave of the arm directed

The father will perhaps be interpreter to the English, the son to the French consulate. By this means, the most private affairs will become known to every member of the department, except the head, and eventually to that best of spy-trainers, the Turkish government. This explains how a subordinate, whose pay is 900*l.* per annum, and who spends double that sum, can afford, after twelve or thirteen years' service, to purchase a house for 2000*l.* and to furnish it for as much more. Besides which the condition, the ideas, and the very nature of these dragomans are completely Oriental. The most timid and cringing of men, they dare not take the proper tone with a government to which, in case of the expulsion of a consul, they and their families would become subject. And their prepossessions are utterly Oriental. Hanna Massara, dragoman to the consul-general at Cairo, in my presence, and before others, advocated the secret murder of a Moslem girl who had fled with a Greek, on the grounds that an adulteress must always be put to death, either publicly or under the rose. Yet this man is an "old and tried servant" of the state.

Such evils might be in part mitigated by employing English youths, of whom an ample supply, if there were any demand, would soon be forthcoming. This measure has been advocated by the best authorities, but without success. Most probably, the reason of the neglect is the difficulty how to begin, or where to end, the Augean labor of consular reform.

me to return to the dragoman, who had the effrontery to ask me four pounds sterling for a Persian passport. I offered one. He derided my offer, and I went away perplexed. On my return to Cairo some months afterwards, he sent to say that had he known me as an Englishman, I should have had the document gratis—a civility for which he was duly thanked.

At last my Shaykh Mohammed hit upon *the* plan. "Thou art," said he, "an Afghan; I will fetch hither the principal of the Afghan college at the Azhar, and he, if thou make it worth his while" (this in a whisper), "will be thy friend." The case was looking desperate; my preceptor was urged to lose no time.

Presently Shaykh Mohammed returned in company with the principal, a little, thin, ragged-bearded, one-eyed, hare-lipped divine, dressed in very dirty clothes, of non-descript cut. Born at Muscat of Afghan parents, and brought up at Mecca, he was a kind of cosmopolite, speaking five languages fluently, and full of reminiscences of toil and travel. He refused pipes and coffee, professing to be ascetically disposed: but he ate more than half my dinner, to reassure me I presume, should I have been fearful that abstinence might injure his health. We then chatted in sundry tongues. I offered certain presents of books, which were rejected (such articles being valueless), and the Shaykh Abd el Wahhab having expressed his satisfaction at my account of myself, told me to call for him at the Azhar Mosque next morning.

Accordingly at six P.M. Shaykh Mohammed and

Abdullah Khan—Khan is a title assumed in India and other countries by all Afghans and Pathans, their descendants, simple as well as gentle—the latter equipped in a gigantic sprigged-muslin turban, so as to pass for a student of theology, repaired to El Azhar. Passing through the open quadrangle we entered the large hall which forms the body of the Mosque. In the northern wall was a dwarf door, leading by break-neck stairs to a pigeon-hole, the study of the learned Afghan Shaykh. We found him ensconced behind piles of musty and greasy manuscripts, surrounded by scholars and scribes, with whom he was cheapening books. He had not much business to transact; but long before he was ready, the stifling atmosphere drove us out of the study, and we repaired to the hall. Presently the Shaykh joined us, and we all rode on away to the citadel, and waited in a mosque till the office hour struck. When the doors were opened we went into the "Divan," and sat patiently till the Shaykh found an opportunity of putting in a word. The officials were two in number; one an old invalid, very thin and sickly-looking, dressed in the Turco-European style, whose hand was being severely kissed by a troop of religious beggars, to whom he had done some small favors; the other was a stout young clerk, whose duty it was to engross, and not to have his hand kissed. My name and other essentials were required, and no objections were offered, for who holier than the Shaykh Abd el Wahhab ibn Yunus el Sulaymani? The clerk filled up a printed paper in the Turkish language, apparently borrowed from the European method for spoiling the traveller; certified me, upon the Shaykh's security, to be one Abdullah, the son of Yusuf (Joseph), originally from Cabool; described my person, and, in exchange for five piastres, handed me the document. I received it with joy.

With bows, and benedictions, and many wishes that Allah might make it the officials' fate to become pilgrims, we left the office, and returned towards El Azhar. When we had nearly reached the Mosque, Shaykh Mohammed lagged behind, and made the sign. I drew near the Afghan, and asked for his hand. He took the hint, and muttering "It is no matter!"—"It is not necessary!"—"By Allah it is not required!" extended his fingers, and brought the musculus guineorum to bear upon three dollars. Poor man! I believe it was his necessity that consented to be paid for doing a common act of Moslem charity; he had a wife and children, and the calling of an Alim is no longer worth much in Egypt.

My departure from Cairo was hastened by an accident. I lost my reputation by a little misfortune which happened in this wise.

At Haji Wali's room in the caravanserai, I met a Yuz-bashi, or captain of Albanian Irregulars, who was in Egypt on leave from El Hejaz. He was a tall, bony, and broad-shouldered mountaineer, about forty years old, with the large "bombé" brow, the fierce eyes, thin lips, lean jaws, and peaky chin of his race. His mustachios were enormously long and tapering, and the rest of his face, like his head, was close shaven. His "Fustan" (kilt) was none of the cleanest, nor was the red cap, which he wore rakishly pulled over his frowning forehead, quite free from stains. Not permitted to carry the favourite pistols, he contented himself with sticking his right hand in the empty belt, and stalking about the house with a most military mien. Yet he was as little of a bully as carpet knight, that same Ali Agha; his body showed many a grisly scar, and one of his shin bones had been broken by a Turkish bullet, when he was playing tricks on the Albanian hills,—an accident inducing a limp, which he attempted to conceal by a heavy swagger. When he spoke, his voice was affectedly gruff; he had a sad knack of sneering, and I never saw him thoroughly sober.

Our acquaintance began with a kind of storm, which blew over, and left fine weather. I was showing Haji Wali my pistols with Damascene barrels when Ali Agha entered the room. He sat down before me with a grin which said intelligibly enough, "What business have *you* with weapons?"—snatched the arm out of my hand, and began to inspect it as a connoisseur. Not admiring this procedure, I wrenched it away from him, and, addressing myself to Haji Wali, proceeded quietly with my dissertation. The captain of Irregulars and I then looked at each other. He cocked his cap on one side, in token of excited pugnacity. I twirled my mustachios to display a kindred emotion. Had he been armed, and in El Hejaz, we should have fought it out at once, for the Arnaouts are "terribili colla pistola," as the Italians say, meaning that upon the least provocation, they pull out a horse-pistol, and fire it in the face of friend or foe. Of course, the only way under these circumstances is to anticipate them; but even this desperate prevention seldom saves a stranger, as whenever there is danger, these men go about in pairs. I never met with a more reckless brood. Upon the line of march Albanian troops are not allowed ammunition; for otherwise there would be half a dozen duels a day. When they quarrel over their cups, it is the fashion for each man to draw a pistol, and to place it against his opponent's breast. The weapons being kept accurately clean seldom miss fire, and if one combatant draw trigger before the other, he would immediately be shot down by the bystanders. In Egypt these men,—who are used as irregulars, and are often quartered upon the hapless villagers, when unable or unwilling to pay taxes,—were the terror of the population. On many occasions they have quarrelled with foreigners, and insulted European women. In El Hejaz their recklessness awes even the Bedawin. The townspeople say of them that "tripe-sellers, and bath-servants at Stambul, they become Pharaohs—tyrants, ruffians—in Arabia." At Jeddah the Arnaouts have amused themselves with firing at the English consul (Mr. Ogilvie) when he walked upon his terrace. And this man-shooting appears a favourite sport with them: at Cairo numerous stories illustrate the sang froid with which they used to knock over the camel-drivers, if any one dared to ride past their barracks. The Albanians vaunt their skill in using weapons, and their pretensions impose upon Arabs as well as Egyptians; yet I have never found them wonderful with any arm (the pistol alone excepted), and our officers, who have visited their native hills, speak of them as tolerable, but by no means first-rate rifle shots.

The captain of Irregulars being unhappily debarred the pleasure of shooting me, after looking fierce for a time, rose, and walked majestically out of the room. A day or two afterwards, he called upon me civilly enough, sat down, drank a cup of coffee, smoked a pipe, and began to converse. But as he knew about a hundred Arabic words, and I as many Turkish, our conversation was carried on under difficulties. Presently he asked me in a whisper for "Raki." I replied that there was none in the house, which induced a sneer, and an ejaculation sounding like "Himar" (ass), the slang synonym amongst fast Moslems for water-drinker.

After rising to depart he seized me waggishly, with an eye to a trial of strength. Thinking that an Indian doctor and a temperance man would not be very dangerous, he exposed himself to what is professionally termed a "cross-buttock," and had his "nut" come in contact with the stone floor instead of my bed, he might not have drunk for many a day. The fall had a good effect upon his temper. He jumped up, patted my head, called for another pipe, and sat down to show me his wounds, and to boast of his exploits. I could not help remarking a ring of English gold, with a bezel of bloodstone, sitting strangely upon his coarse sun-stained hand. He declared that it had been snatched by him from a Konsul (consul) at Jeddah, and he volubly related, in a mixture of Albanian, Turkish, and Arabic, the history of his acquisition. He begged me to supply him with a little poison that "would not lie," for the purpose of quieting a troublesome enemy, and he carefully stowed away in his pouch five grains of calomel, which I gave him for that laudable purpose. Before taking leave he pressed me strongly to go and drink with him: I refused to do so during the day, but, wishing to see how these men sacrifice to Bacchus, promised compliance that night.

About 9 o'clock, when the caravanserai was quiet, I took pipe, and tobacco-pouch, stuck my dagger in my belt, and slipped into Ali Agha's room. He was sitting on a bed spread upon the ground: in front of him stood four wax candles (all Orientals hate drinking in any but a bright light), and a tray containing a basin of stuff like soup maigre, a dish of cold stewed meat, and two bowls of Salatah (sliced cucumber and curds). The "materials" peeped out of an iron pot filled with water; one was a long, thin, white-glass flask of Raki, the other a bottle of some strong perfume. Both were wrapped up in wet rag, the usual refrigerator.

Ali Agha welcomed me politely, and seeing me

admire the preparations, bade me beware how I suspected an Albanian of not knowing how to drink; he made me sit by him on the bed, threw his dagger to a handy distance, signalled me to do the same, and prepared to begin the bout. Taking up a little tumbler, in shape like those from which French postilions used to drink "la goutte," he inspected it narrowly, wiped out the interior with his forefinger, filled it to the brim, and offered it to his guest with a bow. I received it with a low salam, swallowed its contents at once, turned it upside down in proof of fair play, replaced it upon the floor, with a jaunty movement of the arm, somewhat like a pugilist delivering a "rounder," bowed again, and requested him to help himself. The same ceremony followed on his part. Immediately after each glass,—and rapidly the cup went about,—we swallowed a draught of water, and ate a spoonful of the meat or the Salatah in order to cool our palates. Then we reapplied ourselves to our pipes, emitting huge puffs,—a sign of being "fast" men,—and looked facetiously at each other,—drinking being considered by Moslems a funny and pleasant sort of sin.

The Albanian captain was at least half seas over when we began the bout, yet he continued to fill and to drain without showing the least progress towards ebriety. I in vain for a time expected the "bad-masti," (as the Persians call it,) the horse play, and the gross facetiæ, which generally accompany southern and eastern tipsiness. Ali Agha, indeed, occasionally took up the bottle of perfume, filled the palm of his right hand, and dashed it in my face; I followed his example, but our pleasantries went no further.

Presently my companion started a grand project, namely, that I should entice the respectable Haji Wali into the room, where we might force him to drink. The idea was facetious: it was making a Bow-street magistrate polk at a casino. I started up to fetch the Haji: and when I returned with him Ali Agha was found in a new stage of "freshness." He had stuck a green-leaved twig upright in the floor, and had so turned over a goblet of water, that its contents trickled slowly, in a tiny stream under the verdure; whilst he was sitting before it mentally gazing, with an outward show of grim Quixotic tenderness, upon the shady trees and the cool rills of his fatherland. Possibly he had peopled the place with "young barbarians at play;" for verily I thought that a tear "which had no business there" was glistening in his stony eye.

The appearance of Haji Wali suddenly changed the scene. Ali Agha jumped up, seized the visitor by the shoulder, compelled him to sit down, and, ecstasied by the good man's horror at the scene, filled a tumbler, and with the usual grotesque grimaces insisted upon its being drunk off. Haji Wali stoutly refused; then Ali Agha put it to his own lips, and drained it with a hurt-feeling and reproachful aspect. We made our unconvivial friend smoke a few puffs, and then we returned to the charge. In vain the Haji protested that throughout life he had avoided the deadly sin; in vain he promised to drink with us to-morrow,—in vain he quoted Koran, and alternately coaxed, and threatened us with the police. We were inexorable. At last the Haji started upon his feet, and rushed away, regardless of any thing but escape, leaving his Tarbush, his slippers, and his pipe, in the hands of the enemy. The host did not dare to pursue his recreant guest beyond the door, but returning he carefully sprinkled the polluting liquid on the cap, pipe, and shoes, and called the Haji an ass in every tongue he knew.

Then we applied ourselves to supper, and dispatched the soup, the stew, and the Salatah. A few tumblers and pipes were exhausted to obviate indigestion, when Ali Agha arose majestically, and said that he required a troop of dancing girls to gladden his eyes with a ballet.

I represented that such persons are no longer admitted into caravanserais. He inquired, with calm ferocity, "who hath forbidden it?" I replied "the Pasha;" upon which Ali Agha quietly removed his cap, brushed it with his dexter fore-arm, fitted it on his forehead, raking forwards, twisted his mustachios to the sharp point of a single hair, shouldered his pipe, and moved towards the door, vowing, that he would make the Pasha himself come, and dance before us.

I foresaw a brawl, and felt thankful that my boon companion had forgotten his dagger. Prudence whispered me to return to my room, to bolt the door, and to go to bed, but conscience suggested that it would be unfair to abandon the Albanian in his present helpless state. I followed him into the outer gallery, pulling him, and begging him, as a despairing wife might urge a drunken husband, to return home. And he, like the British husband, being greatly irritated by the unjovial advice, instantly belaboured with his pipe-stick the first person he met in the gallery, and sent him flying down the stairs with fearful shouts of "O Egyptians! O ye accursed! O genus of Pharaoh! O race of dogs! O Egyptians!"

He then burst open a door with his shoulder, and reeled into a room where two aged dames were placidly reposing by the side of their spouses, who were basket-makers. They immediately awoke, seeing a stranger, and hearing his foul words, they retorted with a hot volley of vituperation.

Put to flight by the old women's tongues, Ali Agha, in spite of all my endeavours, reeled down the stairs, and fell upon the sleeping form of the night porter, whose blood he vowed to drink—the Oriental form of threatening "spiflication." Happily for the assaulted, the Agha's servant, a sturdy Albanian lad, was lying on a mat in the doorway close by. Roused by the tumult he jumped up, and found the captain in a state of fury. Apparently the man was used to the master's mood. Without delay he told us all to assist, and we lending a helping hand, half dragged and half carried the Albanian to his room. Yet even in this ignoble plight, he shouted with all the force of his lungs the old war-cry, "O Egyptians! O race of dogs! I have dishonored all Sikandariyah—all Kahirah—all Suways,"

—Anglicè, Alexandria, Cairo, and Suez,—an extensive field of operations. And in this vaunting frame of mind he was put to bed. No Welsh undergraduate at Oxford, under similar circumstances, ever gave more trouble.

"You had better start on your pilgrimage at once," said Haji Wali, meeting me the next morning with a "goguenard" smile.

He was right. Throughout the caravanserai nothing was talked of for nearly a week but the wickedness of the captain of Albanian Irregulars, and the hypocrisy of the staid Indian doctor. Thus it was, gentle reader, that I lost my reputation of being a "serious person" at Cairo. And all I have to show for it is the personal experience of an Albanian drinking-bout.

I wasted but little time in taking leave of my friends, telling them by way of precaution, that my destination was Mecca viâ Jeddah, and firmly determining, if possible, to make El Medina viâ Yambu. "Conceal," says the Arab's proverb, "thy tenets, thy treasure, and thy travelling."

CHAPTER VIII.

From Cairo to Suez.

SHAYKH NASSAR, a Bedawi of Tur (Mount Sinai), being on his way homewards, agreed to let me have two dromedaries for the sum of 50 piastres, or about ten shillings each. Being desirous to set out with a certain display of respectability, I accepted these terms; a man of humbler pretensions would have travelled with a single animal, and a camel-man running behind him. But, besides ostentation, I wanted my attendant to be mounted, that we might make a forced march in order to ascertain how much a four years' life of European effeminacy had impaired my powers of endurance. The reader may believe the assertion that there are few better tests than an eighty-four-mile-ride in midsummer, on a bad wooden saddle, borne by a worse dromedary, across the Suez desert. Even the Squire famed for being copper-sheeted might not have disdained a trial of the kind.

I started my Indian boy and heavy luggage for Suez two days before the end of the Eed,—laden camels generally taking fifty-five or sixty hours to do the journey, and I spent the intermediate time with Haji Wali. He advised me to mount about 3 P.M., so that I might arrive at Suez on the evening of the next day, and assisted me in making due preparations of water, tobacco, and provisions. Early on the morning of departure the Afghan Shaykh came to the caravanserai, and breakfasted with us, "because Allah willed it." After a copious meal he bestowed upon me a stately benediction, and would have embraced me, but I humbly bent over his hand: sad to relate, immediately that his back was turned, Haji Wali raised his forefinger to a right angle with the palm, and burst into a shout of irreverent laughter. At 3 o'clock Nassar, the Bedawi, came to announce that the dromedaries were saddled. I dressed myself, sticking a pistol in my belt, and passing the crimson silk cord of the Hamail or pocket Koran over my shoulder, in token of being a pilgrim. Then distributing a few trifling presents to friends and servants, and, accompanied by the Shaykh Mohammed, and Haji Wali, I descended the stairs with an important gait. In the court-yard squatted the camels, (dromedaries they could not be called,) and I found that a second driver was going to accompany us. I objected to this, as the extra Bedawi would, of course, expect to be fed by me; but Nassar swore that the man was his brother, and, as you rarely gain by small disputes with these people, he was allowed to have his own way.

Then came the preparatory leave-takings. Haji Wali embraced me heartily, and so did my poor old Shaykh, who, despite his decrepitude and my objections, insisted upon accompanying me to the city gate. I mounted the camel, crossed my legs before the pommel—stirrups are not used in Egypt—and, preceding my friend, descended the street leading towards the desert. As we emerged from the huge gateway of the caravanserai all the bystanders, except only the porter, who believed me to be a Persian, and had seen me with the drunken captain, exclaimed, "Allah bless thee, Y'al Hajj (O pilgrim!), and restore thee to thy country and thy friends!" And passing through the Bab el Nasr, where I addressed the salutation of peace to the sentry, and to the officer commanding the guard, both gave me God-speed with great cordiality—the pilgrim's blessing in Asia, like the old woman's in Europe, being supposed to possess peculiar efficacy. Outside the gate my friends took a final leave of me, and I will not deny having felt a tightening of heart as their honest faces and forms faded in the distance.

But Shaykh Nassar switches his camel's shoulder, and appears inclined to take the lead. This is a trial of manliness. There is no time for emotion. Not a moment can be spared, even for a retrospect. I kick my dromedary, who steps out into a jog-trot. The Bedawin with a loud ringing laugh attempt to give me the go-by. I resist, and we continue like children till the camels are at their speed, though we have eighty-four miles before us, and above us an atmosphere like a furnace blast. The road is deserted at this hour, otherwise grave Moslem travellers would have believed the police to be nearer than convenient to us.

Presently we drew rein, and exchanged our pace for one more seasonable, whilst the sun began to tell on man and beast. High raised as we were above the ground, the reflected heat struck us sensibly, and the glare of a macadamised road added a few extra degrees of caloric. The Bedawin, to refresh themselves, prepare to smoke. They fill my chibouque, light it with a flint and steel, and cotton dipped in a solution of gunpowder, and pass it over to me. After a few puffs I return it to them, and they use it turn by turn. Then they begin to while away the tedium of the road by asking questions, which passe-temps is not easily exhausted; for they are never satisfied till they know as much of you as you do of yourself. They next resort to talking about victuals; for with this hungry race, food, as a topic of conversation, takes the place of money in happier lands. And lastly, even this engrossing subject being exhausted for the moment, they take refuge in singing: and, monotonous and droning as it is, their Modinha has yet an artless plaintiveness, which admirably suits the singer and the scenery. If you listen to the words, you will surely hear allusions to bright verdure, cool shades, bubbling rills, or something which hereabouts man hath not, and yet which his soul desires.

And now while Nassar and his brother are chaunting a duet, the refrain being,

"W'al arz mablul bi matar,"
"And the earth wet with rain,"—

I must crave leave to say a few words, despite the triteness of the subject, about the modern Sinaitic race of Arabs.

Besides the tribes occupying the northern parts of the peninsula, five chief clans are enumerated by Burckhardt. Nassar, and other authorities at Suez, divided them into six, namely:—

1. Karashi, who, like the Gara in Eastern Arabia, claim an apocryphal origin from the great Koraysh tribe.

2. Salihi, the principal family of the Sinaitic Bedawin.

3. Arimi: according to Burckhardt this clan is merely a sub-family of the Sawalihahs.

4. Saidi. Burckhardt calls them Welad Said, and derives them also from the Sawalihahs.

5. Aliki, and lastly, the

6. Muzaynah, generally pronounced M'zaynah. This class is an off-shoot from the great Jehaynah tribe inhabiting the barrens about Yambu'. According to oral tradition five persons, the ancestors of the present Muzaynah race, were forced by a blood-feud to fly their native country. They landed at the Shurum or Creek-ports, and have now spread themselves over the eastern parts of the peninsula. In El Hejaz the Muzaynah is an old and noble tribe. It produced Kaab el Ahbar, the celebrated poet, to whom Mohammed gave the cloak which the Ottomans believe to have been taken by Sultan Selim from Egypt, and to have been converted under the name of Khirkah Sherif into the national Oriflamme.

There are some interesting ethnographical points about these Sinaitic clans—interesting at least to those who would trace the genealogy of the great Arabian family. Any one who knows the Bedawin can see that the Muzaynah are pure blood. Their brows are broad, their faces narrow, their features regular, and their eyes of a moderate size: whereas the other Tawarah (Sinaitic) clans are as palpably Egyptian. These have preserved that roundness of face which may still be seen in the Sphinx as in the modern Copt, and their eyes have that peculiar size, shape, and look which the old Egyptian painters attempted to express by giving to the profile, the form of the full organ. Upon this feature, so characteristic of the Nilotic race, I would lay great stress. No traveller familiar with the true, Egyptian eye, long, almond-shaped, deeply fringed, slightly raised at the outer corner and dipping in front like the Chinese, can ever mistake it. It is to be seen in half-castes, and, as I have before remarked, families originally from the banks of the Nile, but settled for generations in the Holy Land, El Hejaz, retain the peculiarity.

I therefore believe the Turi Bedawin to be an impure race, Egypto-Arab, whereas his neighbour the Hejazi is the pure Syrian or Mesopotamian. "And he (Ishmael) dwelt in the wilderness of Paran (Wady Firan?), and his mother took him a wife, out of the land of Egypt." (Gen. xxi. 21.) I wonder that some geographers have attempted to identify Massa the son of Ishmael (Gen. xxv. 14.) with Mecca, when in verse 18 of the same chapter we read, "And they (the twelve princes, sons of Ishmael) *dwelt from Havilah unto Shur*."

This asserts, as clearly as language can, that the posterity of, or the race typified by, Ishmael,—the Egypto-Arab,—occupied only the northern parts of the peninsula. Their habitat is not even included in Arabia by those writers who bound the country on the north by an imaginary line drawn from Ras Mohammed to the mouths of the Euphrates.

Dr. Wilson (Lands of the Bible), repeated by Eliot Warburton, (Crescent and Cross,) lays stress upon the Tawarah tradition, that they are Beni-Israel converted to El-Islam, considering it a fulfilment of the prophecy, "that a remnant of Israel shall dwell in Edom." With due deference to so illustrious an orientalist and Biblical scholar as Dr. Wilson, I believe that most modern Moslems, being ignorant that Jacob was the first called "prince with God," apply the term Beni-Israel to all the posterity of Abraham, not to Jews only.

A wonderful change has taken place in the Tawarah tribes, whilome portrayed by Sir John Mandeville as "folke fulle of alle evylle condiciouns." Niebuhr notes the trouble they gave him, and their perpetual hankering for both murder and pillage. Even in the late Mohammed Ali's early reign, no governor of Suez dared to flog, or to lay hands upon a Turi, whatever offence he might have committed within the walls of the town. Now the wild man's sword is taken from him, before he is allowed to enter the gates, and my old acquaintance, Giaffar Bey, would think no more of belabouring a Bedawi than of flogging a Fellah. Such is the result of Mohammed Ali's rigorous policy, and such the effects of even semi-civilisation, when its influence is brought to bear direct upon barbarism.

To conclude this subject, the Tawarah still retain many characteristics of the Bedawi race. The most good-humoured and sociable of men, they delight in a jest, and may readily be managed by kindness and courtesy. Yet they are passionate, nice upon points of honor, revengeful and easily offended where their peculiar prejudices are misunderstood. I have always found them pleasant companions, and deserving of respect, for their hearts are good, and their courage is beyond a doubt. Those travellers who complain of their insolence and extortion may have been either ignorant of their language or offensive to them by assumption of superiority,—in the Desert man meets man,—or physically unfitted to acquire their esteem.

We journeyed on till near sunset through the wilderness without ennui. It is strange how the mind can be amused by scenery that presents so few objects to occupy it. But in such a country every slight modification of form or color rivets observation: the senses are sharpened, and the perceptive faculties, prone to sleep over a confused mass of objects, act vigorously when excited by the capability of embracing each detail. Moreover desert views are eminently suggestive; they appeal to the Future, not to the Past; they arouse because they are by no means memorial. To the solitary wayfarer there is an interest in the wilderness unknown to Cape seas and Alpine glaciers, and even to the rolling Prairie,—the effect of continued excitement on the mind, stimulating its powers to their pitch. Above, through a sky terrible in its stainless beauty, and the splendors of a pitiless blinding glare, the Simum caresses you like a lion with flaming breath. Around lie drifted sand-heaps, upon which each puff of wind leaves its trace in solid waves; flayed rocks, the very skeletons of mountains, and hard unbroken plains, over which he who rides is spurred by the idea that the bursting of a water-skin, or the pricking of a camel's hoof would be a certain death of torture,—a haggard land infested with wild beasts, and wilder men,—a region whose very fountains murmur the warning words "Drink and away!" What can be more exciting? what more sublime? Man's heart bounds in his breast at the thought of measuring his puny force with Nature's might, and of emerging triumphant from the trial. This explains the Arab's proverb, "Voyaging is a Victory." In the Desert even more than upon the ocean, there is present death: hardship is there, and piracies, and shipwreck—solitary, not in crowds, where, as the Persians say, "Death is a Festival,"—and this sense of danger, never absent, invests the scene of travel with an interest not its own.

Let the traveller who suspects exaggeration leave the Suez road for an hour or two, and gallop northwards over the sands: in the drear silence, the solitude, and the fantastic desolation of the place, he will feel what the Desert may be. And then the Oases, and little lines of fertility—how soft and how beautifull—even though the Wady el Ward (the Vale of Flowers) be the name of some stern flat upon which a handful of wild shrub blossoms while struggling through a cold season's ephemeral existence.

In such circumstances the mind is influenced through the body. Though your mouth glows, and your skin is parched, yet you feel no languor, the effect of humid heat; your lungs are lightened, your sight brightens, your memory recovers its tone, and your spirits become exuberant; your fancy and imagination are powerfully aroused, and the wildness and sublimity of the scenes around you stir up all the energies of your soul—whether for exertion, danger, or strife. Your morale improves: you become frank and cordial, hospitable and single-minded: the hypocritical politeness and the slavery of civilisation are left behind you in the city. Your senses are quickened: they require no stimulants but air and exercise,—in the Desert spirituous liquors excite only disgust. There is a keen enjoyment in mere animal existence. The sharp appetite disposes of the most indigestible food, the sand is softer than a bed of down, and the purity of the air suddenly puts to flight a dire cohort of diseases. Hence it is that both sexes, and every age, the most material as well as the most imaginative of minds; the tamest citizen, the parson, the old maid, the peaceful student, the spoiled child of civilisation, all feel their hearts dilate, and their pulses beat strong, as they look down from their dromedaries upon the glorious Desert. Where do we hear of a traveller being disappointed by it? It is another illustration of the ancient truth that Nature returns to man, however unworthily he has treated her. And believe me, when once your tastes have conformed to the tranquillity of such travel, you will suffer real pain in returning to the turmoil of civilisation. You will anticipate the bustle and the confusion of artificial life, its luxury and its false pleasures, with repugnance. Depressed in spirits, you will for a time after your return feel incapable of mental or bodily exertion. The air of cities will suffocate you, and the care-worn and cadaverous countenances of citizens will haunt you like a vision of judgment.

As the black shadow mounted in the Eastern sky, I turned off the road, and was suddenly saluted by a figure rising from a little hollow with an "As' Salamo Alaykum" of truly Arab sound. I looked at the speaker for a moment without recognising him. He then advanced with voluble expressions of joy, invited me to sup, seized my camel's halter without waiting for an answer, "nakh'd" it (*i. e.* forced it to kneel), led me hurriedly to a carpet spread in a sandy hollow, pulled off my slippers, gave me cold water for ablution, told me that he had mistaken me at a distance for a "Sherif" or Prince of the Arabs, but was delighted to find himself in error, and urged me to hurry over ablution, otherwise that night would come on before we could say our prayers. It was Mohammed el Basyuni, the Meccan boy of whom I had bought my pilgrim-garb at Cairo. There I had refused his companionship, but here for reasons of his own—one of them was an utter want of money—he would take no excuse. When he prayed he stood behind me, thereby proving pliancy of conscience, for he suspected me from the first of being at least a heretic. There are many qualifications necessary for an Imam, a leader of prayer; the first condition, of course, is orthodoxy.

After devotions he lighted a pipe, and immediately placed the snake-like tube in my hand; this is an argument which the tired traveller can rarely resist. He then began to rummage my saddle-bags; he drew forth stores of provisions, rolls, water-melons, boiled eggs, and dates and, whilst lighting the fire and boiling the coffee, he managed to distribute his own stock, which was neither plentiful nor first-rate, to the camelmen. Shaykh Nassar and his brother looked aghast at this movement, but the boy was inexorable. They tried a few rough hints, which he noticed by singing a Hindostani couplet that asserts the impropriety of anointing rats' heads with jasmine oil. They suspected abuse, and waxed cross; he acknowledged this by deriding them. "I have heard of Nasrs and Nasirs, and Mansúrs, but may Allah spare me the mortification of a Nassár!" said the boy, relying upon my support. And I urged him on, wanting to see how the city Arab treats the countryman. He then took my tobacco-pouch from the angry Bedawin, and in a stage-whisper reproved me for entrusting it to such thieves; insisting, at the same time, upon drinking all the coffee, so that the poor guides had to prepare some for themselves. He improved every opportunity of making mischief. "We have eaten water-melon!" cried Nassar, patting its receptacle in token of repletion. "Dost thou hear, my lord, how they grumble? the impudent ruffians!" remarked Mohammed. "*We have eaten water-melon!* that is to say, we ought to have eaten meat!" The Bedawin, completely out of temper, told him not to trust himself among their hills. He seized a sword, began capering about after the fashion of the East-Indian school of arms, and boasted that he would attack single-handed the whole clan—which elicited an ironical "Allah! Allah!" from the hearers.

After an hour most amusingly spent in this way I arose, much to the dissatisfaction of my guides, who wished to sleep there, and insisted upon mounting. Shaykh Nassar and his brother had reckoned upon living gratis, for at least three days, judging it improbable that a soft Effendi would hurry himself. When they saw the fair vision dissolve, they began to finesse: they induced the camel-man, who ran by the side of Mohammed's dromedary, to precede the animal —a favourite manœuvre to prevent overspeed. Ordered to fall back, the fellow pleaded fatigue, and inability to walk. The boy Mohammed immediately asked if I had any objection to dismount one of my guides, and to let his weary attendant ride for an hour or so.

I at once assented, and the Bedawin obeyed me with ominous grumblings. When we resumed our march the melancholy Arabs had no song left in them, whereas Mohammed chanted vociferously, and quoted bad Hindostani and worse Persian till silence was forcibly imposed upon him. The camel-men lagged behind, in order to prevent my dromedary advancing too fast, and the boy's guide, after dismounting, would stride in front of us, under pretext of showing the way. And so we jogged on, now walking, then trotting, till the dromedaries began to grunt with fatigue, and the Arabs clamoured for a halt.

At midnight we reached the Central Station, and lay down under its walls to take a little rest. The dews fell heavily, wetting the sheets that covered us; but who cares for such trifles in the Desert? The moon shone bright; the breeze blew coolly, and the jackal sang a lullaby which lost no time in inducing the soundest sleep. As the Wolf's Tail, the first brushes of grey light which appear as forerunners of dawn, showed in the heavens we arose. Grey mists floating over the hills northwards gave the Dar el Bayda, the Pasha's Palace, the look of some old feudal castle. There was a haze in the atmosphere, which beautified even the face of Desolation. The swift-flying Kata (sand-grouse) sprang in noisy coveys from the road, and a stray gazelle paced daintily over the stony plain. As we passed by the Pilgrim's tree, I added another rag to its coat of tatters. We then invoked the aid of the holy saint El Dakruri from his cream-colored abode, mounted our camels, and resumed the march in real earnest. The dawn passed away in its delicious coolness, and sultry morning came on. Then day glared in its fierceness, and the noontide sun made the plain glow with terrible heat. Still we pressed onwards.

At 3 P.M. we turned off the road into a dry watercourse, which is not far from No. 13 station. The sand, was dotted with the dried-up leaves of the Datura, and was strongly perfumed by "Shih" a kind of Absinthe, sweetest herb of the desert. A Mimosa was there, and although its shade at this season is little better than a cocoa tree's, the Bedawin would not neglect it. We lay down upon the sand, to rest among a party of Maghrabi pilgrims travelling to Suez. These wretches, who were about a dozen in number, appeared to be of the lowest class; their garments consisted of a Burnus-cloak and a pair of sandals, their sole weapon a long knife, and their only stock a bag of dry provisions. Each had his large wooden bowl, but none carried water with him. It was impossible to help pitying their state, nor could I eat, seeing them hungry, thirsty, and wayworn. Nassar served out about a pint of water and a little bread to each man. Then they asked for more. None was to be had, so they cried out that money would do as well. I had determined upon being generous to the extent of a few pence. Custom, as well as inclination, was in favor of the act; but when the alms became a demand, and the demand was backed by fierce looks and a derisive sneer, and a kind of reference to their knives, gentle Charity took the alarm and fled. My pistols kept them at bay, for they were only making an attempt to intimidate, and, though I took the precaution of sitting apart from them, there was no real danger. The Suez road, by the wise regulations of Mohammed Ali, has become as safe to European travellers as that between Hampstead and Highgate, and even Easterns have little to fear but what their fears create. My Indian servant was full of the dangers he had run, but I did not believe in them. I afterwards heard that the place where the Maghrabis attempted to frighten what they thought a timid Turk was once notorious for plunder and murder. Here the spurs of two opposite hills almost meet upon the plain, a favorable ground for Bedawi ambuscade. Of the Maghrabis I shall have more to say when relating my voyage in the Pilgrim Ship: they were the only travellers from whom we experienced the least annoyance. Numerous parties of Turks, Arabs, and Afghans, and a few East-Indians were on the same errand as ourselves. All, as we passed them, welcomed us with the friendly salutation that becomes men engaged in a labor of religion.

About half an hour before sunset, I turned off the road leftwards and, under pretext of watering the dromedaries, rode up to inspect the fort El Ajrudi. It is a quadrangle with round towers at the gateway and at the corners, newly built of stone and mortar; the material is already full of crevices, and would not stand before a twelve-pounder. Without guns or gunners, it was occupied by about a dozen Fellahs who act as hereditary "Ghafirs" (guardians); they were expecting at that time to be reinforced by a party of Bashi Buzuks—irregulars from Cairo. The people of the country were determined that an English fleet would soon appear in the Red Sea, and this fort is by them ridiculously considered the key of Suez. As usual in these Vauban-lacking lands, the well supplying the stronghold is in a detached and distant building, which can be approached by an enemy with the greatest security. Over the gateway was an ancient inscription reversed; the water was brackish, and of bad quality.

We resumed our way: Suez was now near. In the azure distance the castellated peaks of Jebel Rahah, and the wide sand-tracts over which lies the land-route to El Hejaz. Before us the sight ever dear to English eyes,—a strip of sea gloriously blue, with a gallant steamer walking the waters. On the right-hand side the broad slopes of Jebel Mukattam, a range of hills which flanks the road all the way from Cairo. It was at this hour a spectacle not easily to be forgotten. The near range of chalk and sand-stone wore a russet suit, gilt where the last rays of the sun seamed it with light, and the deep folds were shaded with the richest purple; whilst the background of the higher hills, Jebel Taweri, generally known as Abu Deráj' (the Father of Steps), was sky-blue streaked with the lightest plum color. We drew up at a small building called Bir Suways (well of Suez), and under pretext of watering the cattle, I sat for half an hour admiring the charms of the Desert. The eye never tires of such loveliness of hue, and the memory of the hideousness of this range, when a sun in front exposed each gaunt and barren feature, supplied the evening view with another element of attraction.

It was already night when we passed through the tumbling six-windowed gateway of Suez; and still remained the task of finding my servant and effects. After wandering in and out of every Wakaleh in the village, during which peregrination the boy Mohammed proved himself so useful that I determined at all risks to make him my companion, we accidentally heard that a Hindi had taken lodgings at a hostelry bearing the name of Jirjis el Zahr, the "George:" so called after its owner, a Copt, Consular Agent for Belgium. On arriving there our satisfaction was diminished by the intelligence that the same Hindi, after locking the door, had gone out with his friends to a ship in the harbour; in fact, that he had made all preparations for running away. I dismounted, and tried to persuade the porter to break open the wooden bolt, but he absolutely refused, and threatened the police. Meanwhile Mohammed had found a party of friends, men of El Medinah, returning to the pilgrimage after a begging tour through Egypt and Turkey. The meeting was characterised by vociferous inquiries, loud guffaws, and warm embraces. I was invited to share their supper, and their dormitory,—an uncovered platform projecting from the gallery over the square court below,

—but I had neither appetite nor spirits enough to be sociable. The porter, after much persuasion, showed me an empty room, in which I spread my carpet. That was a sad night. My eighty-four (85?) mile ride had made every bone ache; I had lost much epidermis, and the sun had seared every portion of skin exposed to it. So, lamenting my degeneracy and the ill effects of four years' domicile in Europe, and equally disquieted in mind about the fate of my goods and chattels, I fell into an uncomfortable sleep.

CHAPTER IX.

Suez.

EARLY on the morning after my arrival, I arose, and consulted my new acquaintances about the means of recovering the missing property. They unanimously advised a visit to the governor, whom, however, they described to be a "Kalb ibn kalb," (dog, son of a dog,) who never returned Moslems' salutations, and who thought all men dirt to be trodden under foot by Turks. The boy Mohammed showed his savoir faire by extracting from his huge Sahharah-box a fine embroidered cap, and a grand peach-coloured coat, with which I was instantly invested; he dressed himself with similar magnificence, and we then set out to the "palace."

Giaffar Bey,—he has since been deposed,—then occupied the position of judge, officer commanding, collector of customs, and magistrate of Suez. He was a Mir-liwa, or brigadier-general, and had some reputation as a soldier, together with a slight tincture of European science and language. The large old Turk received me most superciliously, disdained all return of salam, and fixing upon me two little eyes like gimlets, demanded my business. I stated that one Shaykh Nur, my Hindi servant, had played me false; therefore I required permission to break into the room supposed to contain my effects. He asked my profession. I replied the medical. This led him to inquire if I had any medicine for the eyes, and being answered in the affirmative, he sent a messenger with me to enforce obedience on the part of the porter. The obnoxious measure was, however, unnecessary. As we entered the caravanserai, there appeared at the door the black face of Shaykh Nur, looking, though accompanied by sundry fellow-countrymen, uncommonly as if he merited and expected the bamboo. He had, by his own account, been seduced into the festivities of a coal-hulk manned by Lascars, and the vehemence of his self-accusation saved him from the chastisement which I had determined to administer.

I must now briefly describe the party of Mecca and Medina men into which fate threw me: their names will so frequently appear in the following pages, that a few words about their natures will not be misplaced.

First of all comes Umar Effendi,—so called in honor,—a Daghistani or Circassian, the grandson of a Hanafi Mufti at El Medinah, and the son of a Shaykh Rakb, an officer whose duty it is to lead dromedary-caravans. He sits upon his cot, a small, short, plump body, of yellow complexion and bilious temperament, grey-eyed, soft-featured, and utterly beardless—which affects his feelings—he looks fifteen, and he owns to twenty-eight. His manners are those of a student; he dresses respectably, prays regularly, hates the fair sex, like an Arab, whose affections and aversions are always in extremes, is serious, has a mild demeanour, an humble gait, and a soft slow voice. When roused he becomes furious as a Bengal tiger. His parents have urged him to marry, and he, like Camaralzaman, has informed his father that he is "a person of great age, but little sense." Urged moreover by a melancholy turn of mind, and the want of leisure for study at El Medinah, he fled the paternal domicile, and entered himself a pauper Talib ilm (student) in the Azhar Mosque. His disconsolate friends and afflicted relations sent a confidential man to fetch him home by force, should it be necessary; he has yielded, and is now awaiting the first opportunity of travelling gratis, if possible, to El Medinah.

That confidential man is a negro-servant, called Sa'ad, notorious in his native city as El Jinni, the Demon. Born and bred a slave in Umar Effendi's family, he obtained manumission, became a soldier in El Hejaz, was dissatisfied with pay perpetually in arrears, turned merchant, and wandered far and wide, to Russia, to Gibraltar, and to Baghdad. He is the pure African, noisily merry at one moment, at another silently sulky; affectionate and abusive, brave and boastful, reckless and crafty, exceedingly quarrelsome, and unscrupulous to the last degree. The bright side of his character is his love and respect for the young master Umar Effendi; yet even him he will scold in a paroxysm of fury, and steal from him whatever he can lay his hands on. He is generous with his goods, but is ever borrowing and never paying money; he dresses like a beggar, with the dirtiest Tarbush upon his tufty poll, and only a cotton shirt over his sooty skin, whilst his two boxes are full of handsome apparel for himself and the three ladies, his wives, at El Medinah. He knows no fear but for those boxes. Frequently during our search for a vessel he forced himself into Giaffar Bey's presence, and there he demeaned himself so impudently, that we expected to see him lamed by the bastinado; his forwardness, however, only amused the dignitary. He wanders all day about the bazar, talking about freight and passage, for he has resolved, cost what it will, to travel free, and, with doggedness like his, he must succeed.

Shaykh Hamid el Samman derives his cognomen, the "Clarified-Butter-Seller," from a celebrated saint and Sufi of the Kadiriyyeh order, who left a long line of holy descendants at El Medinah. This Shaykh squats upon a box full of presents for the daughter of his paternal uncle, his wife, a perfect specimen of the town Arab. His poll is crowned with a rough Shushah or tuft of hair; his face is of a dirty brown; his little goatee straggles untrimmed; his feet are bare, and his only garment is an exceedingly unclean, ochre-colored blouse, tucked into a leathern girdle beneath it. He will not pray, because he is unwilling to take pure clothes out of his box; but he smokes when he can get other people's tobacco, and groans between the whiffs, conjugating the verb all day, for he is of active mind. He can pick out his letters, and he keeps in his bosom a little dog's-eared MS. full of serious romances and silly prayers, old and exceedingly ill-written: this he will draw forth at times, peep into for a moment, devoutly kiss, and restore to its proper place with the veneration of the vulgar for a book. He can sing all manner of songs, slaughter a sheep with dexterity, deliver a grand call to prayer, shave, cook, fight, and he excels in the science of vituperation: like Sa'ad, he never performs his devotions, except when necessary to "keep up appearances," and though he has sworn to perish before he forgets his vow to the "daughter of his uncle," I shrewdly suspect he is no better than he should be. His brow crumples at the word wine, but there is quite another expression about the region of the mouth; Stamboul, where he has lived some months, without learning ten words of Turkish, is a notable place for displacing prejudice. And finally, he has not more than a piastre or two in his pocket, for he has squandered the large presents given to him at Cairo and Constantinople by noble ladies, to whom he acted as master of the ceremonies, at the tomb of the Prophet.

Stretched on a carpet, smoking a Persian Kaliun all day, lies Salih Shakkar, a Turk on the father's, and an Arab on the mother's side, born at El Medinah. This lanky youth may be 16 years old, but he has the ideas of 46; he is thoroughly greedy, selfish, and ungenerous, coldly supercilious as a Turk, 'and energetically avaricious as an Arab. He prays more often, and dresses more respectably, than the descendant of the Clarified-Butter-Seller; he affects the Constantinople style of toilette, and his light yellow complexion makes people consider him a "superior person." We were intimate enough on the road, when he borrowed from me a little money. But at El Medinah he cut me pitilessly, as a "town man" does a continental acquaintance accidentally met in Hyde Park, and of course he tried, though in vain, to evade repaying his debt. He had a tincture of letters, and appeared to have studied critically the subject of "largesse." "The generous is Allah's friend, ay, though he be a sinner, and the miser is Allah's foe, ay, though he be a saint," was a venerable saying always in his mouth. He also informed me that Pharaoh, although the quintessence of impiety, is mentioned by name in the Koran, by reason of his liberality, whereas Nimrod, another monster of iniquity, is only alluded to, because he was a stingy tyrant. It is almost needless to declare that Salih Shakkar was, as the East-Indians say, a very "flysucker." There were two other men of El Medinah in the Wakalet Girgis; but I omit description, as we left them, they being penniless, at Suez. One of them, Mohammed Shiklibha, I afterwards met at Mecca, and seldom have I seen a more honest and warm-hearted fellow. When we were embarking at Suez, he fell upon Hamid's bosom, and both of them wept bitterly, at the prospect of parting even for a few days.

All the individuals above mentioned lost no time in opening the question of a loan. It was a lesson in oriental metaphysics to see their condition. They had a twelve days' voyage, and a four days' journey, before them; boxes to carry, custom-houses to face, and stomachs to fill; yet the whole party could scarcely, I believe, muster two dollars of ready money. Their boxes were full of valuables, arms, clothes, pipes, slippers, sweetmeats, and other "notions," but nothing short of starvation would have induced them to pledge the smallest article.

Foreseeing that their company would be an advantage, I hearkened favourably to the honeyed request for a few crowns. The boy Mohammed obtained six dollars; Hamid about five pounds,—I intended to make his house at El Medinah my home; Umar Effendi three dollars; Sa'ad the Demon, two—I gave the money to him at Yambu',—and Salih Shakkar fifty piastres. But since in these lands, as a rule, no one ever lends coins, or borrowing ever returns them, I took care to exact service from the first, to take two rich coats from the second, a handsome pipe from the third, a "bala" or yataghan from the fourth, and from the fifth an imitation Cashmere shawl. After which, we sat down and drew out the agreement. It was favorable to me: I lent them Egyptian money, and bargained for repayment in the currency of El Hejaz, thereby gaining the exchange, which is sometimes 16 per cent. This was done, not so much for the sake of profit, as with the view of becoming a Hatim, a well-known Arab chieftain, whose name has come to stand for generosity itself, by a "never mind" on settling day.

My companions having received these small sums, became affectionate, and eloquent in my praise: they asked me for the future to make one of their number at meals, overwhelmed me with questions, insisted upon a present of sweetmeats, detected in me a great man under a cloud—perhaps my claims to being a Dervish assisted them to this discovery—and declared that I should perforce be their guest at Mecca and El Medinah. On all occasions precedence was forced upon me; my opinion was the first consulted, and no project was settled without my concurrence: briefly, Abdullah the Dervish suddenly found himself a person of consequence.

This elevation led me into an imprudence which might have cost me dear; it aroused the only suspicion about me ever expressed during the summer's tour. My friends had looked at my clothes, overhauled my medicine-chest, and criticised my pistols; they sneered at my copper-cased watch, and remembered having seen a compass at Constantinople. Therefore I imagined they would think little about a sextant. This was a mistake. The boy Mohammed I afterwards learned waited only my leaving the room to declare that the would-be Haji was one of the Infidels from India, and a council sat to discuss the case.

Fortunately for me Umar Effendi had looked over a letter which I had written to Haji Wali that morning, and he had at various times received categorical replies to certain questions in high theology. He felt himself justified in declaring, ex cathedrâ, the boy Mohammed's position perfectly untenable. And Shaykh Hamid, who looked forward to being my host, guide, and debtor in general, and probably cared scantily for catechism or creed, swore that the light of El Islam was upon my countenance, and consequently that the boy Mohammed was a pauper, a "fakir," an owl, a cut-off-one (scil., from the pleasures and the comforts of life), a stranger, and a Wahhabi heretic, for daring to impugn the faith of a brother believer. The scene ended with a general abuse of the acute youth, who was told on all sides that he had no shame, and was directed to fear Allah. I was struck with the expression of my friends' countenances when they saw the sextant, and, determining with a sigh to leave it behind, I prayed five times a day for nearly a week.

We all agreed not to lose an hour in securing places on board some vessel bound for Yambu', and my companions, hearing that my passport as a British Indian was scarcely "en règle," earnestly advised me to have it signed by the governor without delay, whilst they occupied themselves about the harbour. They warned me that if I displayed the Turkish Tezkirah given to me at the citadel of Cairo, I should infallibly be ordered to await the caravan, and lose their society and friendship. Pilgrims arriving at Alexandria, be it known to the reader, are divided into bodies, and distributed by means of passports to the three great roads, namely Suez, Cosseir, and the Hajj route by land round the Gulf of Akabah. After the division has once been made, government turns a deaf ear to the representations of individuals. The Bey of Suez has an order to obstruct pilgrims as much as possible till the end of the season, when they are hurried down that way, lest they should arrive at Mecca too late. As most of the Egyptian high officials have boats, which sail up the Nile laden with pilgrims and return freighted with corn, the government naturally does its utmost to force the delays and discomforts of this line upon strangers. And as those who travel by the Hajj route must spend money in the Egyptian territories, at least fifteen days longer than they would if allowed to embark at once for Suez, the Bey very properly assists them in the former, and obstructs them in the latter case.

Knowing these facts, I felt that a difficulty was at hand. The first thing was to take Shaykh Nur's passport, which was "en règle," and my own which was not, to the Bey for signature. He turned the papers over and over, as if unable to read them, and raised false hopes high by referring me to his clerk. The under official at once saw the irregularity of the document, asked me why it had not been visé at Cairo, swore that under such circumstances nothing would induce the Bey to let me proceed, and when I tried persuasion, waxed insolent. I feared that it would be necessary to travel viâ Cosseir, for which there was scarcely time, or to transfer myself on camel back to the harbour of Tur, and there to await the chance of finding a place in some half-filled vessel to El Hejaz,—which would have been relying upon an accident.

My last hope at Suez was to obtain assistance

from Mr. West, then H. B. M.'s vice-consul and since then consul. I therefore took the boy Mohammed with me, choosing him on purpose, and excusing the step to my companions by concocting an artful fable about my having been, in Afghanistan, a benefactor to the British nation. We proceeded to the consulate. Mr. West, who had been told by imprudent Augustus Bernal to expect me, saw through the disguise, despite jargon assumed to satisfy official scruples, and nothing could be kinder than the part he took. His clerk was directed to place himself in communication with the Bey's factotum, and when objections to signing the Alexandrian Tezkirah were offered, the vice-consul said that he would, at his own risk, give me a fresh passport as a British subject from Suez to Arabia. His firmness prevailed, and on the second day, the documents were returned to me in a satisfactory state. I take pleasure in owning this obligation to Mr. West: in the course of my wanderings, I have often received from him open-hearted hospitality and the most friendly attentions.

Whilst these passport difficulties were being solved, the rest of the party was as busy in settling about passage and passage-money. The peculiar rules of the port of Suez require a few words of explanation.*

---

* The account here offered to the reader was kindly supplied to me by Henry Levick, Esq., (late vice-consul, and afterwards postmaster at Suez), and it may be depended upon, as coming from a resident of 16 years' standing. All the passages marked with inverted commas are extracts from a letter with which that gentleman favored me. The information is obsolete now (1873), but it may be interesting as a specimen of the things that were.

"About thirty-five years ago (1853), the ship-owners proposed to the then government, with the view of keeping up freight, a Farzah, or system of rotation. It might be supposed that the Pasha, whose object notoriously was to retain all monopolies in his own hands, would have refused his sanction to such a measure. But it so happened in those days that all the court had ships at Suez: Ibrahim Pasha alone owned four or five. Consequently they expected to share profits with the merchants, and thus to be compensated for the want of port-dues. From that time forward all the vessels in the harbour were registered, and ordered to sail in rotation. This arrangement benefits the owner of the craft 'en départ,' giving him in his turn a temporary monopoly, with the advantage of a full market; and freight is so high that a single trip often clears off the expense of building and the risk of losing the ship—a sensible succedaneum for insurance companies. On the contrary, the public must always be a loser by the 'Farzah.' Two of a trade do not agree elsewhere; but at Suez even the Christian and the Moslem ship-owner are bound by a fraternal tie, in the shape of this rotation system. It injures the general merchant, and the Red Sea trader, not only by perpetuating high freight, but also by causing at one period of the year a break in the routine of sales and in the supplies of goods for the great Jeddah market.* At this moment (Nov. 1853),

* Note to Second Edition. The "Farzah," I may here observe, has been abolished by Said Pasha since the publication of these lines: the effects of "free-trade" are exactly what were predicted by Mr. Levick.

the vessel to which the turn belongs happens to be a large one; there is a deficiency of export to El Hejaz,—her owner will of course wait any length of time for a full cargo; consequently no vessel with merchandise has left Suez for the last seventy-two days. Those who have bought goods for the Jeddah market at three months' credit will therefore have to meet their acceptances for merchandise still warehoused at the Egyptian port. This strange contrast to 'free-trade' principle is another proof that protection benefits only one party, the protected, while it is detrimental to the interests of the other party, the public." To these remarks of Mr. Levick's, I have only to add that the government supports the Farzah with all the energy of protectionists. A letter from Mr. J. Drummond Hay was insufficient to induce the Bey of Suez to break through the rule of rotation in favour of certain princes from Morocco. The recommendations of Lord Stratford de Redcliffe met with no better fate; and all Mr. West's good will could not procure me a vessel out of her turn.

We were forced to rely upon our own exertions, and the activity of Sa'ad the Demon. This worthy, after sundry delays and differences, mostly caused by his own determination to travel gratis, and to make us pay too much, finally closed with the owner of the Golden Thread. He took places for us upon the poop, the most eligible part of the vessel at this season of the year; he premised that we should not be very comfortable, as we were to be crowded with Maghrabi pilgrims, but "Allah makes all things easy!" Though not penetrated with the conviction that this would happen in our case, I paid for two deck passages eighteen Riyals (dollars), my companions seven each, whilst Sa'ad secretly entered himself as an able seaman. Mohammed Shiklibha we were obliged to leave behind, as he could not or would not afford the expense, and none of us might afford it for him. Had I known him to be the honest, true-hearted fellow he was—his kindness at Mecca quite won my heart— I should not have grudged the small charity.

Nothing more comfortless than our days and nights in the "George" Inn. The ragged walls of our rooms were clammy with dirt, the smoky rafters foul with cobwebs, and the floor, bestrewed with kit in terrible confusion, was black with hosts of cockroaches, ants and flies. Pigeons nestled on the shelf, cooing amatory ditties the live-long day, and cats like tigers crawled through a hole in the door, making night hideous with their cat-a-waulings. Now a curious goat, then an inquisitive jackass, would walk stealthily into the room, remark that it was tenanted, and retreat with dignified demeanour, and the mosquitoes sang Io Pæans over our prostrate forms throughout the twenty-four hours.

I spare the reader the enumeration of the other Egyptian plagues that infested the place. After the first day's trial, we determined to spend the hours of light in the passages, lying upon our boxes or rugs, smoking, wrangling, and inspecting one another's chests. The latter occupation was a fertile source of disputes, for nothing was more common than for a friend to seize an article belonging to another, and to swear by the Prophet's beard that he admired it, and, therefore, would not return it. The boy Mohammed and Shaykh Nur, who had been intimates the first day, differed in opinion on the second, and on the third, came to pushing each other against the wall.

Sometimes we went into the bazar, a shady street flanked with poor little shops, or we sat in the coffee-house, drinking hot saltish water tinged with burnt bean, or we prayed in one of the three tumble-down old Mosques, or we squatted upon the pier, lamenting the want of Hammams, and bathing in the tepid sea. I presently came to the conclusion that Suez as a "watering-place" is duller even than Dover.

The only society we found—excepting an occasional visitor—was that of a party of Egyptian women, who with their husbands and families occupied some rooms adjoining ours. At first they were fierce, and used bad language, when the boy Mohammed and I, whilst Umar Effendi was engaged in prayer, and the rest were wandering about the town, ventured to linger in the cool passage, where they congregated, or to address a facetious phrase to them. But hearing that I was a Hakim-bashi—for fame had promoted me to the rank of a "Physician General" at Suez—all discovered some ailments. They began prudently with requesting me to display the effects of my drugs by dosing myself, but they ended submissively by swallowing the nauseous compounds. To this succeeded a primitive form of flirtation, which mainly consisted of the demand direct. The most charming of the party was one Fattúmah, a plump-personed dame fast verging upon her thirtieth year, fond of a little flattery, and possessing, like all her people, a most voluble tongue. The refrain of every conversation was "Marry me, O Fattúmah! O daughter! O female pilgrim!" In vain the lady would reply, with a coquettish movement of the sides, a toss of the head, and a flirting manipulation of her head-veil, "I am mated, O young man!"—it was agreed that she, being a person of polyandrous propensities, could support the weight of at least three matrimonial engagements.

Sometimes the entrance of the male Fellahs interrupted these little discussions, but people of our respectability and nation were not to be imposed upon by such husbands. In their presence we only varied the style of conversation—inquiring the amount of "Mahr," or marriage settlement, deriding the cheapness of womanhood in Egypt, and requiring to be furnished on the spot with brides at the rate of ten shillings a head.

More often the amiable Fattúmah—the fair sex in this country, though passing frail, have the best tempers in the world—would laugh at our impertinences. Sometimes vexed by our imitating her Egyptian accent, mimicking her gestures, and depreciating her countrywomen, she would wax wroth, and order us to be gone, and stretch out her forefinger, a sign that she wished to put out our eyes, or adjure Allah to cut the hearts out of our bosoms. Then the "Marry me, O Fattúmah, O daughter, O female pilgrim!" would give way to Y'al Ago-o-oz! (O old woman and decrepit!) "O daughter of sixty sires, and fit only to carry wood to market!"—whereupon would burst a storm of wrath, at the tail of which all of us, like children, starting upon our feet, rushed out of one another's way. But —"qui se dispute, s'adore"—when we again met all would be forgotten, and the old tale be told over de novo.

This was the amusement of the day. At night we, men, assembling upon the little terrace, drank tea, recited stories, read books, talked of our travels, and indulged in various pleasantries. The great joke was the boy Mohammed's abusing all his companions to their faces in Hindostani, which none but Shaykh Nur and I could understand; the others, however, guessed his intention, and revenged themselves by retorts of the style uncourteous in the purest Hejazi.

I proceed to offer a few more extracts from Mr. Levick's letter about Suez and the Suezians. "It appears that the number of pilgrims who pass through Suez to Mecca has of late been steadily on the decrease. When I first came here (in 1838) the pilgrims who annually embarked at this port amounted to between 10,000 and 12,000, the shipping was more numerous, and the merchants were more affluent.

"I have ascertained from a special register kept in the government archives that in the Moslem year 1268 (from 1851 to 1852) the exact number that passed through was 4893. In 1299 A.H. it had shrunk to 3136. The natives assign various causes to the falling off, which I attribute chiefly to the indirect effect of European civilisation upon the Moslem powers immediately in contact with it. The heterogeneous mass of pilgrims is composed of people of all classes, colors, and costumes. One sees among them, not only the natives of countries contiguous to Egypt, but also a large proportion of central Asians from Bokhara, Persia, Circassia, Turkey and the Crimea, who prefer this route by way of Constantinople to the difficult, expensive, and dangerous caravan-line through the desert from Damascus and Baghdad. The West sends us Moors, Algerines, and Tunisians, and Inner Africa a mass of sable Takrouri, and others from Bornou, the Sudan, Ghedamah near the Niger, and Jabarti from the Habash.

"The Suez ship-builders are an influential body of men, originally Candiots and Alexandrians. When Mohammed Ali fitted out his fleet for the Hejaz war, he transported a number of Greeks to Suez, and the children now exercise their fathers' craft. There are at present three great builders at this place. Their principal difficulty is the want of material. Teak comes from India viâ Jeddah, and Venetian boards, owing to the expense of camel-transport, are a hundred per cent. dearer here than at Alexandria. Trieste and Turkey supply spars, and Jeddah, canvass: the sail-makers are Suez men, and the crews a mongrel mixture of Arabs and Egyptians; the Rais, or captain, being almost invariably, if the vessel be a large one, a Yambu man. There are two kinds of craft, distinguished from each other by tonnage, not by build. The Baghlah (buggalow) is a vessel above 50 tons burden, the Sambuk (a classical term) from 15 to 50. The ship-owner bribes the Amir el Bahr, or port-captain, and the Nazir el Safayn, or the captain commanding the government vessels, to rate his ship as high as possible—if he pay the price, he will be allowed 9 ardebbs (each 300 lbs.) to the ton. The number of ships belonging to the port of Suez amounts to 92; they vary from 25 to 250 tons. The departures in A.H. 1269 (1852 and 1853) were 38, so that each vessel, after returning from a trip, is laid up for about two years. Throughout the passage of the pilgrims, that is to say, during four months, the departures average twice a week; during the remainder of the year from 6 to 10 vessels may leave the port. The homeward trade is carried on principally in Jeddah bottoms, which are allowed to convey goods to Suez, but not to take in return-cargo there: they must not interfere with, nor may they partake in any way of the benefits of the rotation system.

"During the present year the imports were contained in 41,395 packages, the exports in 15,988. Specie makes up in some manner for this preponderance of imports: a sum of from 30,000*l.* to 40,000*l.*, in crown, or Maria Theresa, dollars annually leaves Egypt for Arabia, Abyssinia, and other parts of Africa. I value the imports at about 350,000*l.*; the export trade to Jeddah at 300,000*l.* per annum. The former consists principally of coffee and gum Arabic; of these there were respectively 17,460 and 15,132 bales, the aggregate value of each article being from 75,000*l.* to 80,000*l.*, and the total amount 160,000*l.* In the previous year the imports were contained in 36,840 packages, the exports in 13,498: of the staple articles —coffee and gum Arabic—they were respectively 15,499 and 14,129 bales, each bale being valued at about 5*l.* Next in importance comes wax from Yemen and the Hejaz, mother-of-pearl from the Red Sea, sent to England in rough, pepper from Malabar, cloves brought by Moslem pilgrims from Java, Borneo, and Singapore, cherry pipe-sticks from Persia and Bussora, and Persian or Surat 'Timbak' (tobacco). These I value at 20,000*l.* per annum. There were also (A. D. 1853) of cloves 708 packages and of Malabar pepper 948: the cost of these two might be 7000*l.* Minor articles of exportation are, general spiceries (ginger, cardamoms, &c.), Eastern perfumes, such as aloes wood, ottar of rose, ottar of pink and others, tamarinds from India and Yemen, Banca tin, hides supplied by the nomade Bedawin, senna leaves from Yemen and the Hejaz, and blue chequered cotton Melayahs (women's mantillas), manufactured in southern Arabia. The total value of these smaller imports may be 20,000*l.* per annum.

"The exports chiefly consist of English and native 'grey domestics,' bleached Madipilams, Paisley lappets, and muslins for turbans; the remainder being Manchester prints, antimony, Syrian soap, iron in bars, and common ironmongery, Venetian or Trieste beads, used as ornaments in Arabia and Abyssinia, writing paper, Tarbooshes, Papooshes (slippers), and other minor articles of dress and ornaments.

"The average annual temperature of the year at Suez is 67° Fahrenheit. The extremes of heat and cold are found in January and August; during the former month the thermometer ranges from a minimum of 38° to a maximum of 68°; during the latter the variation extends from 68° to 102°, or even to 104°, when the heat becomes oppressive. Departures from these extremes are rare. I never remember to have seen the thermometer rise above 108° during the severest Khamsin, or to have sunk below 34° in the rawest wintry wind. Violent storms come up from the south in March. Rain is very variable: sometimes three years have passed without a shower, whereas in 1841 torrents poured for nine successive days, deluging the town, and causing many buildings to fall.

"The population of Suez now numbers about 4800. As usual in Mohammedan countries no census is taken here. Some therefore estimate the population at 6000. Sixteen years ago it was supposed to be under 3000. After that time it rapidly increased till 1850, when a fatal attack of cholera reduced it to about half its previous number. The average mortality is about twelve a month. The endemic diseases are fevers of typhoid and intermittent types in spring, when strong northerly winds cause the waters of the bay to recede,*

---

* During these North winds the sandy bar is exposed and allows men to

and leave a miasma-breeding swamp exposed to the rays of the sun. In the months of October and November febrile attacks are violent; ophthalmia more so. The eye-disease is not so general here as at Cairo, but the symptoms are more acute; in some years it becomes a virulent epidemic, which ends either in total blindness or in a partial opacity of the cornea, inducing dimness of vision, and a permanent weakness of the eye. In one month three of my acquaintances lost their sight. Dysenteries are also common, and so are bad boils, or rather ulcers. The cold season is not unwholesome, and at this period the pure air of the Desert restores and invigorates the heat-wasted frame.

"The walls, gates, and defences of Suez are in a ruinous state, being no longer wanted to keep out the Sinaitic Bedawin. The houses are about 500 in number, but many of the natives prefer occupying the upper stories of the Wakalehs, the rooms on the ground floor serving for stores to certain merchandise, wood, dates, cotton, &c.

"The Suezians live well, and their bazar is abundantly stocked with meat and clarified butter brought from Sinai, and fowls, corn, and vegetables from the Sharkiyah province; fruit is supplied by Cairo as well as by the Sharkiyah, and wheat conveyed down the Nile in flood to the capital is carried on camel-back across the Desert. At sunrise they eat the Fatur, or

---

cross, which may explain the passage of the Israelites. Similarly as Jeddah, the bars are covered during the South and bare during the North winds.

breakfast, which in summer consists of a 'fatireh,' a kind of muffin, or of bread and treacle. In winter it is more substantial, being generally a mixture of lentils and rice, with clarified butter poured over it, and a 'kitchen' of pickled lime or stewed onions. At this season they greatly enjoy the 'Ful mudammas,' (boiled horsebeans), eaten with an abundance of linseed oil, into which they steep bits of bread. The beans form, with carbon-generating matter, a highly nutritive diet, which, if the stomach can digest it,—the pulse is never shelled,—gives great strength. About the middle of the day comes 'El Ghada,' a light dinner of wheaten bread, with dates, onions or cheese: in the hot season melons and cooling fruits are preferred, especially by those who have to face the sun. 'El Asha,' or supper, is served about half an hour after sunset; at this meal all but the poorest classes eat meat. Their favourite flesh, as usual in this part of the world, is mutton; beef and goat are little prized."[*]

The people of Suez are a finer and a fairer race than the Cairenes. The former have more the appearance of Arabs: their dress is more picturesque, their eyes are carefully darkened with Kohl, and they wear sandals, not slippers. They are, according to all accounts, a turbulent and somewhat fanatic set, fond of quarrels, and slightly addicted to "pronunciamientos." The general programme of one of these latter diversions is said to be as follows. The boys will first be

[*] Here concludes Mr. Levick's letter. For the following observations, I alone am answerable.

sent by their fathers about the town in a disorderly mob, and ordered to cry out "Long live the Sultan!" with its usual sequel, "Death to the Infidels!" The Infidels, Christians or others, must hear and may happen to resent this; or possibly the governor, foreseeing a disturbance, orders an ingenous youth or two to be imprisoned, or to be caned by the police. Whereupon some person, rendered influential by wealth or religious reputation, publicly complains that the Christians are all in all, and that in these evil days El Islam is going to destruction. On this occasion the speaker conducts himself with such insolence, that the governor perforce consigns him to confinement, which exasperates the populace still more. Secret meetings are now convened, and in them the chiefs of corporations assume a prominent position. If the disturbance be intended by its main spring to subside quietly, the conspirators are allowed to take their own way; they will drink copiously, become lions about midnight, and recover their hare-hearts before noon next day. But if mischief be intended, a case of bloodshed is brought about, and then nothing can arrest the torrent of popular rage. The Egyptian, with all his good humour, merriment, and nonchalance, is notorious for doggedness, when, as the popular phrase is, his "blood is up." And this, indeed, is his chief merit as a soldier. He has a certain mechanical dexterity in the use of arms, and an Egyptian regiment will fire a volley as correctly as a battalion at Chobham. But when the head, and not the hands, is required, he notably fails.

The reason of his superiority in the field is his peculiar stubbornness, and this, together with his powers of digestion and of enduring hardship on the line of march, is the quality that makes him terrible to his old conqueror, the Turk.

Note to Third Edition. I revisited Suez in September 1869, and found it altered for the better. The population had risen from 6000 to 20,000. The tumble-down gateway was still there, but of the old houses—including the "George Inn" whose front had been repaired—I recognized only four, and they looked mean by the side of the fine new buildings. In a few years ancient Suez will be no more. The bazars are not so full of filth and flies, now that pilgrims pass straight through and hardly even encamp. The sweet-water canal renders a Hammám possible; coffee is no longer hot saltish water; and presently irrigation will cover with fields and gardens the desert plain extending to the feet of Jebel Atakah. The noble works of the "Canal Maritime," which should in justice be called the "Lesseps Canal," shall soon transform Clysma into a modern and civilized city. The Railway station close to the hotel, the new British hospital; the noisy Greek casino; the Frankish shops; the puffing steamers and the ringing of morning bells, gave me a novel impression. Even the climate has been changed by filling up the Timsah Lakes. Briefly, the *kaf* is now at home in Suez.

CHAPTER X.

The Pilgrim Ship.

The larger craft anchor some three or four miles from the Suez pier, so that it is necessary to drop down in a skiff or shore-boat.

Immense was the confusion at the eventful hour of our departure. Suppose us gathered upon the beach, on the morning of a fiery July day, carefully watching our hurriedly-packed goods and chattels, surrounded by a mob of idlers, who are not too proud to pick up waifs and strays, whilst pilgrims are rushing about apparently mad, and friends are weeping, acquaintances are vociferating adieux, boatmen are demanding fees, shopmen are claiming debts, women are shrieking and talking with inconceivable power, and children are crying—in short, for an hour or so we stand in the thick of a human storm. To confound confusion, the boatmen have moored their skiff half a dozen yards away from the shore, lest the porters should be unable to make more than double their fare from the Hajis. Again the Turkish women make a hideous noise, as they are carried off struggling vainly in brawny arms; the children howl because their mothers howl; and the men scold and swear, because in such scenes none may be silent. The moment we had embarked, each individual found that he or she had missed something of vital importance—a pipe, a child, a box, or a water-melon; and naturally all the servants were in the bazars, when they should have been in the boat. Therefore, despite the rage of the sailors, who feared being too late for a second trip, we stood for some time on the beach before putting off.

From the shore we poled to the little pier, where sat the Bey in person to perform a final examination of our passports. Several were detected without the necessary document. Some were bastinadoed, others were peremptorily ordered back to Cairo, and the rest were allowed to proceed. At about 10 A.M. (July 6) we hoisted sail, and ran down the channel leading to the roadstead. On our way we had a specimen of what we might expect from our fellow passengers, the Maghrabi—men of the Maghrab, or Western Africa. A boat crowded with these ruffians ran alongside of us, and, before we could organise a defence, about a score of them poured into our vessel. They carried things too with a high hand, laughed at us, and seemed quite ready to fight. My Indian boy, who happened to let slip the word "Mu'arras," narrowly escaped a blow with a palm-stick, which would have felled a camel. They outnumbered us, and they were armed; so that, on this occasion, we were obliged to put up with their insolence.

Our Pilgrim Ship, the Silk el Zahab, or the "Golden Wire," was a Sambuk of about fifty tons, with narrow wedge-like bows, a clean water line, a sharp keel, undecked except upon the poop, which was high enough to act sail in a gale of wind. She carried two masts, raking imminently forwards, the main being considerably larger than the mizen; the former was provided with a huge triangular latine, very deep in the tack, but the second sail was unaccountably wanting. She had no means of reefing, no compass, no log, no sounding lines, no spare ropes, nor even the suspicion of a chart: in her box-like cabin and ribbed hold there was something which savoured of close connexion between her model and that of the Indian Toni (dug-out). Such, probably, were the craft which carried old Sesostris across the Red Sea to Deir; such were the cruisers which once every three years left Ezion-Geber for Tarshish; such the transports of which 130 were required to convey Ælius Gallus, with his 10,000 men.

"Bakhshish" was the last as well as the first odious sound I heard in Egypt. The owner of the shore-boat would not allow us to climb the sides of our vessel before paying him his fare, and when we did so, he asked for Bakhshish. If Easterns would only imitate the example of Europeans—I never yet saw an Englishman give Bakhshish to a soul—the nuisance would soon be abated. But on this occasion all my companions complied with the request, and at times it is unpleasant to be singular.

The first look at the interior of our vessel showed a hopeless sight; for Ali Murad, the greedy owner, had promised to take sixty passengers in the hold, but had stretched the number to ninety-seven. Piles of boxes and luggage in every shape and form filled the ship from stem to stern, and a torrent of Hajis was pouring over the sides like ants into the East-Indian sugar-basin. The poop, too, where we had taken our places, was covered with goods, and a number of pilgrims had established themselves there by might, not by right.

Presently, to our satisfaction, appeared Sa'ad the Demon, equipped as an able seaman, and looking most unlike the proprietor of two large boxes full of valuable merchandise. This energetic individual instantly prepared for action. With our little party to back him, he speedily cleared the poop of intruders and their stuff by the simple process of pushing or rather throwing them off it into the pit below. We then settled down as comfortably as we could; three Syrians, a married Turk with his wife and family, the Rais or captain of the vessel, with a portion of his crew, and our seven selves, composing a total of eighteen human beings, upon a space certainly not exceeding 10 feet by 8. The cabin—a miserable box about the size of the poop, and three feet high—was stuffed, like the hold of a slaver, with fifteen wretches, women and children, and the other ninety-seven were disposed upon the luggage, or squatted on the bulwarks. Having some experience in such matters, and being favoured by fortune, I found a spare bed-frame slung to the ship's side; and giving a dollar to its owner, a sailor —who flattered himself that, because it was his, he would sleep upon it—I instantly appropriated it, preferring any hardship outside, to the condition of a packed herring inside, the place of torment.

Our Maghrabis were fine-looking animals from the deserts about Tripoli and Tunis; so savage that, but a few weeks ago, they had gazed at the cock-boat, and wondered how long it would be growing to the size of the ship that was to take them to Alexandria. Most of them were sturdy young fellows, round-headed, broad-shouldered, tall and large-limbed, with frowning eyes, and voices in a perpetual roar. Their manners were rude, and their faces full of fierce contempt or insolent familiarity. A few old men were there, with countenances expressive of intense ferocity; women as savage and full of fight as men; and handsome boys with shrill voices, and hands always upon their daggers. The women were mere bundles of dirty white rags. The males were clad in Burnus, brown or striped woollen cloaks with hoods; they had neither turban nor Tarbush, trusting to their thick curly hair or to the prodigious hardness of their scalps as a defence against the sun; and there was not a slipper nor a shoe amongst the party. Of course all were armed; but, fortunately for us, none had anything more formidable than a cut-and-thrust dagger about ten inches long. These Maghrabis travel in hordes under a leader who obtains the temporary title of "Maula,"—the master. He has generally performed a pilgrimage or two, and has collected a stock of superficial information which secures for him the respect of his followers, and the profound contempt of the heaven-made Ciceroni of Meccah and El Medinah. No people endure greater hardships when upon the pilgrimage than these Africans, who trust almost entirely to alms and to other such dispensations of Providence. It is not therefore to be wondered at that they rob whenever an opportunity presents itself. Several cases of theft occurred on board the "Golden Wire;" and as such plunderers seldom allow themselves to be baulked by insufficient defence, they are accused perhaps deservedly of having committed some revolting murders.

The first thing to be done after gaining standing-room was to fight for greater comfort; and never a Holyhead packet in the olden time showed a finer scene of pugnacity than did our pilgrim ship. A few Turks, rugged old men from Anatolia and Caramania, were mixed up with the Maghrabis, and the former began the war by contemptuously elbowing and scolding their wild neighbours. The Maghrabis under their head man, "Maula Ali," a burly savage, in whom I detected a ridiculous resemblance to the Rev. Charles Delafosse, an old and well-remembered schoolmaster, retorted so willingly that in a few minutes nothing was to be seen but a confused mass of humanity, each item indiscriminately punching and pulling, scratching and biting, butting and trampling whatever was obnoxious to such operations, with cries of rage, and all the accompaniments of a proper fray. One of our party on the poop, a Syrian, somewhat incautiously leapt down to aid his countrymen by restoring order. He sank immediately below the surface of the living mass;

and when we fished him out, his forehead was cut open, half his beard had disappeared, and a fine sharp set of teeth belonging to some Maghrabi had left their mark in the calf of his leg. The enemy showed no love of fair play, and never appeared contented unless five or six of them were setting upon a single man. This made matters worse. The weaker of course drew their daggers, and a few bad wounds were soon given and received. In a few minutes five men were completely disabled, and the victors began to dread the consequences of their victory.

Then the fighting stopped, and, as many could not find places, it was agreed that a deputation should wait upon Ali Murad, the owner, to inform him of the crowded state of the vessel. After keeping us in expectation at least three hours, he appeared in a rowboat, preserving a respectful distance, and informed us that any one who pleased might quit the ship and take back his fare. This left the case exactly as it was before; none would abandon his party to go on shore: so Ali Murad rowed off towards Suez, giving us a parting injunction to be good boys, and not fight; to trust in Allah, and that Allah would make all things easy to us.

His departure was the signal for a second fray, which in its accidents differed a little from the first. During the previous disturbance we kept our places with weapons in our hands. This time we were summoned by the Maghrabis to relieve their difficulties, by taking about half a dozen of them on the poop.

Sa'ad the Demon at once rose with an oath, and threw amongst us a bundle of "Nebút"—goodly ashen staves six feet long, thick as a man's wrist, well greased, and tried in many a rough bout. He shouted to us, "Defend yourselves if you don't wish to be the meat of the Maghrabis!" and to the enemy, "Dogs and sons of dogs! now shall you see what the children of the Arab are,"—"I am Umar of Daghistan!" "I am Abdullah the son of Joseph!" "I am Sa'ad the Demon!" we exclaimed, "renowning it" by this display of name and patronymic. To do our enemies justice, they showed no sign of flinching; they swarmed towards the poop like angry hornets, and encouraged each other with loud cries of "Allahu akbar!" But we had a vantage ground about four feet above them, and their palm-sticks and short daggers could do nothing against our terrible quarter-staves. In vain the "Jacquerie" tried to scale the poop and to overpower us by numbers; their courage only secured them more broken heads.

At first I began to lay on load with "main morte," really fearing to kill some one with such a weapon; but it soon became evident that the Maghrabis' heads and shoulders could bear and did require the utmost exertion of strength. Presently a thought struck me. A large earthen jar full of drinking water—in its heavy frame of wood the weight might have been 100 lbs.—stood upon the edge of the poop, and the thick of the fray took place beneath. Seeing an opportunity I crept up to the jar, and, without attracting attention, rolled it down by a smart push with the shoulder upon the swarm of assailants. The fall caused a shriller shriek to rise above the ordinary din, for heads, limbs, and bodies were sorely bruised by the weight, scratched by the broken potsherds, and wetted by the sudden discharge. A fear that something worse might be coming made the Maghrabis slink off towards the end of the vessel. After a few minutes, we, sitting in grave silence, received a deputation of individuals in whity-brown Burnus, spotted and striped with what Mephistopheles calls a "curious juice." They solicited peace, which we granted upon the condition that they would pledge themselves to keep it. Our heads, shoulders, and hands were penitentially kissed, and presently the fellows returned to bind up their hurts in dirty rags.

We owed this victory entirely to our own exertions, and the meek Umar was by far the fiercest of the party. Our Rais, as we afterwards learned, was an old fool who could do nothing but call for the Fatihah, or opening chapter of the Koran, claim Bakhshish at every place where we moored for the night, and spend his leisure hours in the "Caccia del Mediterraneo." Our crew consisted of half a dozen Egyptian lads, who, not being able to defend themselves, were periodically chastised by the Maghrabi, especially when any attempt was made to cook, to fetch water, or to prepare a pipe.

At length, about 3 P.M. on the 6th July, 1853, we shook out the sail and, when it bellied in the favourable wind, we recited the Fatihah with upraised hands which we afterwards drew down our faces. As the "Golden Wire" started from her place, I could not help casting one wistful look upon the British flag floating over the Consulate. But the momentary regret was stifled by the heart-bounding which prospects of an adventure excite, and by the real pleasure of leaving Egypt. I had lived there a stranger in the land, and a hapless life it had been: in the streets every man's face, as he looked upon the Persian, was the face of a foe. Whenever I came in contact with the native officials, insolence marked the event; and the circumstance of living within hail of my fellow countrymen, and yet finding it impossible to enjoy their society, still throws a gloom over the memory of my first sojourn in Egypt.

The ships of the Red Sea—infamous region of rocks, reefs, and shoals—cruise along the coast by day, and at night lay to in the first cove they find; they do not sail when it blows hard, and as in winter time the weather is often stormy and the light of day does not last long, the voyage is intolerably slow. At sunset we stayed our adventurous course and, still within sight of Suez, we anchored comfortably under the lee of Jebel Atakah, the "Mountain of Deliverance," the butt-end of Jebel Joshi. We were now on classic waters. The Eastern shore was dotted with the little grove of palm-trees which clusters around the Uyun Musa, or Moses' Wells; and on the west, between two towering ridges, lay the mouth of the valley (Badia or

Wadi Tawarik or Wadi Musa) down which, according to Father Sicard, the Israelites fled to the Sea of Sedge. The view was by no means deficient in a sort of barbarous splendour. Verdure there was none, but under the violet and orange tints of the sky the chalky rocks became heaps of topazes, and the brown-burnt ridges masses of amethyst. The rising mists, here silvery white, there deeply rosy, and the bright blue of the waves, lining long strips of golden sand, compensated for the want of softness by a semblance of savage gorgeousness.

Next morning (July 7), before the cerulean hue had vanished from the hills, we set sail. It was not long before we came to a proper sense of our position. The box containing my store of provisions, and, worse still, my opium, was at the bottom of the hold, perfectly unapproachable; we had, therefore, the pleasure of breaking our fast on "Mare's skin,"* and a species of biscuit, hard as a stone and quite as tasteless. During the day, whilst unsufferable splendor reigned above, the dashing of the waters below kept my nest in a state of perpetual drench. At night rose a cold bright moon, with dews falling so thick and clammy that the skin felt as though it would never be dry again. It is, also, by no means pleasant to sleep upon a broken cot about four feet long by two broad, with the certainty that a false movement would throw

* Jild el Faras (or Kamar el din), a composition of apricot paste, dried, spread out, and folded into sheets, exactly resembling the article after which it is named. Turks and Arabs use it when travelling; they dissolve it in water, and eat it as a relish with bread or biscuit.

you over-board, and a conviction that if you do fall from a Sambuk under sail, no mortal power can save you. And as under all circumstances in the East, dozing is one's chief occupation, the reader will understand that the want of it left me in utter, utter idleness.

The gale was light that day, and the sunbeams were fire; our crew preferred crouching in the shade of the sail to taking advantage of what wind there was. In spite of our impatience we made but little way: near evening time we anchored on a tongue of sand, about two miles distant from the well-known and picturesque heights called by the Arabs Hammam Far'aun, "Pharaoh's Hot Baths," which

> "Like giants stand
> To sentinel enchanted land."

The strip of coarse quartz and sandstone gravel is obviously the offspring of some mountain torrent; it stretches southwards, being probably disposed in that direction by the currents as they receive the deposit. The distance of the "Hammam Bluffs" prevented my visiting them, which circumstance I regretted the less as they have been described by pens equal to the task.

That evening we enjoyed ourselves upon clean sand, whose surface, drifted by the wind into small yellow waves, was easily converted by a little digging and heaping up into the coolest and the most comfortable of couches. Indeed, after the canescent heat of the day, and the tossing of our ill-conditioned vessel, we should have been, contented with lodgings far less luxurious. Fuel was readily collected, and while some bathed, others erected a hearth—three large stones and a hole open to leeward—lit the fire, and put on the pot to boil. Shaykh Nur had fortunately brought a line with him; we had been successful in fishing; a little rice also had been bought; with this boiled and rock-cod broiled upon the charcoal, we made a dinner that caused every one to forget the grievance of "mare's skin" and hard biscuit. A few Maghrabis had ventured on shore—the Rais having terrified the others by threatening them with those "bogies," the Bedawin—they offered us Kuskusu in exchange for a little fish. As evening fell we determined, before sleeping, to work upon their morale as effectually as we had attacked their physique. Shaykh Hamid stood up and indulged them with the Azan, or call to prayers, pronounced after the fashion of El Medinah. They performed their devotions in lines ranged behind us as a token of respect, and when worship was over we were questioned about the Holy City till we grew tired of answering. Again our heads and shoulders, our hands and knees, were kissed, but this time in devotion, not in penitence. My companions could scarcely understand half the rugged words which the Maghrabis used, as this dialect was fresh from the distant desert: still we succeeded in making ourselves intelligible to them, vaunting our dignity as the Sons of the Prophet, and the sanctity of our land which should protect its children from every description of fraud and violence. We benignantly promised to be their guides at El Medinah, and the boy Mohammed would conduct their devotions at Mecca, always provided that they repented their past misdeeds, avoided any repetition of the same, and promised to perform the duties of good and faithful pilgrims.

Presently the Rais joined our party, and the usual story-telling began. The old man knew the name of each hill, and had a legend for every nook and corner in sight. He dwelt at length upon the life of Abu Zulaymah, the patron saint of these seas, whose little tomb stands at no great distance from our bivouac place, and told us how he sits watching over the safety of pious mariners in a cave among the neighbouring rocks, and sipping his coffee, which is brought in a raw state from Mecca by green birds, and prepared in the usual way by the hands of ministering angels. He showed us the spot where the terrible king of Egypt, when close upon the heels of the children of Israel, was whelmed in the "hell of waters," and he warned us that next day our way would be through breakers, and reefs, and dangerous currents, over whose troubled depths, since that awful day, the Ifrit of the storm has never ceased to flap his sable wing. The wincing of the hearers proved that the shaft of the old man's words was sharp; but as night was advancing, we unrolled our rugs, and fell asleep upon the sand, all of us happy, for we had fed and drunk, and—the homo sapiens is a hopeful animal—we made sure that on the morrow the Ifrit would be merciful, and allow us to eat fresh dates at the harbour of Tur.

Fair visions of dates doomed to the Limbo of things which should have been! The grey dawn (July 8) looked down upon us in difficulties. The water is deep near this coast; we had anchored at high tide close to the shore, and the ebb had left us high and dry. As the fact became apparent, a storm was upon the point of breaking. The Maghrabis, but for our interference, would have bastinadoed the Rais, who, they said with some reason, ought to have known better. When this phase of feeling passed away, they applied themselves to physical efforts. All except the women and children, who stood on the shore encouraging their relatives with shrill quaverings, threw themselves into the water; some pushed, others applied their shoulders to the vessel's side, and all used their lungs with might and main. But the "Golden Wire" was firmly fixed, and their exertions were too irregular. Physical force failed, upon which they changed their tactics. At the suggestion of their "Maula," they prepared to burn incense in honor of the Shaykh Abu Zulaymah. The material not being forthcoming, they used coffee, which perhaps accounts for the shortcomings of that holy man. After this the Rais remembered that their previous exertions had not begun under the auspices of the Fatihah. Therefore they prayed, and then re-applied themselves to work. Still they failed. Finally, each man called aloud upon his own particular saint or spiritual guide, and rushed forward as if he alone sufficed for the exploit. Shaykh Hamid unwisely quoted the name, and begged the assistance of his great ancestor, the "Clarified-Butter-Seller;" the obdurate "Golden Wire" was not moved, and Hamid retired in momentary confusion.

It was now about nine A.M., and the water had risen considerably. My morning had been passed in watching the influx of the tide, and the grotesque efforts of the Maghrabis. When the vessel showed some symptoms of unsteadiness, I arose, walked gravely up to her, ranged the pilgrims around her with their shoulders to the sides, and told them to heave with might when they heard me invoke the revered name of my patron saint. I raised my hands and voice; "Ya Piran Pir! Ya Abd el Kadir Jilani!" was the signal. I thus called upon a celebrated Sufi or mystic, whom many East-Indian Moslems reverence as the Arabs do their Prophet. Each Maghrabi worked like an Atlas, the "Golden Wire" canted half over, and, sliding heavily through the sand, once more floated off into deep water. This was generally voted a minor miracle, and the Effendi was respected—for a day or two.

The wind was fair, but we had all to re-embark, an operation which went on till noon. After starting, I remarked the natural cause which gives this Birket Far'aun, "Pharaoh's Bay," a bad name. Here the gulf narrows, and the winds, which rush down the clefts and valleys of the lofty mountains on the Eastern and Western shores, meeting currents and counter-currents, cause a perpetual commotion. That day the foam-tipped waves repeatedly washed over my cot, by no means diminishing its discomforts. In the evening, or rather late in the afternoon, we anchored, to our infinite disgust, under a ridge of rocks, behind which lies the plain of Tur. The Rais deterred all from going on shore by terrible stories about the Bedawin that haunt the place, besides which there was no sand to sleep upon. We remained, therefore, on board that night, and, making sail early the next morning, we threaded reefs and sand-banks, and we made about noon the intricate and dangerous entrance of Tur.

Nothing can be meaner than the present appearance of the old Phœnician colony, although its position as a harbour, and its plentiful supply of fruit and fresh water, make it one of the most frequented places on the coast. The only remains of any antiquity, except the wells, are the fortifications which the Portuguese erected to keep out the Bedawin. The little town lies upon a plain that stretches with a gradual rise from the sea to the lofty mountain-axis of the Sinaitic group. The country around reminded me strongly of maritime Sind—a flat of clay and sand, clothed with sparse tufts of Salsolæ, and bearing strong signs of a (geologically speaking) recent origin. The town is inhabited principally by Greek and other Christians, who live by selling water and provisions to ships.

A fleecy cloud hung lightly over the majestic head

of Jebel Tur, about eventide, and the outlines of the giant hills stood "picked out" from the clear blue sky. Our Rais, weather-wise man, warned us that these were indications of a gale, and that, in case of rough weather, he did not intend to leave Tur. I was not sorry to hear this. We had passed a pleasant day, drinking sweet water, and eating the dates, grapes, and pomegranates, which the people of the place carry down to the beach for the benefit of hungry pilgrims. Besides which, there were various sights to see, and with these we might profitably spend the morrow. We therefore pitched the tent upon the sand, and busied ourselves with extricating a box of provisions, a labor rendered lighter by the absence of the Maghrabis, some of whom were wandering about the beach, whilst others had gone off to fill their bags with fresh water. We found their surliness insufferable; even when we were passing from poop to forecastle, landing or boarding, they grumbled forth their dissatisfaction.

Our Rais was not mistaken in his prediction. The fleecy cloud on Tur's top had given true warning. When morning (9th July) broke, we found the wind strong, and the sea white with foam. Most of us thought lightly of these terrors, but our valorous captain swore that he dared not for his life cross in such a storm the mouth of ill-omened Akabah. We breakfasted, therefore, and afterwards set out to visit Moses' Hot Baths, mounted on wretched donkeys with pack-saddles, ignorant of stirrups, and without tails, whilst we ourselves suffered generally from boils, which, as usual upon a journey, make their appearance in localities the most inconvenient.

Our road lay northward across the plain towards a long narrow strip of date ground, surrounded by a ruinous mud wall. After a ride of two or three miles, we entered the gardens, and came suddenly upon the Hammam. It is a prim little cockney bungalow, built by the present Pasha of Egypt for his own accommodation, glaringly whitewashed, and garnished with divans and calico curtains of a gorgeous hue. The guardian had been warned of our visit, and was present to supply us with bathing-cloths and other necessaries. One by one, we entered the cistern, which is now in an inner room. The water is about four feet deep, warm in winter, cool in summer, of a saltish-bitter taste, but celebrated for its invigorating qualities, when applied externally.

On one side of the calcareous rock, near the ground, is the hole opened for the spring by Moses' rod, which must have been like the "mast of some tall Ammiral," and near it are the marks of Moses' nails—deep indentations in the stone, which were probably left there by some extinct Saurian. Our cicerone informed us that formerly the finger-marks existed, and that they were long enough for a man to lie in. The same functionary attributed the sanitary properties of the spring to the blessings of the Prophet, and, when asked why Moses had not made sweet water to flow, informed us that the Great Lawgiver had intended the spring for bathing, not for drinking. We sat with him, eating the small yellow dates of Tur, which are delicious, melting like honey in the mouth, and leaving a surpassing arrière goût.

After finishing sundry pipes and cups of coffee, we gave the bath-man a few piastres, and, mounting our donkeys, started eastward for the Bir Musa, "Moses' Well," which we reached in half an hour. It is a fine old shaft, built round and domed over with roughly squared stones, very like what may be seen in some rustic parts of Southern England. The sides of the pit were so rugged that a man could climb down them, and at the bottom was a pool of water, sweet and abundant. We had intended to stay there, and to dine al fresco, but the hated faces of our companions, the Maghrabis, meeting us at the entrance, nipped that project in the bud. Accordingly we retired from the burning sun to a neighbouring coffee-house —a shed of palm-leaves kept by a Tur man, and there, seated on mats, we demolished the contents of our basket. Whilst we were eating, some Bedawin came in and joined us, when invited so to do. They were poorly dressed, and all armed with knives and cheap sabres, hanging to leathern bandoleers: in language and demeanour they showed few remains of their old ferocity. As late as Mohammed Ali's time these people were noted wreckers, and formerly they were dreaded pirates—now they are lions with their fangs and claws drawn.

In the evening, when we returned to our tent, a Syrian, one of our party on the poop, came out to meet us with the information that several large vessels had arrived from Suez, comparatively speaking, empty, and that the captain of one of them would land us at Yambu' for three dollars a head. The proposal was tempting. But, presently it became apparent that my companions were unwilling to shift their precious boxes, and moreover, that I should have to pay for those who could not or would not pay for themselves—that is to say, for the whole party. As such a display of wealth would have been unadvisable, I dismissed the idea with a sigh.

Amongst the large vessels was one freighted with Persian pilgrims, a most disagreeable race of men on a journey or a voyage. They would not land at first, because they feared the Bedawin. They would not take water from the town people, because some of these were Christians. Moreover, they insisted upon making their own call to prayer, which heretical proceeding—it admits five extra words—our party, orthodox Moslems, would rather have died than have permitted. When their crier, a small wizen-faced man, began the Azan with a voice

> "In quel tenore
> Che fa il cappon quando talvolta canta,"

we received it with a shout of derision, and some, hastily snatching up their weapons, offered him an opportunity of martyrdom. The Maghrabis, too, hearing that the Persians were Rafaz (heretics) crowded fiercely round to do a little Jihad, or fighting for the faith. The long-bearded men took the alarm. They were twice the number of our small party, and therefore they had been in the habit of strutting about with nonchalance, and looking at us fixedly, and otherwise demeaning themselves in an indecorous way. But when it came to the point, they showed the white feather.

These Persians accompanied us to the end of our voyage. As they approached the Holy Land, visions of the "Nebút" caused a change for the better in their manners. At Mahar they meekly endured a variety of insults, and at Yambu' they cringed to us like dogs.

CHAPTER XI.

To Yambu'.

On the 11th July 1853, about dawn, we left Tur, after a pleasant halt, with the unpleasant certainty of not touching ground for thirty-six hours. I passed the time in steadfast contemplation of the web of my umbrella, and in making the following meteorological remarks.

Morning. The air is mild and balmy as that of an Italian spring; thick mists roll down the valleys along the sea, and a haze like mother-o'-pearl crowns the headlands. The distant rocks show Titanic walls, lofty donjons, huge projecting bastions, and moats full of deep shade. At their base runs a sea of amethyst, and as earth receives the first touches of light, their summits, almost transparent, mingle with the jasper tints of the sky. Nothing can be more delicious than this hour. But, as

> "—Les plus belles choses
> Ont le pire destin—"

so lovely Morning soon fades. The sun bursts up from behind the main, a fierce enemy, a foe that will force every one to crouch before him. He dyes the sky orange, and the sea incarnadine, where its violet surface is stained by his rays, and he mercilessly puts to flight the mists and haze and the little agate-coloured masses of cloud that were before floating in the firmament. The atmosphere is so clear that now and then a planet is visible. For the two hours following sunrise the rays are endurable; after that they become a fiery ordeal. The morning beams oppress you with a feeling of sickness; their steady glow, reflected by the glaring waters, blinds your eyes, blisters your skin, and parches your mouth: you now become a monomaniac; you do nothing but count the slow hours that must minute by before you can be relieved.

Noon. The wind reverberated by the glowing hills, is like the blast of a lime-kiln. All color melts away with the canescence from above. The sky is a dead milk-white, and the mirror-like sea so reflects the tint that you can scarcely distinguish the line of the horizon. After noon the wind slumbers upon the reeking shore; there is a deep stillness; the only sound heard is the melancholy flapping of the sail. Men are not so much sleeping as half senseless; they feel as if a few more degrees of heat would be death.

Sunset. The enemy sinks behind the deep cerulean sea, under a canopy of gigantic rainbow which covers half the face of heaven. Nearest to the horizon is an arch of tawny orange; above it another of the brightest gold, and based upon these a semicircle of tender sea-green blends with a score of delicate gradations into the sapphire sky. Across the rainbow the sun throws its rays in the form of giant wheel-spokes tinged with a beautiful pink. The Eastern sky is mantled with a purple flush that cloaks the forms of the desert and the hills. Language is a thing too cold, too poor, to express the harmony and the majesty of this hour, which is evanescent, however, as it is lovely. Night falls rapidly, when suddenly the appearance of the zodiacal light restores the scene to what it was. Again the grey hills and the grim rocks become rosy or golden, the palms green, the sands saffron, and the sea wears a lilac surface of dimpling wavelets. But after a quarter of an hour all fades once more; the cliffs are naked and ghastly under the moon, whose light falling upon this wilderness of white crags and pinnacles is most strange, most mysterious.

Night. The horizon is all darkness, and the sea reflects the pale visage of the night-sun as in a mirror of steel. In the air we see giant columns of pallid light, distinct, based upon the indigo-coloured waves, and standing with their heads lost in endless space. The stars glitter with exceeding brilliance. At this hour are

> "River and hill and wood,
>   With all the numberless goings on of life,
> Inaudible as dreams;"

while the planets look down upon you with the faces of smiling friends. You feel the "sweet influence of the Pleiades." You are bound by the "bond of Orion." Hesperus bears with him a thousand things. In communion with them your hours pass swiftly by, till the heavy dews warn you to cover up your face and sleep. And with one look at a certain little Star in the North, under which lies all that makes life worth living through—surely it is a venial superstition to sleep with your face towards that Kiblah!—you fall into oblivion.

Those thirty-six hours were a trial even to the hard-headed Bedawin. The Syrian and his two friends fell ill. Umar Effendi, it is true, had the courage to say his sunset prayers, but the exertion so altered him that he looked another man. Salih Shakkar in despair ate dates till threatened with a dysentery. Sa'ad the Demon had rigged out for himself a cot three feet long, which, arched over with bent bamboo and covered with cloaks, he had slung on to the larboard side; but the loud grumbling which proceeded from his nest proved that his precaution had not been a cure. Even the boy Mohammed forgot to chatter, to scold, to smoke, and to make himself generally disagreeable. The Turkish baby appeared to be dying, and was not strong enough to wail. How the poor mother stood her trials so well, made every one wonder. The most pleasant trait in my companions' characters was the consideration they showed to her, and their attention to her children. Whenever one of the party drew forth a little delicacy—a few dates or a pomegranate—they gave away a share of it to the children, and most of them took their turns to nurse the baby.

This was genuine politeness—kindness of heart.

It would be well for those who sweepingly accuse Easterns of want of gallantry, to contrast this trait of character with the savage scenes of civilisation that take place among the "Overlands" at Cairo and Suez. No foreigner could be present for the first time without bearing' away the lasting impression that the sons of Great Britain are model barbarians. On board the "Golden Wire" Salih Shakkar was the sole base exception to the general geniality of my companions.

As the sun starts towards the west, falling harmlessly upon our heads, we arise, still faint and dizzy, calling for water—which before we had not the strength to drink—and pipes, and coffee, and similar luxuries. Our primitive kitchen is a square wooden box, lined with clay, and filled with sand, upon which three or four large stones are placed to form a hearth. Preparations are now made for the evening meal, which is of the simplest description. A little rice, a few dates, or an onion, will keep a man alive in our position; a single "good dinner" would justify long odds against his seeing the next evening. Moreover, it is impossible in such cases to have an appetite—fortunately, as our store of provisions is a scanty one. Arabs consider it desirable on a journey to eat hot food once in the twenty-four hours; so we determine to cook, despite all difficulties. The operation, however, is by no means satisfactory; twenty expectants surround the single fire, and there is sure to be a quarrel amongst them every five minutes.

As the breeze, cooled by the dew, begins to fan our parched faces, we recover our spirits amazingly. Songs are sung, and tales are told, and rough jests are bandied about, till not unfrequently Oriental sensitiveness is sorely tried. Or, if we see the prospect of storm or calm, we draw forth, and piously peruse, a "Hizb el Bahr." As this prayer is supposed to make all safe upon the ocean wâve, I will not selfishly withhold it from the British reader. To draw forth its virtues, the reciter should receive it from the hands of his Murshid or spiritual guide, and study it during the Chillah, or forty days of fast, of which, I venture to observe, few Sons of Bull are capable.

"O Allah, O Exalted, O Almighty, O All-pitiful, O All-powerful, Thou art my God, and sufficeth to me the knowledge of it! Glorified be the Lord my Lord, and glorified be the Faith my Faith! Thou givest Victory to whom Thou pleasest, and Thou art the Glorious, the Merciful! We pray Thee for Safety in our goings forth and our standings still, in our Words and our Designs, in our Dangers of Temptation and Doubt, and the secret Designs of our Hearts. Subject unto us this Sea, even as Thou didst subject the Deep to Musa (Moses), and as Thou didst subject the Fire to Ibrahim (Abraham), and as Thou didst subject the Iron to Daud (David), and as Thou didst subject the Wind and the Devils and Genii and Mankind to Sulayman (Solomon), and as Thou didst subject the Moon and El Burak to Mohammed, upon whom be Allah's Mercy and His Blessing! And subject unto us all the Seas in Earth and Heaven, in Thy visible and in Thine invisible Worlds, the Sea of this Life, and the Sea of Futurity. O Thou who reignest over everything, and unto whom all Things return, Khyas! Khyas! Khyas!"* And lastly, we lie down upon our cribs, wrapped up in thickly padded cotton coverlets, we forget the troubles of the past day, and we care nought for the discomforts of that to come.

Late on the evening of the 11th July we passed in sight of the narrow mouth of Akabah, whose famosi rupes are a terror to the voyagers of these latitudes. Like the Gulf of Cambay, here a tempest is said to be always brewing, and men raise their hands to pray as they cross it. We had no storm that day from without, but a fierce one was about to burst within our ship. The essence of Oriental discipline is personal respect based upon fear. Therefore it often happens, that the commanding officer, if a mild old gentleman, is the last person whose command is obeyed—his only privilege being that of sitting apart from his inferiors. And such was the case with our Rais. On the present occasion, irritated by the refusal of the Maghrabis to stand out of the steerman's way, and excited by the prospect of losing sight of shore for a whole day, he threatened one of the fellows with his slipper. It required all our exertions, even to a display of the dreaded quarter-staves, to calm the consequent excitement. After passing Akabah, we saw nothing but sea

* These are mystic words, and entirely beyond the reach of dictionaries and vocabularies.

and sky, and we spent a weary night and day tossing upon the waters—our only exercise: every face brightened as, about sunset on the 12th July, we suddenly glided into the mooring-place.

Marsa Damghah—"Damghah Anchorage"—is scarcely visible from the sea. An islet of limestone defends the entrance, leaving a narrow passage on each side. It is not before he enters that the mariner discovers the extent and the depth of this creek, which indents far into the land, and offers 15—20 feet of fine clear anchorage which no swell can reach. Inside it looks more like a lake, and at night its colour is gloriously blue as Geneva itself. I could not help calling to mind, after dinner, the old school lines,

> "Est in secessu longo locus; insula portum
> Efficit objectu laterum; quibus omnis ab alto
> Frangitur, inque sinus scindit sese unda reductos."

Nothing was wanted but the "atrum nemus." Where, however, shall we find such luxury in arid Arabia?

The Rais, as usual, attempted to deter us from landing, by romancing about the "Bedoynes and Ascopards," representing them to be "folke ryghte felonouse and foule and of cursed kynde." To which we replied by shouldering our Nebúts and scrambling into the cock boat. On shore we saw a few wretched-looking beings, Jahaynahs or Juhaynahs, seated upon heaps of dried wood, which they sold to travellers, and three boat-loads of Syrian pilgrims who had preceded us. We often envied them their small swift craft, with their double latine sails disposed in "hare-ears" which, about even-tide in the far distance, looked like a white gull alighting upon the purple wave; and they justified our jealousy by arriving at Yambu' two days before us. The pilgrims had bivouacked upon the beach, and were engaged in drinking their after dinner coffee. They received us with all the rights of hospitality, as natives of the Medinah should everywhere be received; we sat an hour with them, ate a little fruit, satisfied our thirst, smoked their pipes, and when taking leave blessed them. Then returning to the vessel we fed, and lost no time in falling asleep.

The dawn of the next day saw our sail flapping in the idle air. And it was not without difficulty that in the course of the forenoon we entered Wijh Harbour, distant from Damghah but very few miles. Wijh is also a natural anchorage, in no way differing from that where we passed the night, except in being smaller and shallower. From this place to Cairo the road is safe. The town is a collection of huts meanly built of round stones, and clustering upon a piece of elevated rock on the northern side of the creek. It is distant about five miles from the inland fort of the same name, which receives the Egyptian caravan, and which thrives, like its port, by selling water and provisions to pilgrims. The little bazar, almost washed by every high tide, provided us with mutton, rice, baked bread, and the other necessaries of life, at a moderate rate. Luxuries also were to be found: a druggist sold me an ounce of opium at a Chinese price.

With reeling limbs we landed at Wijh, and finding a large coffee-house above and near the beach, we installed ourselves there. But the Persians who preceded us had occupied all the shady places outside, and were correcting their teeth with their case-knives; we were forced to content ourselves with the interior. It was a building of artless construction, consisting of little but a roof supported by wooden posts, roughly hewn from date trees: round the tamped earthen floor ran a raised bench of unbaked brick forming a Divan for mats and sleeping-rugs. In the centre a huge square Mastabeh, or platform, answered a similar purpose. Here and there appeared attempts at long and side walls, but these superfluities had been allowed to admit daylight through large gaps. In one corner stood the apparatus of the "Kahwahji," an altar-like elevation, also of earthen work, containing a hole for a charcoal fire, upon which rested three huge coffee-pots dirtily tinned. Near it were ranged the Shishehs, or Egyptian hookahs, old, exceedingly unclean, and worn by age and hard work. A wooden framework, pierced with circular apertures, supported a number of porous earthenware "gullehs" (monkey jars) full of cold sweet water; the charge for each was, as usual in El Hejaz, five paras. Such was the furniture of the café, and the only relief to the barrenness of the view was a fine mellowing atmosphere composed of smoke, steam, flies, and gnats, in about equal proportions. I have been diffuse in my description of the coffee-house, as it was a type of its class: from Alexandria to Aden the traveller will everywhere meet with buildings of the same kind.

Our happiness in this Paradise—for such it was to us after the "Golden Wire"—was nearly sacrificed by Sa'ad the Demon, whose abominable temper led him at once into a quarrel with the master of the café. And the latter, an ill-looking, squint-eyed, low-browed, broad-shouldered fellow, showed himself no wise unwilling to meet the Demon half way. The two worthies, after a brief bandying of bad words, seized each other's throats leisurely, so as to give the spectators time and encouragement to interfere. But when friends and acquaintances were hanging on to both heroes so firmly that they could not move hand or arm, their wrath, as usual, rose, till it was terrible to see. The little village resounded with the war, and many a sturdy knave rushed in, sword or cudgel in hand, so as not to lose the sport. During the heat of the fray, a pistol which was in Umar Effendi's hand went off —accidentally of course—and the ball passed so close to the tins containing the black and muddy mocha, that it drew the attention of all parties. As if by magic, the storm was lulled. A friend recognised Sa'ad the Demon, and swore that he was no black slave, but a soldier at El Medinah—"no waiter, but a Knight Templar." This caused him to be looked upon as rather a distinguished man, and he proved his right to the honour by insisting that his late enemy should feed with him, and when the other decorously hung back, by dragging him to dinner with loud cries.

My alias that day was severely tried. Besides the Persian pilgrims, sundry nondescripts who came in the same vessel were hanging about the coffeehouse, lying down, smoking, drinking water, bathing, and picking their teeth with their daggers. One inquisitive man was always at my side. He called himself a Pathan; he could speak five or six languages, he knew a number of people everywhere, and he had travelled far and wide over central Asia. These fellows are always good detectors of an incognito. I avoided answering his question about my native place, and after telling him that I had no longer name or nation, being a Dervish, I asked him, when he insisted upon my having been born somewhere, to guess for himself. To my joy he claimed me for a brother Pathan, and in course of conversation he declared himself to be the nephew of an Afghan merchant, a gallant old man who had been civil to me at Cairo. We then sat smoking together with "effusion." Becoming confidential, he complained that he, a Sunni or orthodox Moslem, had been abused, maltreated, and beaten by his fellow-travellers, the heretical Persian pilgrims. I naturally offered to arm my party, to take up our cudgels, and to revenge my compatriot. This thoroughly Sulaymanian style of doing business could not fail to make him sure of his man. He declined, however, wisely remembering that he had nearly a fortnight of the Persians' society still to endure. But he promised himself the gratification, when he reached Mecca, of sheathing his Charay—the terrible Afghan knife—in the chief offender's heart.

At 8 A. M. on the 14th of July we left Wijh, after passing a night, tolerably comfortable by contrast, in the coffee-house. We took with us the stores necessary, for though our Rais had promised to anchor under Jebel Hasan that evening, no one believed him. We sailed among ledges of rock, golden sands, green weeds, and in some places through yellow lines of what appeared to me at a distance foam after a storm. All day a sailor sat upon the mast-head, looking at the water, which was transparent as blue glass, and shouting out the direction. This precaution was somewhat stultified by the roar of voices, which never failed to mingle with the warning, but we wore every half hour, and we did not run aground. About midday we passed by Shaykh Hasan el Marabit's tomb. It is the usual domed and whitewashed building, surrounded by the hovels of its guardians, standing upon a low flat island of yellow rock, vividly reminding me of certain scenes in Sind. Its dreary position attracts to it the attention of passing travellers; the dead saint has a prayer and a Fatiheh for the good of his soul, and the live sinner wends his way with religious refreshment.

Near sunset the wind came on to blow freshly, and we cast anchor together with the Persian pilgrims upon a rock. This was one of the celebrated coral reefs of the Red Sea, and the sight justified Forskal's emphatic description—luxus lususque naturæ. It was a huge ledge or platform rising but little above the level of the deep; the water-side was perpendicular as the wall of a fort, and whilst a frigate might have floated within a yard of it, every ripple dashed over the reef, replenishing the little basins and hollows in the surface. The colour of the waves near it was a vivid amethyst. In the distance the eye rested upon what appeared to be meadows of brilliant flowers resembling those of earth, only brighter far and more lovely. Nor was this land of the sea wholly desolate. Gulls and terns here swam the tide, there, seated upon the coral, devoured their prey. In the air, troops of birds contended noisily for a dead flying fish, and in the deep water they chased a shoal, which, in fright and hurry to escape the pursuers, veiled the surface with spray and foam. And as night came on the scene shifted, displaying fresh beauties. Shadows clothed the background, whose features, dimly revealed, allowed full scope to the imagination. In the forepart of the picture lay the sea, shining under the rays of the moon with a metallic lustre, while its border, where the wavelets dashed upon the reef, was lit by what the Arabs call the "jewels of the deep"—brilliant flashes of phosphoric light giving an idea of splendour which art would vainly strive to imitate. 'Altogether it was a bit of fairy-land, a spot for nymphs and sea-gods to disport upon: you might have heard, without astonishment, old Proteus calling his flocks with the writhed conch; and Aphrodite seated in her shell would have been only a fit and proper climax of its loveliness.

But—as philosophically remarked by Sir Cauline the Knyghte—

> "Every whyte must have its blacke,
> And every sweete its soure—"

this charming coral-garden was nearly being the scene of an ugly accident. The breeze from seaward set us slowly but steadily towards the reef, a fact of which we soon became conscious. Our anchor was not dragging; it had not rope enough to touch the bottom, and vainly we sought for more. In fact the "Golden Wire" was as disgracefully deficient in all the appliances of safety, as any English merchantman in the nineteenth century,—a circumstance which accounts for the shipwrecks and for the terrible loss of life perpetually occurring about the pilgrimage season in these seas. Had she struck upon the razor-like edges of the coral-reef, she would have melted away like a sugar-plum in the ripple, for the tide was rising at the time. Having nothing better to do, we began to make as much noise as possible. Fortunately for us, the Rais commanding the Persians' boat was an Arab from Jeddah, and more than once we had treated him with great civility. Guessing the cause of our distress, he sent two sailors overboard with a cable; they swam gallantly up to us; and in a few minutes we were safely moored to the stern of our useful neighbour.

Which done, we applied ourselves to the grateful task of beating our Rais, and richly had he deserved it. Before noon, when the wind was shifting, he had not once given himself the trouble to wear; and when the breeze was falling he preferred dozing to taking advantage of what little wind remained; with energy we might have been moored that night comfortably under the side of Mount Hasan, instead of floating about on an unquiet sea with a lee-shore of coral reef within a few yards of our counter.

At dawn next day (July 15) we started. We made Jebel Hasan about noon, and an hour or so before sunset we glided into Marsa Mahár. Our resting-place resembled Marsa Damghah at an humble distance; the sides of the cove, however, were bolder and more precipitous. The limestone rocks presented a peculiar appearance; in some parts the base and walls had crumbled away, leaving a coping to project like a canopy; in others the wind and rain had cut deep holes, and pierced the friable material with caverns that looked like the work of art. There was a pretty opening of backwood at the bottom of the cove, and palm trees in the blue distance gladdened our eyes, which pined for the sight of something green. The Rais, as usual, would have terrified us with a description of the Hutaymi tribe that holds these parts, and I knew from Welsted and Moresby that it is a troublesome race. But forty-eight hours of cramps on board ship would make a man think lightly of a much more imminent danger.

Wading on shore we cut our feet with the sharp rocks. I remember to have felt the acute pain of something running into my toe; but after looking at the place and extracting what appeared to be a bit of thorn, I dismissed the subject, little guessing the trouble it was to give me. Having scaled the rocky side of the cove, we found some half-naked Arabs lying in the shade; they were unarmed, and had nothing about them except their villanous countenances wherewith to terrify the most timid. These men still live in limestone caves, like the Thamud tribe of tradition; also they are still Ichthyophagi, existing without any other subsistence but what the sea affords. They were unable to provide us with dates, flesh or milk, but they sold us a kind of fish called in India "Bui:" broiled upon the embers, it proved delicious.

After we had eaten and drunk and smoked, we began to make merry; and the Persians, who, fearing to come on shore, had kept to their conveyance, appeared proper butts for the wit of some of our party: one of us stood up and pronounced the orthodox call to prayer, after which the rest joined in a polemical hymn, exalting the virtues and dignity of the three first Caliphs. Then, as general on such occasions, the matter was made personal by informing the Persians in a kind of rhyme sung by the Meccan gamins, that they were the "slippers of Ali and the dogs of Omar." But as they were too frightened to reply, my companions gathered up their cooking utensils, and returned to the "Golden Wire," melancholy, like disappointed candidates for the honors of Donnybrook.

Our next day was silent and weary, for we were all surly and heartily sick of being on board ship. We should have made Yambu' in the evening but for the laziness of the Rais. Having duly beaten him, we anchored on the open coast, insufficiently protected by a reef, and almost in sight of our destination. In the distance rose Jebel Radhwah or Radhwa, one of the "Mountains of Paradise" in which honored Arabia abounds. It is celebrated by poetry as well as by piety.

> "Did Radhwah strive to support my woes,
> Radhwah itself would be crushed by the weight,"

says Antar. It supplies El Medinah with hones. I heard much of its valleys and fruits and bubbling springs, but afterwards I learned to rank these tales with the superstitious legends which are attached to it. Gazing at its bare and ghastly heights, one of our party, whose wit was soured by the want of fresh bread, surlily remarked that such a heap of ugliness deserved ejection from heaven,—an irreverence too public to escape general denunciation. We waded on shore, cooked there and passed the night; we were short of fresh water, which, combined with other grievances, made us as surly as bears. Sa'ad the Demon was especially vicious; his eyes gazed fixedly on the ground, his lips protruded till you might have lifted his face by them, his mouth was garnished with man who can afford to take a boat must pay in proportion during his land journey. In these countries you perforce go on as you begin: to "break one's expenditure," that is to say, to retrench expenses, is considered all but impossible. We have now left the land of Egypt.

CHAPTER XII.

The Halt at Yambu'.

THE heat of the sun, the heavy dews, and the frequent washings of the waves, had so affected my foot, that on landing at Yambu', I could scarcely place it upon the ground. But traveller's duty was to be done; so, leaning upon my "slave's" shoulder, I started at once to see the town, whilst Shaykh Hamid and the others of our party proceeded to the custom-house.

Yanbu'a el Bahr, Yambu' or fountain of the Sea, identified, by Abyssinian Bruce, with the Iambia village of Ptolemy, is a place of considerable importance, and shares with others the title of "Gate of the Holy City." It is the third quarter of the caravan road from Cairo to Mecca; and here, as well as at El Bedr, pilgrims frequently leave behind them in hired warehouses goods too heavy to be transported in haste, or too valuable to risk in dangerous times. Yambu' being the port of El Medinah, as Jedda is of Mecca, is supported by a considerable transport trade and extensive imports from the harbours on the western coasts of the Red Sea: it supplies its chief town with grain, dates and henna. Here the Sultan's dominion is supposed to begin, whilst the authority of the Pasha of Egypt ceases; there is no Nizam or Regular Army, however, in the town, and the governor is a Sherif or Arab chief. I met him in the great bazar; he is a fine young man of light complexion and the usual high profile, handsomely dressed, with a Cashmere turban, armed to the extent of sword and dagger, and followed by two large fierce-looking Negro slaves leaning upon enormous Nebuts.

The town itself is in no wise remarkable. Built on the edge of a barren plain that extends between the mountains and the sea, it fronts the northern extremity of a narrow winding creek. Viewed from the harbour, it is a long line of buildings, whose painful whiteness is set off by a sky like cobalt and a sea like indigo; behind it lies the flat, here of a bistre-brown, there of a lively tawny; whilst the background is formed by dismal Radhwah,

"Barren and bare, unsightly, unadorned."

Outside the walls are a few little domes and tombs, which by no means merit attention. Inside, the streets are wide, and each habitation is placed at an unsociable distance from its neighbour, except near the port and the bazars, where ground is valuable. The houses are roughly built of limestone and coralline, and their walls full of fossils crumble like almond cake; they have huge hanging windows, and look mean after those in the Moslem quarters of Cairo. There is a "Suk," or market-place, of the usual form, a long narrow lane darkened by a covering of palm leaves, with little shops let into the walls of the houses on both sides. The cafés, which abound here, have already been described in the last chapter; they are rendered dirty in the extreme by travellers, and it is impossible to sit in them without a fan to drive away the flies. The custom-house fronts the landing-place upon the harbour; it is managed by Turkish officials, —men dressed in Tarbushes, who repose the live-long day upon the Divans near the windows. In the case of us travellers they had a very simple way of doing business, charging each person of the party three piastres for each large box, but by no means troubling themselves to meddle with the contents. This, as far as I could learn, is the only tax which the Sultan's government derives from the northern Hejaz; the people declare it to be, as one might expect at this distance from the capital, liable to gross peculation. When the Wahhabis held Yambu', they assessed it, like all other places; for which reason their name is held in the liveliest abhorrence.

Yambu' also boasts of a Hammam or Hot Bath, a mere date-leaf shed, tenanted by an old Turk, who, with his surly Albanian assistant, lives by "cleaning" pilgrims and travellers. Some whitewashed mosques and minarets of exceedingly simple form, a Wakaleh or two for the reception of merchants, and a saint's tomb, complete the list of public buildings.

In one point Yambu' claims superiority over most other towns in this part of El Hejaz. Those who can afford the luxury drink sweet rain-water, collected amongst the hills in tanks and cisterns, and brought on camel-back to the town. Two sources are especially praised, the Ayn el Berkat, and the Ayn Ali, which suffice to supply the whole population: the brackish water of the wells is confined to coarser purposes. Some of the old people here, as at Suez, are said to prefer the drink to which years of habit have accustomed them, and it is a standing joke that, arrived at Cairo, they salt the water of the Nile to make it palatable.

The population of Yambu',—one of the most bigoted and quarrelsome races in El Hejaz—strikes the eye after arriving from Egypt, as decidedly a new feature. The Shaykh or gentleman is over-armed and over-dressed as Fashion, the Tyrant of the Desert as well as of the Court, dictates to a person of his consequence. The civilised traveller from El Medinah sticks in his waist-shawl a loaded pistol, garnished with crimson silk cord, but he partially conceals the butt end under the flap of his jacket. The irregular soldier struts down the street a small armoury of weapons: one look at the man's countenance suffices to tell you what he is. Here and there stalk grim Bedawin, wild as their native wastes, and in all the dignity of pride and dirt; they also are armed to the teeth, and even the presence of the policeman's quarterstaff cannot keep their swords in their scabbards. What we should call the peaceful part of the population never leave the house without a "nebut" (cudgel) over the right shoulder, and the larger, the longer, and the heavier the weapon is, the more gallantry does the bearer claim. The people of Yambu' practise the use of this implement diligently; they become expert in delivering a head blow so violent as to break through any guard, and with it they always decide their trivial quarrels.

The dress of the women differs but little from that of the Egyptians, except in the face veil, which is generally white. There is an independent bearing about the Yambu' men, strange in the East; they are proud without insolence, and they look manly without blustering. Their walk partakes somewhat of the nature of a swagger; owing, perhaps, to the shape of the sandals, not a little assisted by the self-esteem of the wearer, but there is nothing offensive in it; moreover, the population has a healthy appearance, and, fresh from Egypt, I could not help noticing their freedom from ophthalmic disease. The children, too, appear vigorous, nor are they here kept in that state of filth to which fear of the Evil Eye devotes them in the Valley of the Nile.

My companions found me in a coffee-house, where I had sat down to rest from the fatigue of halting on my wounded foot through the town. They had passed their boxes through the custom-house, and were now inquiring in all directions "Where's the Effendi?" After sitting for half an hour, we rose to depart, when an old Arab merchant whom I had met at Suez, politely insisted upon paying for my coffee, still a mark of attention in Arabia as it was whilome in France. We then went to a Wakaleh, near the bazar, in which my companions had secured an airy upper room on the terrace opposite the sea, and tolerably free from Yambu's plague, the flies. It had been tenanted by a party of travellers, who were introduced to me as Umar Effendi's brothers; he had by accident met them in the streets the day before their start for Constantinople, where they were travelling to receive the Ikram.* The family was, as I have said before, from Daghistan (Circassia), and the male members still showed unequivocal signs of a northern origin, in light yellowish skins, grey eyes fringed with dark lashes, red lips, and a very scant beard. They were broad-shouldered, large-limbed men, distinguished only by a peculiar surliness of countenance; perhaps their expression was the result of their suspecting me; for I observed them watching every movement narrowly during Wuzu and prayers. This was a good opportunity for displaying the perfect nonchalance of a True Believer, and my efforts were, I believe, successful, for afterwards they seemed to treat me as a mere stranger, from whom they could expect nothing, and who therefore was hardly worth their notice.

On the afternoon of the day of our arrival we sent for a Mukharrij (hirer of conveyance), and began to treat for camels. One Amm Jemal, a respectable native of El Medinah who was on his way home, undertook to be the spokesman: after a long palaver, (for the Shaykh of the camels and his attendant Bedawin were men that fought for farthings, and we

---

* A certain stipend allowed by the Sultan to citizens of the Haramayn (Meccah and El Medinah). It will be treated of at length in a future chapter.

were not far inferior to them), a bargain was struck. We agreed to pay three dollars for each beast, half in ready money, the other half after reaching our destination, and to start on the evening of the next day, with a grain-caravan, guarded by an escort of irregular cavalry. I hired two animals, one for my luggage and servant, the other for the boy Mohammed and myself, expressly stipulating, that we were to ride the better beast, and that if it broke down on the road, its place should be supplied by another as good.

My friends could not dissemble their uneasiness, when informed by the Mukharrij, that the Hazimi tribe was "out," and that travellers had to fight every day. The Daghistanis also contributed to their alarm. "We met," said they, "between 200 and 300 devils on a Razzia near El Medinah; we gave them the Salam, but they would not reply, although we were all on dromedaries. Then they asked us if we were men of El Medinah, and we replied 'Yes,' and lastly, they wanted to know the end of our journey; so we said Bir Abbas." The not returning "Salam" was a sign on the part of the Bedawin that they were out to fight, and not to make friends; and the dromedary riders, who generally travel without much to rob, thought this behaviour a declaration of desperate designs. The Bedawin asked if they were El Medinah men; because the former do not like, unless when absolutely necessary, to plunder the people of the Holy City. And the Daghistanis said their destination was Bir Abbas, a neighbouring, instead of Yambu', a distant post, because those who travel on a long journey, being supposed to have more funds with them, are more likely to be molested.

The Bedawin who had accompanied the Daghistanis belonged to some tribe unconnected with the Hazimi: the spokesman rolled his head, as much as to say, "Allah has preserved us!". And a young Indian of the party,—I shrewdly suspect him of having stolen my pen-knife that night,—displayed the cowardice of a "Miyan," by looking aghast at the memory of his imminent and deadly risk. "Sir," said Shaykh Nur to me, "we must wait till all this is over." I told him to hold his tongue, and sharply reproved the boy Mohammed, upon whose manner the effect of finding himself suddenly in a fresh country had wrought a change for the worse. "Why, ye were lions at Cairo —and here, at Yambu', you are cats, hens!" It was not long, however, before the youth's impudence returned upon him with increased violence.

We sat through the afternoon in the little room on the terrace, whose reflected heat, together with the fiery winds from the wilderness, seemed to incommode even my companions. After sunset we dined in the open air, a body of twenty: master, servants, children and strangers. All the procurable rugs and pillows had been seized to make a Divan, and we squatted together round a large cauldron of boiled rice, containing square masses of mutton, the whole covered with clarified butter. Sa'ad the Demon was now in his glory. With what anecdotes the occasion supplied him!—his tongue seemed to wag with a perpetual motion—for each man he had a boisterous greeting, and to judge from his whisperings he must have been in every one's privacy and confidence. Conversation over pipes and coffee was prolonged to 10 P.M., a late hour in these lands; then we prayed the Isha, or vespers, and, spreading our mats upon the terrace, we slept in the open air.

The forenoon of the next day was occupied in making sundry small purchases. We laid in seven days' provisions for the journey, repacked our boxes, polished and loaded our arms, and attired ourselves appropriately for the road. By the advice of Amm Jemal I dressed as an Arab, in order to avoid paying the Jizyat, a capitation tax, which upon this road the settled tribes extort from stranger travellers; and he warned me not to speak any language but Arabic, even to my slave, in the vicinity of a village. I bought for my own conveyance a Shugduf or litter, for which I paid two dollars. It is a vehicle appropriated to women and children, fathers of families, married men, "Shelebis" (Exquisites), and generally to those who are too effeminate to ride.

The Shugduf of El Hejaz differs greatly from that used in Syria and other countries. It is composed of two corded cots 5 feet long, slung horizontally about half-way down, and parallel with the camel's sides. These cots have short legs, and at the halt may be used as bedsteads; the two are connected by loose ropes, attached to the inner long sides of the framework, and these are thrown over the camel's pack-saddle. Thick twigs inserted in the ends and the outer long sides of the framework, are bent over the top, bower-fashion, to support matting, carpets, and any other protection against the sun. There is an opening in this kind of wicker-work in front (towards the camel's head), through which you creep, and a similar one behind creates a draught of wind. Outside, towards the camel's tail, are pockets containing gullehs, or earthenware bottles of cooled water. Inside, attached to the wicker-work, hang large provision pouches, similar to those used in old-fashioned travelling chariots. At the bottom are spread the two beds. The greatest disadvantage of the Shugduf is the difficulty of keeping balance. Two men ride in it, and their weights must be made to tally. Moreover, it is liable to be caught and torn by thorn trees, and to be blown off in a gale of wind; while its awkwardness causes the camel repeated falls, which are likely to smash it. Yet it is not necessarily an uncomfortable machine. Those for sale in the bazar are of course worthless, being made of badly seasoned wood. But private litters are sometimes pleasant vehicles, with turned and painted framework, silk cordage, and valuable carpets. The often described "Mahmal" is nothing but a Syrian Shugduf, royally ornamented.

My reason for choosing a litter was that notes are more easily taken in it than on a dromedary's back; the excuse of lameness prevented it detracting from my manhood, and I was careful when entering any populous place to borrow or hire a saddled beast.

Our party dined early that day, for the camels had been sitting at the gate since noon. We had the usual trouble in loading them: the owners of the animals vociferating about the unconscionable weight, the owners of the goods swearing that such weight a child could carry, while the beasts, taking part with their proprietors, moaned piteously, roared, made vicious attempts to bite, and started up with an agility that threw the half-secured boxes or sacks headlong to the ground. About 3 P.M. all was ready; the camels formed into Indian file were placed standing in the streets. But, as usual with Oriental travellers, all the men dispersed about the town: we did not mount before it was late in the afternoon.

I must now take the liberty of presenting to the reader an Arab Shaykh fully equipped for travelling. Nothing can be more picturesque than the costume, and it is with regret that we see it exchanged in the towns and more civilised parts for any other. The long locks or the shaven scalps are surmounted by a white cotton skull-cap, over which is a Kufiyah—a large square kerchief of silk and cotton mixed, and generally of a dull red color with a bright yellow border, from which depend crimson silk twists ending in little tassels that reach the wearer's waist. Doubled into a triangle, and bound with an A'akal or fillet of rope, a skein of yarn or a twist of wool, the kerchief fits the head close behind: it projects over the forehead, shading the eyes, and giving a fierce look to the countenance. On certain occasions one end is brought round the lower part of the face, and is fastened behind the head. This veiling the features is technically called "Lisam:" the chiefs generally fight so, and it is the usual disguise when a man fears the avenger of blood, or a woman starts to take her "Sar."* In hot weather it is supposed to keep the Simum, in cold weather the catarrh, from the lungs.

The body dress is simply a Kamis or cotton shirt: tight sleeved, opening in front, and adorned round the waist and collar, and down the breast, with embroidery like net-work, it extends from neck to foot. Some wear wide trousers, but the Bedawin consider such things effeminate, and they have not yet fallen into the folly of socks and stockings. Over the Kamis is thrown a long-skirted and short-sleeved cloak of camel's hair, called an Aba. It is made in many patterns, and of all materials from pure silk to coarse sheep's wool; some prefer it brown, others white, others striped: in El Hejaz the favourite hue is white, embroidered with gold, tinsel, or yellow thread in two large triangles, capped with broad bands and other figures running down the shoulders and sides of the back. It is lined inside the shoulders and breast with handsome stuffs of silk and cotton mixed, and is tied in front by elaborate strings, and tassels or acorns of silk and gold. A sash confines the Kamis at the waist, and supports the silver-hilted Jambiyah or crooked dagger: the picturesque Arab sandal completes the costume. Finally, the Shaykh's arms are a sword and

* Generally written "Thar," the blood-revenge.

a matchlock slung behind his back; in his right hand he carries a short javelin or a light crooked stick about two feet and a half long, called a Mas'hab, used for guiding camels.

The poorer classes of Arabs twist round their waist, next to the skin, a long plait of greasy leather, to support the back, and they gird the shirt at the middle merely with a cord, or with a coarse sash. The dagger is stuck in this scarf, and a bandoleer slung over the shoulders carries their cartridge-case, powder-flask, flint and steel, priming-horn, and other necessaries. With the traveller, the waist is an elaborate affair. Next to the skin is worn the money-pouch, concealed by the Kamis; the latter is girt with a waist shawl, over which is strapped a leathern belt. This affair should always be well garnished with a pair of long-barrelled and silver-mounted flint pistols, a large and a small dagger, and an iron ramrod with pincers inside; a little leathern pouch fastened to the waist-strap on the right side contains cartridge, wadding, and priming powder. The sword hangs over the shoulder by crimson silk cords and huge tassels: well-dressed men apply the same showy ornaments to their pistols. In the hand may be borne a bell-mouthed blunderbuss, or, better still, a long single-barrel gun with an ounce bore. All these weapons must shine like silver, if you wish to be respected; for the knightly care of arms is here a sign of manliness.

Pilgrims, especially those from Turkey, carry, I have said, a "Hamail," to denote their holy errand.

This is a pocket Koran, in a handsome gold-embroidered crimson velvet or red morocco case, slung by red silk cords over the left shoulder. It must hang down by the right side, and should never depend below the waist-belt. For this I substituted a most useful article. To all appearance a "Hamail," it had inside three compartments, one for my watch and compass, the second for ready money, and the third contained penknife, pencils, and slips of paper, which I could hold concealed in the hollow of my hand. These were for writing and drawing: opportunities of making a "fair copy" into the diary-book, are never wanting to the acute traveller. He must, however, beware of sketching before the Bedawin, who would certainly proceed to extreme measures, suspecting him to be a spy or a sorcerer. Nothing so effectually puzzles these people as the Frankish habit of putting everything on paper; their imaginations are set at work, and then the worst may be expected from them. The only safe way of writing in presence of a Bedawi would be when drawing out a horoscope or preparing a charm; he also objects not, if you can warm his heart upon the subject, to seeing you take notes in a book of genealogies. You might begin with, "And you, men of Harb, on what origin do you pride yourselves?" And while the listeners became fluent upon the, to them, all-interesting theme, you could put down whatever you please upon the margin. The towns-people are more liberal, and years ago the Holy Shrines have been drawn, surveyed, and even lithographed, by Eastern artists: still, if you wish to avoid all suspicion, you must rarely be seen with pen or with pencil in hand.

At 6 P.M. descending the stairs of our Wakaleh, we found the camels standing loaded in the street and shifting their ground in token of impatience. My Shugduf, perched upon the back of a tall strong animal, nodded and swayed about with his every motion, impressing me with the idea that the first step would throw it over the shoulders or the crupper. The camel-men told me I must climb up the animal's neck, and so creep into the vehicle. But my foot disabling me from such exertion, I insisted upon their bringing the beast to squat, which they did grumblingly.

We took leave of Umar Effendi's brothers and their dependents, who insisted upon paying us the compliment of accompanying us to the gate. Then we mounted and started, which was a signal for all our party to disperse once more. Some heard the report of a vessel having arrived from Suez, with Mahommed Shiklibha and other friends on board; these hurried down to the harbour for a parting word. Others, declaring they had forgotten some necessaries for the way, ran off to spend one last hour in gossip at the coffee-house. Then the sun set, and prayers must be said.

The brief twilight had almost faded away before all had mounted.

With loud cries of "Wassit, ya hu!"—go in the middle of the road, O He!—and "Jannib, y'al Jammal!"—keep to the side, O camel-man!—we threaded our way through long, dusty, narrow streets, flanked with whitewashed habitations at considerable intervals, and large heaps of rubbish, sometimes higher than the houses. We were stopped at the gate to ascertain if we were strangers, in which case, the guard would have done his best to extract a few piastres before allowing our luggage to pass; but he soon perceived by my companions' accent, that they were Sons of the Holy City, consequently, that the case was hopeless. While standing here, Shaykh Hamid vaunted the strong walls and turrets of Yambu', which he said were superior to those of Jeddah: they kept Sa'ud, the Wahhabi, at bay in A.D. 1802, but would scarcely, I should say, resist a field battery in A.D. 1853. The moon rose fair and clear, dazzling us with light as we emerged from the shadowy streets, and when we launched into the Desert the sweet air delightfully contrasted with the close offensive atmosphere of the town. My companions, as Arabs will do on such occasions, began to sing.

CHAPTER XIII.

From Yambu' to Bir Abbas.

On the 18th July, about 7 P.M., we passed through the gate of Yambu', and took a due easterly course. Our route lay over the plain between the mountains of Radhwah on the left, and the sea on the right hand; the land was desert, that is to say, a hard level plain, strewed with rounded lumps of granite and greenstone schist, with here and there a dwarf Acacia, and a tuft of rank camel grass. By the light of a glorious moon, nearly at the full, I was able to see the country tolerably well.

Our party consisted of twelve camels, and we travelled in Indian file, head tied to tail, with but one outrider, Umar Effendi, whose rank required him to mount a dromedary with showy trappings. Immediately in front of me was Amm Jemal, whom I had to reprove for asking the boy Mohammed "Where have you picked up that Hindi (Indian)?" "Are we, the Afghans, the Indian-slayers, become Indians?" I vociferated with indignation, and brought the thing home to his feelings, by asking him how he, an Arab, would like to be called an Egyptian, a Fellah? The rest of the party was behind, sitting or dozing upon the rough platforms made by the lids of two huge boxes slung to the sides of their camels. Only one old woman,

El Sitt Maryam (the lady Mary), returning to El Medinah, her adopted country, after a visit to a sister at Cairo, allowed herself the luxury of a half-dollar Shibriyah or cot, fastened crosswise over the animal's load. Moreover, all the party, except Umar Effendi, in token of poverty, were dressed in the coarsest and dirtiest of clothes,—the general suit consisting of a shirt torn in divers places and a bit of rag wrapped round the head. They carried short chibouques without mouth-pieces, and tobacco-pouches of greasy leather. Though the country hereabouts is perfectly safe, all had their arms in readiness, and the unusual silence that succeeded to the singing—even Sa'ad the Demon held his tongue—was sufficient to show how much they feared for their property. After a slow march of two hours facing the moon, we turned somewhat towards the N. E., and began to pass over undulating ground, in which a steady rise was perceptible. We arrived at the halting-place at three in the morning after a short march of about eight hours, during which we could not have passed over more than sixteen miles. The camels were made to kneel; the boxes were taken off and piled together as a precaution against invisible robbers; my little tent, the only one in the party, was pitched; we then spread our rugs upon the ground and lay down to sleep.

We arose at about 9 A.M. (July 19) and after congratulating one another upon being once more in the "dear Desert," we proceeded in exhilarated mood to light the fire for pipes and breakfast. The meal—a biscuit, a little rice, and a cup of milkless tea—was soon despatched, after which I proceeded to inspect our position.

About a mile to the westward lay the little village of Musahhal, a group of miserable mud hovels. On the south was a strip of bright blue sea, and all around, an iron plain producing naught but stones and grasshoppers, and bounded northward by a grisly wall of blackish rock. Here and there a shrub fit only for fuel, or a tuft of coarse grass, crisp with heat, met the eye. All was sun-parched; the furious heat from above was drying up the sap and juice of the land, as the simmering and quivering atmosphere showed; moreover the heavy dews of these regions, forming in large drops upon the plants and stones, concentrate the morning rays upon them like a system of burning-glasses. After making these few observations I followed the example of my companions, and returned to sleep.

At 2 P.M. we were roused to a dinner as simple as the breakfast had been. Boiled rice with an abundance of the clarified butter, in which Easterns delight, some fragments of Kahk, or soft biscuit, and stale bread and a handful of stoned and pressed date-paste, called Ajwah, formed the menu. Our potations began before dinner with a vile-tasted but wholesome drink called Akit, dried sour milk dissolved in water; during the meal we drank the leather-flavoured element, and ended with a large cupful of scalding tea. Enormous quantities of liquid were consumed, for the sun seemed to have got into our throats, and the perspiration trickled as after a shower of rain. Whilst we were eating, a Bedawi woman passed close by the tent, leading a flock of sheep and goats, seeing which I expressed a desire to drink milk. My companions sent by one of the camel-men a bit of bread, and asked in exchange for a cupful of "laban." Thus I learned that the Arabs, even in this corrupt region, still adhere to the meaningless custom of their ancestors, who chose to make the term "Labbán" (milk-seller) an opprobrium and a disgrace. Possibly the origin of the prejudice might be the recognising of a traveller's guest-right to call for milk gratis. However this may be, no one will in the present day sell this article of consumption, even at civilised Mecca, except Egyptians, a people supposed to be utterly without honor. As a general rule in the Hejaz, milk abounds in the spring, but at all other times of the year it is difficult to be procured. The Bedawi woman managed, however, to send me back a cupful.

At 3 P.M. we were ready to start, and all saw, with unspeakable gratification, a huge black nimbus rise from the shoulder of Mount Radhwah, and range itself, like a good Genius, between us and our terrible foe, the sun. We hoped that it contained rain, but presently a blast of hot wind, like the breath of a volcano, blew over the plain, and the air was filled with particles of sand. This is the "dry storm" of Arabia; it appears to depend upon some electrical phenomena which it would be desirable to investigate.

When we had loaded and mounted, my camel-men, two in number, came up to the Shugduf and demanded "Bakhshish," which, it appears, they are now in the habit of doing each time the traveller starts. I was at first surprised to find the word here, but after a few days of Bedawi society, my wonder diminished. The men were Beni-Harb of the great Hejazi tribe, which has kept its blood pure for the last thirteen centuries—how much more we know not, —but they had been corrupted by intercourse with pilgrims, retaining none of their ancestral qualities but greed of gain, revengefulness, pugnacity, and a frantic kind of bravery, displayed on rare occasions. Their nobility, however, did not prevent my quoting the Prophet's saying, "Of a truth, the worst names among the Arabs are the Beni-Kalb (Dog-Sons), and the Beni-Harb (Fight-Sons)"; whilst I taunted them severely with their resemblance to the Fellahs of Egypt. They would have resented this with asperity, had it proceeded from their own people, but the Turkish pilgrim—the character in which they knew me, despite my Arab dress—is a privileged person.

The outer man of these Fight-Sons was contemptible; small chocolate-colored beings, stunted and thin, with mops of coarse bushy hair burned brown by the sun, straggling beards, vicious eyes, frowning brows, screaming voices, and well-made, but attenuated, limbs. On their heads were Kufiyahs (kerchiefs) in the last stage of wear; a tattered shirt, indigo-dyed, and girt with a bit of common rope, composed their clothing;

and their feet were protected from the stones by soles of thick leather, kept in place by narrow thongs tied to the ankle. Both were armed, one with a matchlock, and a Shintiyan or common sword-blade in a leathern scabbard, slung over the shoulder, the other with a Nebut, and both showed at the waist the Arab's invariable companion, the dagger.

These ragged fellows, however, had their pride. They would eat with me, and not disdain, like certain self-styled Caballeros, to ask for more; but of work they would do none. No promise of "Bakhshish," potent as the spell of that word is, would induce them to assist in pitching my tent: they even expected Shaykh Nur to cook for them, and I had almost to use violence, for even the just excuse of a sore foot was insufficient to procure the privilege of mounting my Shugduf while the camel was sitting. It was, they said, the custom of the country from time immemorial to use a ladder when legs would not act. I agreed with them, but objected that I had no ladder. At last, wearied with their thick-headedness, I snatched the nose-string of the camel, and by main force made it kneel.

Our party was now strong enough. We had about 200 beasts carrying grain, attended by their proprietors, truculent looking as the contrabandistas of the Pyrenees. The escort was composed of seven Irregular Turkish cavalry, tolerably mounted, and supplied each with an armoury in epitome. They were privily derided by our party, who, being Arabs, had a sneaking fondness for the Bedawin, however loth they might be to see them amongst the boxes.

For three hours we travelled in a south-easterly direction upon a hard plain and a sandy flat, on which several waters from the highlands find a passage to the sea westward. Gradually we were siding towards the mountains, and at sunset I observed that we had sensibly neared them. We dismounted for a short halt, and, strangers being present, my companions before sitting down to smoke said their prayers—a pious exercise in which they did not engage for three days afterwards, when they met certain acquaintances at El Hamra.

As evening came on, we emerged from a scrub of Acacia and tamarisk and turned due east, traversing an open country with a perceptible rise. Scarcely was it dark before the cry of "Harami" (thieves) rose loud in the rear, causing such confusion as one may see in a boat in the Bay of Naples when suddenly neared by a water-spout. All the camel-men brandished their huge staves, and rushed back vociferating in the direction of the robbers. They were followed by the horsemen, and truly, had the thieves possessed the usual acuteness of the profession, they might have driven off the camels in our van with safety and convenience. But these contemptible beings were only half a dozen in number, and they had lighted their matchlocks, which drew a bullet or two in their direction; whereupon they ran away.

This incident aroused no inconsiderable excitement,

for it seemed ominous of worse things about to happen to us when entangled in the hills, and the faces of my companions, perfect barometers of fair and foul tidings, fell to zero. For nine hours we journeyed through a brilliant moonlight, and as the first grey streak appeared in the Eastern sky we entered a scanty "Misyal," or Fiumara, strewed with pebbles and rounded stones, about half a mile in breadth, and flanked by almost perpendicular hills of primitive formation. I began by asking the names of peaks and other remarkable spots, when I found that a folio volume would not contain a three months' collection: every hill and dale, flat, valley, and water-course here has its proper name or rather names. The ingenuity shown by the Bedawin in distinguishing between localities the most similar, is the result of a high organisation of the perceptive faculties, perfected by the practice of observing a recurrence of landscape features few in number and varying but little amongst themselves. After travelling two hours up this torrent bed, winding in an easterly direction, and crossing some "Harreh," or ridges of rock, "Ri'a," steep descents, "Kita'ah," patches of stony flat and bits of Sahil, dwarf plains, we found ourselves about 8 A.M., after a march of about thirty-four miles, at Bir Sa'id (Sa'id's well), our destination.

I had been led to expect at the "well" a pastoral scene, wild flowers, flocks and flowing waters; so I looked with a jaundiced eye upon a deep hole full of slightly brackish water dug in a tamped hollow—a kind of punch-bowl with granite walls, upon whose grim surface a few thorns of exceeding hardihood braved the heat for a season. Not a house was in sight—it was as barren and desolate a spot as the sun ever "viewed in his wide career." But this is what the Arabian traveller must expect. He is to traverse, for instance, a Vale of Flowers. He indulges in sweet recollections of Indian lakes beautiful with the lotus, and Persian plains upon which Narcissus is the meanest of grasses. He sees a plain like swish-work, where knobs of granite act daisies, and where at every fifty yards some hapless bud or blossom is dying of inanition among the stones.

The sun scorched our feet as we planted the tent, and, after drinking our breakfast, we passed the usual day of perspiration and semi-lethargy. In discomfort man naturally hails a change, even though it be one from bad to worse. When our enemy began slanting towards the west, we felt ready enough to proceed on our journey. The camels were laden shortly after 3 P.M. (July 20), and we started with water jars in our hands through a storm of Simum.

We travelled five hours in a north-easterly course up a diagonal valley, through a country fantastic in its desolation—a mass of huge hills, barren plains, and desert vales. Even the sturdy Acacias here failed, and in some places the camel grass could not find earth enough for its root. The road wound among mountains, rocks and hills of granite, and over broken ground, flanked by huge blocks and boulders, piled up as if man's art had aided Nature to disfigure herself. Vast clefts seamed like scars the hideous face of earth; here they widened into dark chasms, there they were choked with glistening drift sand. Not a bird nor a beast was to be seen or heard; their presence would have argued the vicinity of water, and though my companions opined that Bedawin were lurking among the rocks, I decided that these Bedawin were the creatures of their fears. Above, a sky like polished blue steel with a tremendous blaze of yellow light glared upon us without the thinnest veil of mist cloud. Below, the brass-coloured circle scorched the face and dazzled the eyes, mocking them the while with offers of water that was but air. The distant prospect appeared more attractive than the nearer view, because it borrowed a bright azure tinge from the intervening atmosphere; but the jagged peaks and the perpendicular streaks of shadow down the flanks of the mountainous background showed that yet in store for us was no change for the better.

Between 10 and 11 P.M., we reached human habitations—a phenomenon unseen since we left Musahhal—in the shape of a long straggling village. It is called El Hamra, from the redness of the sands near which it is built, or El Wasitah, the "half-way," because it is the middle station between Yambu' and El Medinah. It is therefore considerably out of place in Burckhardt's map, and those who copy from him make it much nearer the sea-port than it really is. We wandered nearly an hour in search of an encamping place, for the surly villagers ordered us off every flatter bit of ground, without, however, deigning to show us where the jaded beasts might rest. At last, after long wrangling, we found the usual spot; the camels were unloaded, the boxes and baggage were disposed in a circle for greater security against the petty pilferers in which this part of the road abounds, and my companions spread their rugs so as to sleep upon their valuables. I was invited to follow the general example, but I absolutely declined the vicinity of so many steaming and snoring fellow-travellers. Some wonder was excited by the Afghan Haji's obstinacy and recklessness; but resistance to these people is sometimes bien placé, and a man from Cabool is allowed to say and to do strange things. In answer to their warnings of nightly peril I placed a drawn sword by my side and a cocked pistol under my pillow, the saddle-bag; a carpet spread upon the cool loose sand, formed by no means an uncomfortable couch, and upon it I enjoyed a sound sleep till day-break.

Rising at dawn (July 21), I proceeded to visit the village. It is built upon a narrow shelf at the top of a precipitous hill to the North, and on the South runs a sandy Fiumara about half a mile broad. On all sides are rocks and mountains rough and stony; so you find yourself in another of those punch-bowls which the Arabs seem to consider choice sites for settlements. The Fiumara, hereabouts very winding, threads the high grounds all the way down from the plateau of El Medinah: during the rainy season it becomes a raging torrent, carrying westwards to the Red Sea the drainage of a hundred hills. Water of good quality is readily found in it by digging a few feet below the surface at the angles where the stream forms the deepest hollows, and in some places the stony sides give out bubbling springs.

El Hamra itself is a collection of stunted houses or rather hovels, made of unbaked brick and mud, roofed over with palm leaves, and pierced with airholes, which occasionally boast a bit of plank for a shutter. It appears thickly populated in the parts where the walls are standing, but, like all settlements in the Holy Land El Hejaz, it abounds in ruins. It is well supplied with provisions, which are here cheaper than at El Medinah,—a circumstance that induced Sa'ad the Demon to overload his hapless camel with a sack of wheat. In the village are a few shops where grain, huge plantains, ready-made bread, rice, clarified butter, and other edibles are to be purchased. Palm orchards of considerable extent supply it with dates. The bazar is, like the generality of such places in the villages of Eastern Arabia, a long lane, here covered with matting, there open to the sun, and the narrow streets—if they may be so called—are full of dust and glare.

Near the encamping ground of caravans is a fort for the officer commanding a troop of Albanian cavalry, whose duty it is to defend the village, to hold the country, and to escort merchant travellers. The building consists of an outer wall of hewn stone, loopholed for musketry, and surmounted by "Shararif,"—"remparts coquets,"—about as useful against artillery as the sugar gallery round a Twelfth-cake. Nothing would be easier than to take the place: a false attack would draw off the attention of the defenders, who in these latitudes know nothing of sentry-duty, whilst scaling-ladders or a bag full of powder would command a ready entrance into the other side. Around the El Hamra fort are clusters of palm-leaf huts, where the soldiery lounge and smoke, and near it is the usual coffee-house, a shed kept by an Albanian. These places are frequented probably on account of the intense heat inside the fort.

We passed a comfortless day at the "Red Village." Large flocks of sheep and goats were being driven in and out of the place, but their surly shepherds would give no milk, even in exchange for bread and meat. The morning was spent in watching certain Bedawin, who, matchlock in hand, had climbed the hills in pursuit of a troop of cranes: not one bird was hit of the many fired at—a circumstance which did not say much for their vaunted marksmanship. Before breakfast I bought a moderately sized sheep for a dollar. Shaykh Hamid butchered it, according to rule, and my companions soon prepared a feast of boiled mutton. But that sheep proved a "bone of contention." The boy Mohammed had, in a fit of economy, sold its head to a Bedawi for three piastres, and the others, disappointed in their anticipations of "haggis," lost temper. With the Demon's voluble tongue and impudent countenance in the van, they opened such a volley of raillery and sarcasm upon the young "tripe-seller," that he in his turn became excited—furious. I had some difficulty to keep the peace, for it did not suit my interests that they should quarrel. But to do the Arabs justice, nothing is easier for a man who knows them than to work upon their good feelings. "He is a stranger in your country—a guest!" acted as a charm; they listened patiently to Mohammed's gross abuse, only promising to answer him when in *his* land, that is to say, near Meccah. But what especially soured our day was the report that Sa'ad, the great robber-chief, and his brother were in the field; consequently that our march would be delayed for some time: every half-hour some fresh tattle from the camp or the coffee-house added fuel to the fire of our impatience.

A few particulars about this Schinderhans of El Hejaz may not be unacceptable. He is the chief of the Sumaydah and the Mahamid, two influential sub-families of the Hamidah, the principal family of the Beni-Harb tribe of Bedawin. He therefore aspired to rule all the Hamidah, and through them the Beni-Harb, in which case he would have been, de facto, monarch of the Holy Land. But the Sherif of Meccah, and Ahmed Pasha, the Turkish governor of the chief city, for some political reason degraded him, and raised up a rival in the person of Shaykh Fahd, another ruffian of a similar stamp, who calls himself chief of the Beni-Amr, the third sub-family of the Hamidah family. Hence all kinds of confusion.

Sa'ad's people, who number it is said 5000, resent, with Arab asperity, the insult offered to their chief, and beat Fahd's, who do not amount to 800. Fahd, supported by the government, cuts off Sa'ad's supplies. Both are equally wild and reckless, and — nowhere doth the glorious goddess, Liberty, show a more brazen face than in this Eastern

"Inviolate land of the brave and the free:"—

both seize the opportunity of shooting troopers, of plundering travellers, and of closing the roads.

This state of things continued till I left the Hejaz, when the Sherif of Meccah proposed, it was said, to take the field in person against the arch-robber. And, as will afterwards be seen in these pages, Sa'ad had the audacity to turn back the Sultan's Mahmal or litter —the ensign of Imperial power—and to shut the road against its cortége, because the Pashas of El Medinah and of the Damascus caravan would not guarantee his restitution to his former dignity.

That such vermin is allowed to exist proves the imbecility of the Turkish government. The Sultan pays pensions in corn and cloth to the very chiefs who arm their varlets against him, and the Pashas, aftes purloining all they can, hand over to their enemies the means of resistance. It is more than probable, that Abdul Mejid has never heard a word of truth concerning El Hejaz, and that fulsome courtiers persuade him that men there tremble at his name. His government, however, is desirous, if report speaks truth, of thrusting El Hejaz upon the Egyptian, who on his side would willingly pay a large sum to avert such calamity. The Holy Land drains off Turkish gold and blood in abundance, and the lords of the country hold in it a contemptible position. If they catch a thief, they dare not hang him. They must pay black mail, and yet be shot at in every pass. They affect superiority over the Arabs, hate them, and are despised by them.

Such in El Hejaz are the effects of the charter of Gulkhaneh, a panacea like Holloway's pills for all the evils to which Turkish, Arab, Syrian, Greek, Egyptian, Persian, Armenian, Kurd, and Albanian flesh is heir to. Such the results of the Tanzimat, the silliest copy of Europe's folly—bureaucracy and centralisation—that the pen of empirical statecraft ever traced.* Under a strong-handed and strong-hearted despotism, like Mohammed Ali's, El Hejaz, in one generation, might be purged of its pests. By a proper use of the blood feud; by vigorously supporting the weaker against the stronger classes; by regularly defeating every Bedawi who earns a name for himself, and, above all, by the exercise of unsparing, unflinching, justice, the few thousands of half naked bandits, who now make the land a fighting field, would soon sink into utter insignificance.

But to effect such end, the Turks require the old

---

* The greatest of all its errors was that of appointing to the provinces, instead of the single Pasha of the olden time, three different governors, civil, military, and fiscal, all depending upon the supreme council at Constantinople. Thus, each province has three plunderers instead of one, and its affairs are referred to a body that can take no interest in it.

stratocracy, which, bloody as it was, worked with far less misery than the charter and the new code. What Milton calls

"The solid rule of civil government"

has done wonders for the race that nurtured and brought to perfection an idea spontaneous to their organisation. The world has yet to learn that the admirable exotic will thrive amongst the country gentlemen of Monomotapa or the ragged nobility of El Hejaz.*

Sa'ad, the Old Man of the Mountains, was described to me as a little brown Bedawi, contemptible in appearance, but remarkable for courage and ready wit. He has for treachery a keen scent which he requires to keep in exercise. A blood feud with Abdel Muttalib, the present Sherif of Meccah, who slew his nephew, and the hostility of several Sultans has rendered his life eventful. He lost all his teeth by poison, which would have killed him, had he not, after swallowing the potion, corrected it by drinking off a large pot-full of clarified butter. Since that time he has lived entirely upon fruits, which he gathers for himself, and coffee which he prepares with his own hands. In Sultan Mahmud's time he received from Constantinople a gorgeous purse, which he was told to open, as it contained something for his private inspection. Suspecting treachery, he gave it for this purpose to a slave, bidding him carry it to some distance; the

* These remarks were written in 1853: I see no reason to change them in 1870.

bearer was shot by a pistol cunningly fixed, like Rob Roy's, in the folds of the bag.

Whether this far-known story be "true or only well found," it is certain that Shaykh Sa'ad now fears the Turks, even when they bring gifts. The Sultan sends, or is supposed to send him presents of fine horses, robes of honor, and a large quantity of grain. But the Shaykh, trusting to his hills rather than to steeds, sells them; he gives away the dresses to his slaves, and he distributes the grain among his clansmen. Of his character men as usual tell two tales: some praise his charity, and call him the friend of the poor, as certainly as he is a foe to the rich. Others on the contrary describe him as cruel, cold-blooded, and notably, even among Arabs, revengeful and avaricious. The truth probably lies between these two extremes, but I observed that those of my companions who spoke most highly of the robber chief when at a distance seemed to be in the sudori freddi whilst under the shadow of his hills.

El Hamra is the third station from El Medinah in the Darb Sultani—the Sultan's or High Road,—the westerly line leading to Meccah along the sea coast. When the robbers permit, the pilgrims prefer this route on account of its superior climate, the facility of procuring water and supplies, the vicinity of the sea, and the circumstance of its passing through "Bedr," the scene of the Prophet's greatest military exploit.

After mid-day on the 21st July, when we had made up our minds that Fate had determined we should halt at El Hamra, a caravan arrived from Mecca, and the new travellers had interest to procure an escort, and permission to proceed without delay towards El Medinah. The good news filled us with joy. A little after 4 P.M. we urged our panting camels over the fiery sands to join the Meccans, who were standing ready for the march, on the other side of the torrent bed, and an hour afterwards, we started in an easterly direction.

My companions having found friends and relations in the Meccan caravan,—the boy Mohammed's elder brother, about whom more anon, was of the number; —were full of news and excitement. At sunset they prayed with unction: even Sa'ad and Hamid had not the face to sit their camels during the halt, when all around were washing, sanding themselves,* and busy with their devotions. We then ate our suppers, remounted, and started once more. Shortly after night set in, we came to a sudden halt. A dozen different reports rose to account for this circumstance; it was occasioned by a band of Bedawin, who had manned a gorge, and sent forward a "parliamentary" ordering us forthwith to stop. They at first demanded money to let us pass; but at last, hearing that we were Sons of the Holy Cities, they granted us transit on the sole condition that the military—whom they, like Irish peasants, hate and fear—should return to whence they came. Upon this, our escort, 200 men, wheeled

---

* When water cannot be obtained for ablution before prayers, Moslems clap the palms of their hands upon the sands, and draw them down the face and both fore-arms. This operation, which is performed once or twice—it varies in different schools—is called Tayammum.

their horses round and galloped back to their barracks.

We moved onwards, without, however, seeing any robbers; my camel-man pointed out their haunts, and showed me a small bird hovering over a place where he supposed water trickled from the rock. The fellow had attempted a sneer at my expense when the fray was impending. "Why don't you load your pistols, Effendi," he cried, "and get out of your litter, and show fight?" "Because," I replied as loudly, "in my country, when dogs run at us, we thrash them with sticks." This stopped Mansur's mouth for a time, but he and I were never friends. Like the lowest orders of Orientals he required to be ill-treated; gentleness and condescension he seemed to consider proofs of cowardice or of imbecility. I began with kindness, but was soon compelled to use hard words at first, and then threats, which, though he heard them with frowns and mutterings, produced manifest symptoms of improvement.

> "Oignez vilain, il vous poindra !
> Poignez vilain, il vous oindra !"

says the old French proverb, and the lesson is more valuable in the East even than in the West.

Our night's journey had no other incident. We travelled over rising ground with the moon full in our faces, and about midnight we passed through another long straggling line of villages, called Jadaydah,* or

---

* I write this word as my companions pronounced it. Burckhardt similarly gives it "Djedeyde," and Ali Bey "Djidelda." Giovanni Finati wrongly calls

El Khayf. The principal part of it lies on the left of the road going to El Medinah; it has a fort like that of El Hamra, springs of tolerable drinking water, a Nakhil or date ground, and a celebrated (dead) saint, Abd el Rahim el Burai. A little beyond it lies the Bughaz, or defile, where in A.D. 1811 Tussún Bey and his 8000 Turks were totally defeated by 25,000 Harbi Bedawin and Wahhabis. This is a famous attacking point of the Beni-Harb. In former times both Jezzar Pasha, the celebrated "butcher" of Syria, and Abdullah Pasha of Damascus, were baffled at the gorge of Jadaydah; and this year the commander of the Syrian caravan, afraid of risking an attack at a place so ill-omened, avoided it by marching upon Meccah by the desert road of Nejd. At 4 A.M., having travelled about twenty-four miles due east, we encamped at Bir Abbas.

_{the place "Jedeed Bughaz," which Mr. Bankes, his editor, rightly translates the "new opening or pass."}

CHAPTER XIV.

From Bir Abbas to El Medinah.

THE 22nd of July was a grand trial of temper to our little party. The position of Bir Abbas exactly resembles that of El Hamra, except that the bulge of the hill-girt Fiumara is at this place about two miles wide. There are the usual stone forts and palm-leaved hovels for the troopers, stationed here to hold the place and to escort travellers, with a coffee-shed, and a hut or two, called a bazar, but no village. Our encamping ground was a bed of loose sand, with which the violent Simum filled the air: not a tree nor a bush was in sight; a species of hardy locust and swarms of flies were the only remnants of animal life: the scene was a caricature of Sind. Although we were now some hundred feet, to judge by the water-shed, above the level of the sea, the mid-day sun scorched even through the tent; our frail tenement was more than once blown down, and the heat of the sand made the work of re-pitching it painful.

Again my companions, after breakfasting, hurried to the coffee-house, and returned one after the other with dispiriting reports. Then they either quarrelled desperately about nothing, or they threw themselves on their rugs, pretending to sleep in very sulkiness. The lady Maryam soundly rated her surly son, for refusing to fill her chibouque for the twelfth time that morning, with the usual religious phrases, "Ali direct thee into the right way, O my son!"—meaning that he was going to the bad,—and "O my calamity, thy mother is a lone woman, O Allah!"—equivalent to the European parental plaint about grey hairs being brought down in sorrow to the grave.

Before noon a small Caravan which followed us came in with two dead bodies—a trooper shot by the Bedawin, and an Albanian killed by sun-stroke, or the fiery wind. Shortly after mid-day a Caravan, travelling in an opposite direction, passed by us; it was composed chiefly of Indian pilgrims, habited in correct costume, and hurrying towards Meccah in hot haste. They had been allowed to pass unmolested, because probably a pound sterling could not have been collected from a hundred pockets, and Sa'ad the Robber sometimes does a cheap good deed. But our party having valuables with them did not seem to gather heart from this event.

In the evening we all went out to see some Arab Shaykhs who were travelling to Bir Abbas in order to receive their salaries. Without such douceurs, it is popularly said and believed, no stone walls could enable a Turk to hold El Hejaz against the hill-men. Such was our system in Afghanistan—most unwise, teaching in limine the subject to despise rulers subject to black-mail. Besides which these highly paid Shaykhs do no good. When a fight takes place or a road is shut, they profess inability to restrain their clansmen, and the richer they are, of course the more formidable they become.

The party looked well; they were Harb, dignified old men in the picturesque Arab costume, with erect forms, fierce thin features, and white beards, well armed, and mounted upon high-bred and handsomely equipped dromedaries from El Shark, the Eastern Region. Preceded by their half-naked clansmen, carrying spears twelve or thirteen feet long, garnished with single or double tufts of black ostrich feathers, and ponderous matchlocks, which were discharged on approaching the fort, they were not without a kind of barbaric pomp.

Immediately after the reception of these Shaykhs, there was a parade of the Arnaut Irregular Horse. About 500 of them rode out to the sound of a Nakus or little kettle-drum, whose puny notes strikingly contrasted with this really martial sight. The men, it is true, were mounted on lean Arab and Egyptian nags, ragged-looking as their clothes, and each trooper was armed in his own way, though all had swords, pistols, and matchlocks, or firelocks of some kind. But they rode hard as Galway buckeens, and there was a gallant reckless look about the fellows which prepossessed me strongly in their favour. Their animals, too, though notable "screws," were well trained, and their accoutrements were intended for use, not show.

I watched their manœuvres with curiosity. They left their cantonments one by one, and, at the sound of the tom-tom, by degrees formed a "plump" or "herse"—*column* it could not be called—all huddled together in confusion. Presently the little kettle-drum changed its note and the parade its aspect. All the serried body dispersed as Light Infantry would, now continuing their advance, then hanging back, then making a rush, and all the time keeping up a hot fire upon the enemy. At another signal they suddenly put their horses to full speed, and, closing upon the centre, again advanced in a dense mass. After three quarters of an hour parading, sometimes charging singly, often in bodies, to the right, to the left, and straight in front, halting when requisite, and occasionally retreating, Parthian-like, the Arnauts turned en masse towards their lines. As they neared them all broke off and galloped in, ventre à terre, discharging their shotted guns with much recklessness against objects assumed to denote the enemy. But ball cartridge seemed to be plentiful hereabouts; during the whole of this and the next day, I remarked that bullets, notched for noise, were fired away in mere fun.

Barbarous as these movements may appear to the Cavalry Martinet of the "good old school," yet to something of the kind will the tactics of that arm, I humbly opine, return, when the perfect use of the rifle, the revolver, and field artillery shall have made the present necessarily slow system fatal. Also, if we adopt the common-sense opinion of a modern writer —the late Captain Nolan—and determine that "individual prowess, skill in single combats, good horsemanship, and sharp swords render cavalry formidable," these semi-barbarians are wiser in their generation than the civilised, who never practise arms (properly so called), whose riding-drill never made a good rider, whose horses are over-weighted, and whose swords are worthless. They have yet another point of superiority over us—they cultivate the individuality of the soldier, whilst we strive to make him a mere automaton. In the days of European chivalry, battles were a system of well fought duels. This was succeeded by the age of discipline, when, to use the language of Rabelais, "men seemed rather a consort of organ-pipes, or mutual concord of the wheels of a clock, than an infantry and cavalry, or army of soldiers." Our aim should now be to combine the merits of both systems; to make men individually excellent in the use of weapons, and still train them to act naturally and habitually in concert. The French have given a model to Europe in the Chasseurs de Vincennes—a body capable of most perfect combination, yet never more truly soldier-like than when each man is fighting alone. We, I suppose, shall imitate them at some future time.

A distant dropping of fire-arms ushered in the evening of our first melancholy day at Bir Abbas. This, said my companions, was a sign that the troops and the hill-men were fighting. They communicated the intelligence, as if it ought to be an effectual check upon my impatience to proceed; it acted, however, in the contrary way. I supposed that the Bedawin, after battling out the night, would be less warlike the next day; the others, however, by no means agreed in opinion with me. At Yambu' the whole party had boasted loudly that the people of El Medinah could keep their Bedawin in order, and had twitted the boy Mohammed with their superiority in this respect to his townsmen, the Meccans. But now that a trial was impending I saw none of the fearlessness so conspicuous when peril was only possible. The change was charitably to be explained by the presence of their valuables; the "Sahharehs," like conscience, making cowards of them all. But the young Meccan, who, having sent on his box by sea from Yambu' to Jeddah, felt merry, like the empty traveller, would not lose the opportunity to pay off old scores. He taunted the Medinites till they stamped and raved with fury. At last, fearing some violence, and feeling answerable to his family for the boy's safety, I seized him by the nape of his neck and the upper posterior portion of his nether garments, and drove him before me into the tent.

When the hubbub had subsided and all sat after supper smoking the pipe of peace in the cool night air, I rejoined my companions, and found them talking, as usual, about old Shaykh Sa'ad. The scene was appropriate for the subject. In the distance rose the blue peak said to be his eyrie, and the place was pointed out with fearful meaning. As it is inaccessible to strangers, report has converted it into another garden of Irem. A glance, however, at its position and formation satisfied me that the bubbling springs, the deep forests, and the orchards of apple trees, quinces and pomegranates, with which my companions furnished it, were a "myth," whilst some experience in Arab ignorance of Vauban suggested to me strong doubts about the existence of an impregnable fortress on the hill-top. The mountains, however, looked beautiful in the moonlight, and distance gave them a semblance of mystery well suited to the grisly themes which they inspired.

That night I slept within my Shugduf, for it would have been mere madness to lie on the open plain in a place so infested by banditti. The being armed is but a poor precaution near this robbers' den. If you wound a man in the very act of plundering, an exorbitant sum must be paid for blood-money. If you kill him, even to save your life, then adieu to any chance of escaping destruction. Roused three or four times during the night by jackals and dogs prowling about our little camp, I observed that my companions, who had agreed amongst themselves to keep watch by turns, had all fallen into a sound sleep. However, when we awoke in the morning, the usual inspection of goods and chattels showed that nothing was missing.

The next day (July 23) was a forced halt, a sore stimulant to the traveller's ill-humour; and the sun, the sand, the dust, the furious Simum, and the want of certain small supplies, aggravated our grievance. My sore foot had been inflamed by a dressing of onion skin which the lady Maryam had insisted upon applying to it. Still, being resolved to push forward by any conveyance that could be procured, I offered ten dollars for a fresh dromedary to take me on to El Medinah. Shaykh Hamid also declared he would leave his box in charge of a friend and accompany me. Sa'ad the Demon flew into a passion at the idea of any member of the party escaping the general evil, and he privily threatened Mohammed to cut off the legs of any camel that ventured into the camp. This, the boy—who, like a boy of the world as he was, never lost an opportunity of making mischief—instantly communicated to me, and it brought on a furious dispute. Sa'ad was reproved and apologised for by the rest of the party, and presently he himself was pacified, principally, I believe, by the intelligence that no camel was to be hired at Bir Abbas. One of the Arnaut garrison, who had obtained leave to go to El Medinah, came to ask us if we could mount him, as otherwise he should be obliged to walk the whole way. With him we debated the propriety of attempting a passage through the hills by one of the many by-paths that traverse them: the project was amply discussed, and duly rejected.

We passed the day in the usual manner; all crowded together for shelter under the tent. Even Maryam joined us, loudly informing Ali, her son, that his mother was no longer a woman but a man, whilst our party generally, cowering away from the fierce glances of the sun, were either eating or occasionally smoking, or were occupied in cooling and drinking water.

About sunset-time came a report that we were to start that night. None could believe that such good was in store for us; before sleeping, however, we placed each camel's pack apart, so as to be ready for loading at a moment's notice, and we took care to watch that our Bedawin did not drive their animals away to any distance.

At last about 11 P.M., as the moon was beginning to peep over the eastern wall of rock, was heard the glad sound of the little kettle-drum calling the Albanian troopers to mount and march. In the shortest possible time all made ready, and hurriedly crossing the sandy flat, we found ourselves in company with three or four caravans, forming one large body for better defence against the dreaded Hawamid.* By dint of much manœuvring, arms in hand—Shaykh Hamid and the "Demon" took the prominent parts—we, though the last comers, managed to secure places about the middle of the line. On such occasions all push forward recklessly, as an English mob in the strife of sight-seeing; the rear, being left unguarded, is the place of danger, and none seek the honor of occupying it.

We travelled that night up the Fiumara in an easterly direction, and at early dawn (July 24) we found ourselves in an ill-famed gorge called Shu'ab el Hajj (the "Pilgrim's Pass"). The loudest talkers became silent as we neared it, and their countenances showed apprehension written in legible characters. Presently from the high precipitous cliff on our left, thin blue curls of smoke—somehow or other they caught every eye—rose in the air, and instantly afterwards rang the

* Hawamid is the plural of Hamidah, Shaykh Sa'ad's tribe.

sharp cracks of the hill-men's matchlocks echoed by the rocks on the right. My Shugduf had been broken by the camel falling during the night, so I called out to Mansur that we had better splice the frame-work with a bit of rope: he looked up, saw me laughing, and with an ejaculation of disgust disappeared. A number of Bedawin were to be seen swarming like hornets over the crests of the hills, boys as well as men carrying huge weapons, and climbing with the agility of cats. They took up comfortable places on the cut-throat eminence, and began firing upon us with perfect convenience to themselves.

The height of the hills and the glare of the rising sun prevented my seeing objects very distinctly, but my companions pointed out to me places where the rock had been scarped, and where a kind of rough stone breastwork—the Sangah of Afghanistan—had been piled up as a defence, and a rest for the long barrel of the matchlock. It was useless to challenge the Bedawin to come down and fight us like men upon the plain; they will do this on the eastern coast of Arabia, but rarely, if ever, in El Hejaz. And it was equally unprofitable for our escort to fire upon a foe ensconced behind stones. Besides which, had a robber been killed, the whole country would have risen to a man; with a force of 3000 or 4000, they might have gained courage to overpower a caravan, and in such a case not a soul would have escaped.

As it was, the Bedawin directed their fire principally against the Albanians. Some of these called for assistance to the party of Shaykhs that accompanied us from Bir Abbas, but the dignified old men, dismounting and squatting in council round their pipes, came to the conclusion that, as the robbers would probably turn a deaf ear to their words, they had better spare themselves the trouble of speaking. We had therefore nothing to do but to blaze away as much powder, and to veil ourselves in as much smoke, as possible; the result of the affair was that we lost twelve men, besides camels and other beasts of burden. Though the bandits showed no symptoms of bravery, and confined themselves to slaughtering the enemy from their hill-top, my companions seemed to consider this questionable affair a most gallant exploit.

After another hour's hurried ride through the Wady Sayyalah appeared Shuhada, to which we pushed on,

> "Like nighted swain on lonely road,
> When close behind fierce goblins tread."

Shuhada, "The Martyrs," is so called because here are supposed to be buried forty braves that fell in one of Mohammed's many skirmishes. Some authorities consider it only the cemetery of the Wady Sayyalah people. The once populous valley is now desert and barren, and one might easily pass by the consecrated spot without observing a few ruined walls and a cluster of rude Bedawi graves, each an oval of rough stones lying beneath the thorn trees on the left of and a little off the road. Another half hour took us to a favourite halting-place, Bir el Hindi, so called from some forgotten Indian who dug a well there. But we left it behind, wishing to put as much space as we could between our tents and the nests of the Hamidah.

Then quitting the Fiumara, we struck northwards into a well-trodden road running over stony rising ground. The heat became sickening; here, and in the East generally, at no time is the sun more dangerous than between 8 and 9 A.M. Still we hurried on. It was not before 11 A.M. that we reached our destination, a rugged plain covered with stones, coarse gravel, and thorn trees in abundance, and surrounded by inhospitable rocks, pinnacle-shaped, of granite below, and in the upper parts fine limestone. The well was at least two miles distant, and not a hovel was in sight: a few Bedawi children belonging to an outcast tribe fed their starveling goats upon the hills. This place is called "Suwaykah;" it is, I was told, the site of the foray celebrated in the history of El Islam. Yet not for this reason did my comrades look lovingly upon its horrors: their boxes were safe, and with the eye of imagination they could now behold their homes. That night we must have travelled about twenty-two miles; the direction of the road was due east, and the only remarkable feature in the ground was its steady rise.

We pitched the tent under a villanous Mimosa, the tree whose shade is compared by poetic Bedawin to the false friend who deserts you in your utmost need. I enlivened the hot dull day by a final affair with Sa'ad the Demon. His alacrity at Yambu' obtained for him the loan of a couple of dollars: he had bought grain at El Hamra, and now we were near El Medinah; still there was not a word about repayment. And knowing that an Oriental debtor discharges his debt as he pays his rent—with the greatest unwillingness —and that, on the other hand, an Oriental creditor will devote the labor of a year to recovering a sixpence, I resolved to act like a native of the country placed in my position, and by dint of sheer dunning and demanding pledges to recover my lawful property. About noon Sa'ad the Demon, after a furious rush, bare-headed, through the burning sun, flung the two dollars down upon my carpet: however, he presently recovered temper, and, as subsequent events showed, I had chosen the right part. Had he not been forced to repay his debt, he would have despised me for a "freshman," and would have coveted more. As it was, the boy Mohammed bore the brunt of unpopular feeling, my want of liberality being traced to his secret and perfidious admonitions. He supported his burden the more philosophically, because, as he notably calculated, every dollar saved at El Medinah would be spent under his stewardship at Meccah.

At 4 P.M. (July 24) we left Suwaykah, all of us in the worst of bad humours, and travelled in a N.E. direction. So "out of temper" were my companions, that at sunset, of the whole party, Umar Effendi was the only one who would eat supper. The rest sat upon the ground, pouting, grumbling, and—they had been allowed to exhaust my stock of Latakia—smoking Syrian tobacco as if it were a grievance. Such a game at naughty children, I have seldom seen played even by Oriental men. The boy Mohammed privily remarked to me that the camel-men's beards were now in his fist—meaning that we were out of their kinsmen, the Harb's, reach. He soon found an opportunity to quarrel with them; and, because one of his questions was not answered in the shortest possible time, he proceeded to abuse them in language which sent their hands flying in the direction of their swords. Despite, however, this threatening demeanour, the youth, knowing that he now could safely go to any lengths, continued his ill words, and Mansur's face was so comically furious, that I felt too much amused to interfere.

At last the camel-men disappeared, thereby punishing us most effectually for our sport. The road lay up rocky hill and down stony vale; a tripping and stumbling dromedary had been substituted for the usual monture: the consequence was that we had either a totter or a tumble once per mile during the whole of that long night. In vain the now fiery Mohammed called for the assistance of the camel-men with the full force of his lungs: "Where be those owls, those oxen of the oxen, those beggars, those cut-off ones, those foreigners, those Sons of Flight!* withered be their hands! palsied be their fingers! the foul mustachioed fellows, basest of the Arabs that ever hammered tent-peg, sneaking cats, goats of El Akhfash!

* A popular but not a bad pun—"*H*arb" (Fight) becomes, by the alteration of the H, "Harb" (Flight).

(a noted wiseacre). Truly I will torture them the torture of the oil (*i. e.* burn them alive), the mines of infamy! the cold of countenance!" (fools).

The Bedawi brotherhood of the camel-men looked at him wickedly, muttering the while "By Allah! and by Allah! and by Allah! O boy, we will flog thee like a hound when we catch thee in the Desert!" All our party called upon him to desist, but his temper had got completely the upper hand over his discretion, and he expressed himself in such classic and idiomatic Hejazi, that I had not the heart to stop him. Some days after our arrival at El Medinah, Shaykh Hamid warned him seriously never again to go such perilous lengths, as the Beni-Harb were celebrated for shooting or poniarding the man who ventured to use even the mild epithet "O jack-ass!" to them. And in the quiet of the city the boy Mohammed, like a sobered man shuddering at dangers braved when drunk, hearkened with discomposure and penitence to his friend's words. The only immediate consequence of his abuse was that my broken Shugduf became a mere ruin, and we passed the dark hours perched like two birds upon the only entire bits of frame-work the cots contained.

The sun had nearly risen (July 25) before I shook off the lethargic effects of such a night. All around me were hurrying their camels, regardless of rough ground, and not a soul spoke a word to his neighbour. "Are there robbers in sight?" was the natural question. "No!" replied Mohammed; "they are walking with their eyes, they will presently see their homes!" Rapidly we passed the Wady el Akik, of which,

> "O my friend, this is Akik, then stand by it,
> Endeavouring to be distracted by love, if not really a lover," *

and a thousand other such pretty things, have been said by the Arab poets. It was as "dry as summer's dust," and its "beautiful trees" appeared in the shape of vegetable mummies. Half an hour after leaving the "Blessed Valley" we came to a huge staircase roughly cut in a long broad line of black scoriaceous basalt. This is the Mudarraj or flight of steps traversing the western ridge of the so-called El Harratayn. It is holy ground; for the Prophet spoke well of it. Arrived at the top, we passed through a lane of dark lava, with steep banks on both sides, and after a few minutes El Medinah suddenly opened upon our dazed vision.

We halted our beasts as if by word of command. All of us descended, in imitation of the pious of old and sat down, jaded and hungry as we were, to feast our eyes with a view of the Holy City. "O Allah! this is the Haram (sanctuary) of Thy Prophet; make it to us a Protection from Hell Fire, and a Refuge from Eternal Punishment! O open the Gates of Thy Mercy, and let us pass through them to the Land of Joy!" and "O Allah, bless the last of Prophets, the Seal of Prophecy, with Blessings in number as the

---

* The esoteric meaning of this couplet is, "Man! this is a lovely portion of God's creation: then gaze upon it, and here learn to love the perfections of thy Supreme Friend."

Stars of Heaven, and the Waves of the Sea, and the Sands of the Waste—bless him, O Lord of Might and Majesty, as long as the Corn-field and the Date-grove continue to feed Mankind!"* And again, "Live, for ever, O Most Excellent of Prophets!—live in the Shadow of Happiness during the Hours of Night and the Times of Day, whilst the Bird of the Tamarisk (the dove) moaneth like the childless Mother, whilst the West-wind bloweth gently over the Hills of Nejd, and the Lightning flasheth bright in the Firmament of El Hejaz!"

Such were the poetical exclamations that rose all around me, showing how deeply tinged with imagination becomes the language of the Arab under the influence of strong passion or religious enthusiasm. I now understood the full value of a phrase in the Moslem ritual, "And when his (the pilgrim's) eyes shall *fall upon the Trees of El Medinah*, let him raise his Voice and bless the Prophet with the choicest of Blessings." In all the fair view before us nothing was more striking, after the desolation through which we had passed, than the gardens and orchards about the town. It was impossible not to enter into the spirit of my companions, and truly I believe that for some minutes my enthusiasm rose as high as theirs. But presently, when we remounted, the traveller returned strong upon me: I made a rough sketch of the town,

---

* That is to say, "throughout all ages and all nations." The Arabs divide the world into two great bodies, first themselves, and, secondly, "Ajam," *i. e* all that are not Arabs. Similar bi-partitions are the Hindus and Mlenchhas the Jews and Gentiles, the Greeks and Barbarians, &c. &c.

put questions about the principal buildings, and in fact collected materials for the next chapter.

The distance traversed that night was about twenty-two miles in a direction varying from easterly to north-easterly. We reached El Medinah on the 25th July, thus taking nearly eight days to travel over little more than 130 miles. This journey is performed with camels in four days, and a good dromedary will do it without difficulty in half that time.*

* The following is a synopsis of our stations:
1. From Yambu' 18th July to Musahhal, N.E. . . . . 16 miles ⎫
2. From Musahhal 19th July to Bir Sa'id, S. and E. . . 34 ,, ⎬ 64 miles.
3. From Bir Sa'id 20th July to El Hamra, N.E. . . . 14 ,, ⎭
4. From El Hamra 21st July to Bir Abbas, E. . . . . 24 ,, ⎫
5. From Bir Abbas 23d July to Suwaykah, E. . . . . 22 ,, ⎬ 68 miles.
6. From Suwaykah 24th July to El Medinah, N. and E. 22 ,, ⎭

Total English miles 132.

END OF VOL. I.

www.ingramcontent.com/pod-product-compliance
Lightning Source LLC
Chambersburg PA
CBHW031331230426
43670CB00006B/311